# BUT DELIVER US FROM EVIL

# BUT DELIVER US FROM EVIL

*An introduction to the demonic dimension
in pastoral care*

JOHN RICHARDS

*A Crossroad Book*
THE SEABURY PRESS · New York

*This book is gratefully dedicated to the many priests, ministers and lay people who have told me of their experiences, shared their insights, and given me their friendship—among whom are many who have not had formal acknowledgment in the text but who have contributed so much.*

The Seabury Press
815 Second Avenue
New York, N.Y. 10017

© *John Richards, 1974*
Printed in the United States of America

LIBRARY OF CONGRESS CATALOGING IN PUBLICATION DATA

Richards, John.
    But deliver us from evil.

    "A Crossroads book."
    Bibliography: p.
    1. Exorcism. 2. Demoniac possession. 3. Occult sciences. I. Title.
BV873.E8R52  1974           265'9           74–10845
ISBN 0–8164–1184–0

# CONTENTS

| | | |
|---|---|---|
| Notes | | vi |
| Preface | | vii |
| Acknowledgments | | ix |
| 1 | The Healing Church | 1 |
| 2 | The Occult Explosion | 19 |
| 3 | The Occult Journey | 38 |
| 4 | The Occult Journey—continued | 58 |
| 5 | The Problem of Possession | 91 |
| 6 | Deliverance | 119 |
| 7 | Exorcism | 155 |
| 8 | Places | 192 |
| | A Postscript | 215 |
| | Appendix: Exorcism of the Possessed | 222 |
| | Bibliography | 226 |
| | Indexes | 241 |

# NOTES

1. I have only used the title 'Doctor' for those working or qualified in some sphere of medicine. I apologise to holders of other doctorates, but I know they will readily understand my reasons for doing so in a study where qualified medical and psychiatric opinion is so important.

2. All names in case-histories have been changed, and sufficient details altered to make identification impossible, except in cases which have previously appeared in the press or other publication.

3. Quotations from my private tape-recordings of interviews or talks have been preceded by an asterisk(*), to distinguish them from quotations of written sources.

# PREFACE

Had I, even in the nineteen sixties, ventured to suggest that exorcism should be a small but real part of the Church's ministry of healing, most opinion—even informed opinion—would have dismissed the suggestion as medieval superstition. I would have been under great pressure to justify taking such a stand within both a church and a society in which the supernatural was out of fashion.

Today the task is much easier. While the spiritual and supernatural still remain unfashionable in many quarters of the Church, no informed opinion would hold that they are unfashionable in the contemporary society which the Church exists to serve. In the 'Age of Aquarius' it is not only youth club leaders, but the police and even psychiatrists that talk more freely than many churchmen about evil influences in peoples' lives.

What follows will not fit easily into the contemporary theological scene, but I have no doubt whatever that it is, and increasingly will be, in tune with the contemporary pastoral situation. Whether it will contribute constructively to this situation time alone will tell. If it does, it will not primarily be due to the work of other writers (although my bibliography indicates my debt to them) but to my many friends in this country and elsewhere who are actively engaged in the 'ministry of deliverance', who have given their time and shared both their experiences and their confidences with me. With very few exceptions my reading has done little more than underline what I have learnt from them. I hesitate to say that it is *their* book, lest I appear to avoid taking full responsibility for its many weaknesses, yet not to say so would be misleading. It would have been a prodigious, and, I believe, an unnecessary undertaking to have documented all that they have shared with me at conferences and in private in the last eight years, in an attempt to give 'credit where credit is due'. I know them well enough to be convinced that they share my desire that if anyone is helped by this book neither they nor I are thought of, but only Him in whose Name the ministry here related is undertaken; who taught us to pray:

> Our Father, who art in heaven,
> hallowed by thy name;
> thy kingdom come;
> thy will be done;
> on earth as it is in heaven.
> Give us this day our daily bread.
> And forgive us our trespasses,
> as we forgive those who trespass against us.
> And lead us not into temptation;
> *but deliver us from evil.*
>
>                    Amen.

Michaelmas Day 1973                    JOHN RICHARDS
                                        *Cambridge*

# ACKNOWLEDGMENTS

I WISH TO express my deep gratitude to the Queen's Theological College, Birmingham, for awarding me a year's Research Fellowship to study exorcism, and for inviting me to lecture on the Church's Healing Ministry—the content of which I have incorporated into my first chapter.

My thanks are also due to the many people who responded to an appeal I made in the press for details of experiences related to my studies. Their names are not mentioned because so many entrusted me with accounts of a personal nature.

Many individuals and organisations supplied me with tape-recordings of talks, and thus enabled me to draw more deeply on the insights of Pastor Richard Bolt, Prebendary Henry Cooper, the Rev. Jean Darnell, the Rev. Oswald Guinness, Dr Kurt Koch, Derek Prince, Peter Scothern, the late Fr Gilbert Shaw, the late Edgar Trout, the Rev. David Watson and H. A. Maxwell Whyte—far too few of whom have written at any length on this subject, about which they know so much. For this material I am grateful to Mrs Richard Bolt, the Rev. Fr Leslie Giddens, the Rev. Fr Kenneth Leech, the Rev. Alan McCabe, the Rev. J. Maitland Moir and to the Fountain Trust, the Guild of Health, the L'Abri Fellowship, the London Healing Mission and the Voice of Deliverance.

Among those who allowed me to inverview them and also to record the session in order that I might more accurately and conveniently use their opinions were—the Rev. George Bennett (Divine Healing Mission), the Rev. Martin Gouldthorpe, the Rev. Alan Harrison (Guild of Health), Captain Barry Irons (Church Army), Dr Kenneth McAll, the Rev. J. Christopher Neil-Smith, Dr Cicely Newman and Mrs Jean Orr (both of the Columban Community of Healing, N. Ireland) and the Revs Dennis Peterson, George Tarleton, Tom Walker and Tom Willis. So much of what they shared with me was of a confidential nature, however, that I have only been able to use a little of their material directly. I alone know the extent of their indirect contribution to this book—and I am deeply grateful.

In my endeavour to make an objective assessment of occultism, I have been greatly helped by Françoise Strachan, but I remain responsible for the opinions expressed below.

I received useful advice for reading matter from the Rev. Dr Hugh Trowell (then Study Group Secretary of the Institute of Religion and Medicine). Dr Joan FitzHerbert kindly endorsed Dr Alfred Lechler's essay on distinguishing between disease and the demonic—an assessment which I had no medical qualifications to make. With these I am grateful also to Mrs Esther Langrish for translating Dr Jean Lhermitte's article in *Ecclesia* No. 67 'Les Possédés sont-ils des fous?', and I share with many others an immense debt of gratitude to Dr Kenneth McAll whose friendship I have long valued and who has been a constant source of inspiration and knowledge in the undertaking of this study.

It is a joy for me to be able in this way to express my thanks to my family; to the Rev. Donald Anders Richards for advising me about so many things and for checking the manuscripts; to my mother for transcribing a number of my lectures, and to Rosemary, my wife, without whose constant 'Love, joy, peace, . . .' this book would never have been completed.

I owe a great debt of gratitude to those who introduced me to this ministry, and particularly to the Rev. Dom Robert Petitpierre, O.S.B. who, in 1964, asked me to become the Secretary of the Study Group on Exorcism of which, until very recently, he was Chairman. He thus placed me in a position where I knew something had to be written, but it has been a constant source of astonishment that, together with our present Chairman, the Rev. Alan Harrison, he should have so encouraged and helped me to do the work myself.

# CHAPTER ONE

# THE HEALING CHURCH

THE WHOLE IDEA of exorcism will appal some and fascinate others. Most people's view of it comes from the picture papers or from horror films; others' from history books.

It is understandable that the mass media, for reasons of impact, usually omit the *context* of exorcism in the same way that they so successfully portray violence outside the context of frustration, and sex outside the context of love—it makes 'better' news. Many of those whose knowledge of exorcism comes from history books are likely to have a no less imperfect view of it, for far too many historians display more relish for the sensational than real understanding of the subject. The demonic must be one of the few subjects where a writer's essential qualification should be that he is not fascinated by it.

In many respects this book is not about demons; medieval woodcuts of them will not leer at you between the chapters. What follows is more about God and about people than it is about the demonic, for I share Karl Barth's mistrust of looking for too long or too systematically at demons.

The title of this book strikes a somewhat defensive and negative note if taken by itself. I hope that its very familiarity will encourage people to see it in the context of the Lord's Prayer, where deliverance is one, but only one, aspect of the Kingdom of God. In thinking about deliverance from evil (of which exorcism is a part) it is worth noting that our prayer for deliverance comes after, not before, the forgiveness of our sins. While this may not be a very important factor in an exegesis of the Lord's Prayer, it illustrates a point which those who see evil as more than the absence of good would do well to note.

Some who view evil in this way are inclined, if they use demonic terminology, so to elevate the demonic that 'our trespasses' become '*their* trespasses', and ourselves merely pawns in an eternal chess game. This is heresy and (if it is permissible so to grade heresy) a bad one; one that has dissuaded many intelligent people who would otherwise wish to be true to the New Testament from using its demonic concepts or language altogether.

The petition about deliverance from evil in the Lord's Prayer has a unique position; it is either, as with St Luke, omitted altogether, or it is last! Popular usage follows it by one of two things—either an ascription of the kingdom, the power and the glory to God, or—Amen, full-stop. This conveniently symbolises the only two advisable progressions from the word 'evil'.

There are those who in their thinking about deliverance from evil are apt to create for themselves, as it were, another alternative ending to the prayer. They either ascribe the kingdom, the power and the glory to created beings and not to the Creator, or, like a cat shaking a dying rat, postpone the 'Amen, full-stop', as if Christ's victory was somehow in question. The Lord's Prayer illustrates what our Lord's life so clearly shows, that deliverance from evil is a *part* of the Gospel; a part, but *only* a part, of the establishment of God's Rule in individuals and in society. Although for the synoptic Gospel-writers at any rate, our Lord's exorcisms seemed obvious foci of the Kingdom, neither Luke, nor (as one would particularly expect) the author of Matthew, felt it necessary to introduce in any 'spiritualised' way the prophet's hopes for the 'liberation of the captives' (Isaiah 61:1) into the programme of the Messianic age outlined for John's disciples.

> . . . the blind see again, and the lame walk, lepers are cleansed, and the deaf hear, and the dead are raised to life and the Good News is proclaimed to the poor; (Matthew 11:5 and Luke 7:22)

Although the scope of the 'Good News' is spiritual as well as physical, corporate as well as individual, political as well as personal, the theme of healing—even in a narrow sense—is a dominant one. The early Church continued our Lord's ministry:

> I have neither silver nor gold, but I will give you what I have: In the name of Jesus Christ the Nazarene, walk! (Acts 3:5)

Peter has no money, but he does have power to heal. The opposite of the situation today, not least among those who attach greatest importance to the Apostolic Succession!

Is society any less sick?

Douglas Webster begins his thought-provoking Bible Studies entitled *The Healing Christ* with these words:

> There is one remarkable area of agreement between most modern writers, even non-Christian writers, and the Bible. It is in describing the human condition as one of sickness.

While there appears some agreement about the condition, there is less agreement about the cure. The vastness of the problem, together with the scope of the Gospel have tended to lead to fragmentation and distortion. Thus a person suffering from malnutrition may, in current terminology, be 'completely healed' while there has been no healing whatever of the economic, social or domestic factors of which his illness may have been a symptom. Whether we tend to think primarily of a 'spiritual' or a 'social' Gospel we are equally distorting the New Testament, which knows no rigid distinction between 'saving' and 'healing'. It is a common but narrow view of the healing-Gospel that excludes Zacchaeus' story from the 'healing miracles'. Not infrequently healings of priorities, of relationships and of timetable are of a far deeper nature than the temporary relief of physical suffering—so much of which is caused by a selfish distortion of one or more of these three things. The New Testament uses the same basic word for the wholeness which the witnesses testify had come to the Gerasene demoniac and for the transformation which had come to Zacchaeus and his household.[1] Although there is need to write about the ministry to demoniacs, there is an even greater need to write about the relevance of the Gospel to the Zacchaeuses of today—who far outnumber the former. 'Healing', in general conversation, is used almost exclusively of certain physical states of individuals, yet the writer of the Apocalypse could look forward to the *healing* of the nations (Revelation 22:2). If the Church exists to mediate God's answer to the sickness of the human condition, then it is well to think of her Healing Ministry with the scope of the New Testament writers rather than the limits of popular usage.

While the *Church's Ministry of Healing* was recommended by

[1] Luke 19:9 and 8:36 (Greek *sōteria* and *esōthē*).

the Archbishop's Commission because it was a less misleading title than 'Faith Healing', 'Divine Healing' and 'Spiritual Healing', it has the one disadvantage of appearing to departmentalise activities which are 'healing' ones, and others which (presumably) are not. I have been accused more than once of stretching language too far when I have asserted that 'Christ was always healing'; that his action in the Temple and his criticism of the Pharisees were the acts of a Healer no less than his restoration of sight or hearing. Whether we actually use the word 'healing' or not, is less important than whether our concept of healing, of wholeness, of salvation is great enough. For we have not simply to take into account what is generally termed Christ's 'earthly ministry' but also the Cross.

> It was God who reconciled us to himself through Christ and gave us the work of handing on this reconciliation. In other words, God in Christ was reconciling the world to himself . . .
> (2 Corinthians 5:18–19)

Whatever terminology we use, the title of Dr Michael Wilson's book *The Church is Healing* (SCM) is a useful reminder that what has become recognised as the 'Ministry of Healing' is *one* aspect only of the corporate life and work of Christ's Church. This has repeatedly been said by writers on this subject. The Rev. A. H. Purcell Fox, for instance, warns:

> We must not allow the healing ministry to be lifted out of its setting in the larger ministry of the Church, for to do so would be to let it degenerate into a cult. It is but one aspect of God's redemptive power, and although it has been neglected and therefore needs to be brought back to its rightful place, it cannot be made into a sole end in itself without grievous distortion of the whole content of the Christian faith.[1]

If a 'grievous distortion' comes when the 'healing ministry' is divorced from the total Gospel of which it is a part, the dangers and distortions facing those who might divorce the ministry of deliverance and exorcism from the healing ministry are *immeasurably* greater. I have never, in fact, encountered anybody who *wanted* to do this, but I have met a good number whose ministry could not be integrated into the life of the local worshipping community because of apathy, ignorance or prejudice,

---

[1] *The Church's Ministry of Healing* (Longmans).

or who, because of (unsought) publicity and lack of understanding or co-operation from other clergy, had to spend a disproportionate amount of time on it.

Whatever breadth of meaning we give to the word 'healing',
the ministry of deliverance is such a small part of the Church's
ministry of healing that some reminder of its context is
necessary. Firstly, however, a word about the use of 'exorcism'
and 'deliverance'.

'Exorcism' is disliked by many for two reasons: because it
does not arise in the New Testament in a truly Christian context,
i.e. it is never used of our Lord or of his disciples, and because
of the many erroneous and superstitious practices that, as I
mentioned above, are commonly attached to the word. Strictly
speaking it is only the *demonic* that can be 'exorcised' *from*
people or places, although general usage is rarely so precise.
Deliverance is a much wider term—it is Biblical and it has none
of the erroneous connotations of the word 'exorcism'. There is a
great deal within society and within individuals which is not
demonic but from which they need to be delivered. One might
illustrate the usage by saying that—'Exorcism is the necessary
part of the ministry of deliverance to someone who is known to
be afflicted in some way by the demonic.' (For a further discussion of terms see Chapter Six.)

The Church's Ministry, is, of course, Christ's Ministry. I shall
presume that no reader would think that any Christian minister
or congregation ever brought Christian healing to anyone other
than through the healing power of Christ working through
them. If it were literally only the Church's ministry, there would
be no ministry at all, because humanly speaking the people of
God share all the sickness and distortion of the society to which
they minister. The Church's ministry of healing is, in many
ways, the blind leading the blind, but with one important
addition—our Lord leading the blind leading the blind. Paul
Tillich when addressing graduating students at the New York
Union Theological Seminary in a talk entitled 'Heal the Sick;
Cast out Demons' said:

> Should you ask me "Can we heal without being healed our-
> selves?" I would answer "You can!" For neither the disciples
> nor you could ever say "We are healed so let us heal others." He
> who would believe this of himself is least fit to heal others. (*The
> Eternal Now*)

It is not the place here, when there is available a wide range of books dealing with the healing ministry, to set out in detail all its aspects or to try and answer all the misgivings which arise when the subject is mentioned. I would refer the reader to the Archbishops' Commission Report entitled *The Church's Ministry of Healing* (CIO), and to books suggested in my Further Reading list, and mention here only one or two basic points.

A major reservation which many people will rightly have is that this ministry must not suggest that God only works through 'spiritual' means. The reason for the rejection of the term 'Divine Healing' was precisely in order that medicine and its allied disciplines should be seen to be channels of God's healing. A friend of mine who once ran a weekend conference on the Church's Healing Ministry, shared with another such group the fact that during the course of it his child was rushed to hospital for an emergency appendix operation! Clergy–doctor co-operation is now no longer a debating point. This is due to many things, among them the statement issued by the British Medical Association Committee in 1956 on '*Divine Healing and Co-operation between Doctors and Clergy*', and the foundation in 1964 of the Institute of Religion and Medicine (IRM) to provide interdisciplinary dialogue and promote communication between those whose approaches to healing differed. Its description of health as 'a function of the total relationship between the individual and his environment and thus [involving] his physical, mental and spiritual well-being' reflects the thinking of the BMA Committee which asserted that:

As man is body, mind and spirit, and health depends on the harmonious functioning of the whole man, the task of medicine and the Church are inseparable; co-operation thus comes into line with Christ's charge to his disciples to heal and preach.

From a theological view-point our charge to 'heal the sick' cannot be pushed to one side even by radical thinkers. Bishop John Robinson, for instance, states in his book *On Being the Church in the World* that:

There is no preaching of the Gospel consistent with the New Testament which does not include the charge 'Heal the sick'; without that it would simply be a different gospel.

The commission to heal is Christ's charge to the Church, and only to individuals in so far as they are genuine expressions of the Church. No one has put this more clearly than Dr Charrington in his article 'A Medical View of Spiritual Healing' (*Expository Times*, Vol. LXXXI, No. 3).

> It is becoming clear that the Healing Church rather than the healing individual is the logical successor to and continuation of the Healing Christ.

This is more than a theological nicety, for it enables us to have some yard-stick by which to judge the popular 'spiritual healer', on whose ministry—with its mass meetings and almost total disregard for diagnosis and after-care—popular opinion of non-medical factors in healing is so frequently based.

In many respects the Church's ministry of healing is the very antithesis of the popular view of 'spiritual' healing, which sees it as a *specialist's public activity to relieve physical suffering by miraculous or semi-magical means*. The Church's ministry of healing is not dependent on specialist abilities; it is not likely to be undertaken at mass meetings; it is not primarily concerned with the relief of physical suffering; it does not rate its effectiveness by 'miracles', and is accomplished by the generous (and often unpredictable) workings of God, frequently using certain human actions but *not dependent on them*. I have emphasised this last point because there are some who tend to write as if the healing ministry would be greatly extended if we could grasp the 'laws' of spiritual healing and measure and tap the forces at work. That this must be a major concern for those who view healing as a purely natural or psychic phenomenon is clear. What is not clear is why some Christians appear to emphasise the 'forces' rather than the Father.

Mention of natural and psychic healing raises many questions about the nature of non-medical healing, its scope, and the place of the Church's Ministry within this. For clarity we may think of eight types of 'healer' (the list is not conclusive and the categories merge).

(i) *Magical*. The healer uses acquired or created occult power to heal and restore. This concept is basic to white witchcraft.

(ii) *Mediumistic*. The healer is a healing medium through whom spirits, many of whom purport to be 'departed' doctors, are alleged to work. Harry Edwards described the theory of this to the Archbishops' Commission and claims that Pasteur and Lister are 'inspiring his spirit and guiding his fingers'.[1]

(iii) *Psychical*. The healer uses a natural, if inexplicable, force, akin to water-divining. Healing is seen as the action of vibrations, radiations or of 'odic force'. Such natural power is linked with those for whom flowers appear to grow easily, and forms something both of a creed and a pastime among young people who experiment with flower-bulbs and make them wither or advance according to their psychic powers![2]

The remaining five classifications are to be found within the Church's Ministry.

(iv) *Consecrated*. The healer has some natural gift which he or she has consecrated specifically for God's use within a prayerful, corporate and possibly sacramental setting.

(v) *Pastoral*. By far the greatest healing is undertaken by those who would not regard their ministry as a healing one—those who nevertheless bring wholeness at many levels by their friendship and counsel, their support and their encouragement, their prayers and spiritual direction.

(vi) *Sacramental*. Arising out of the Pastoral there are, for many, the sacramental means of healing which belong to the Church. The corporate caring and healing of the Church is mediated both through the Holy Communion and Anointing with Oil, and also through the more personal means of sacramental confession and laying-on of hands.

(vii) *Charismatic*. This is the ministry of someone with a specifically Spirit-given 'gift of healing' (1 Corinthians 12:9, literally 'gifts of healings' which suggests a possible variety of healing-gifts) or with a Spirit-given gift of 'miraculous powers' (verse 10 (Moffat)). Paul's distinction between healings and miracles is interesting here.

(viii) *Mediatory*. Obviously all healers within the Church's ministry of healing are never more than vehicles of God's grace. Or, to put it another way, if God could somehow be removed from the Pastoral, the Consecrated, the Sacramental and the Charismatic there would be little real healing left. Thus they are all mediating God's rule and his love, and yet I think

---

[1] *Powers That Be*, Beverley Nichols, and p. 4, Report.
[2] 'Healing by the Laying on of Hands: Review of Experiments and Implications', Bernard Grad, *Pastoral Psychology*, Vol. 21, No. 206, pp. 19–26 (and other articles in same edition).

it is still necessary to have a specifically 'mediatory' category of healer. By this label I have in mind the Christian minister (using 'minister' in the widest sense of that term) who feels that he or she has no great pastoral gift, no natural ability or charismatic gift, but who finds that his simple presence, without the use of sacraments, is a means of God's bringing greater wholeness to others. This person would, in particular, share Peter's reaction, 'Why are you staring at us as though we had made this man walk by our own power or holiness?' (Acts 3:12)

Something of the variety and range of the Church's Ministry has been implied in the foregoing classification of healing ministries and the earlier remarks about the scope of the Gospel and the extent of Christian 'healing'.

A comprehensive analysis of the healing ministry of the Church would have to concern itself with the majority of the activities of those who are called to be salt and light to the world, and it would certainly have to review at length three topics about which there has been so much discussion—sacraments, intercession and the problem of suffering. Here I shall touch only on prayer, confession, Holy Communion, laying-on of hands and Anointing with Oil.

## PRAYER

One distinctive characteristic of Christian belief about God is the father–child relationship which exists between him and man. Whatever theories are put forward about intercessory prayer, ordinary men and women (and children) have not felt it a meaningless activity to share with such a God their fears and their hopes. Behind this attitude lies a conviction that God cares and that he is capable of acting within our history if he is invited to do so. Would it be natural to invite him in this way if it was thought that he would bring chaos and suffering? No. Prayer, then, is the first item in the healing ministry because it is an expression of invitation to communion with a God whom we believe is a *healing* God. While avoiding any practices which suggest that prayer is making God conform to our will, rather than freeing us to conform to his, it nevertheless remains irrefutable that it is in Christian communities where they take time to *pray* that changes take place. I suspect that *one* reason for the clear relationship between prayer and healing is that where people will regularly gather in prayer for the sick that they are, and increasingly become, the 'caring community' which in recent years has been seen to be so important. For without love the healing ministry, with so much else, is nothing.

Such prayer, even when it is of an intercessory nature will not consist of an amateur medical report submitted to the Almighty for his consideration, but a quiet—even a silent—recollection of God's presence, love and care, and the position of the sick person, together with doctors and family, within his loving purposes. To exclude the medical helpers and relatives would be to disregard the two foremost healing influences in their lives through which God has chosen to work, and through which we must expect him to work—however much we may stress other channels of healing. The phobia of medical aid which is apparent among Christian Scientists is (as many have quipped about their doctrines) 'neither Christian nor scientific'!

Together with other aspects of the healing ministry, the Guild of St Raphael and the Guild of Health have a number of useful leaflets on this subject and I would refer readers to them.

## CONFESSION

> Negative forces such as fear, resentment, jealousy, indulgence and carelessness play no small part in the level of both personal and national health.

The development of our understanding of psychosomatic medicine has underlined this statement which the British Medical Association Committee made twenty-five years ago, although perhaps not all ministers are as aware of this as they might be. Fr Kenneth Leech recently told this story at a conference:

> *I was talking not long ago to a friend who was an analyst, and she said that she had been attending a symposium with two clergymen on the subject of Guilt. The clergymen were saying that guilt was pathological, morbid and unhealthy. She—as an analyst—was saying that guilt was necessary for healthy human lives. She suddenly thought of the absurdity of the situation—it was a psychiatrist who was defending guilt, and the theologians who were objecting to it!

It is difficult to over-emphasise the importance of penitence in healing, not so much because it arises from thinking about ourselves, but because it is really the fruit of thinking about God. It is not, of course, placating an angry Father whom we have upset, but rather cementing a friendship with one from whom we have turned away, renewing our side of a relationship which *we* have spoiled. It is of no great importance whether this happens in private or with another, whether it happens informally or formally. A moment's thought on the Parable of the Prodigal Son will remind us of the healing nature of the process. A renewed emphasis on Confession among Evangelicals and others may in part be due to their realisation of the great element of *conversion* in such a process. When, as we shall consider later, people wish to come out of Black Magic, Satanism or witchcraft, their freedom from these enslaving activities very much depends on whether they can really renounce the 'Devil and all his works' and 'turn to Christ'. In this process, which is in the most literal way a 'conversion', confession in some manner or other is usually essential. Absolution is very much part of the ministry of deliverance, and not simply because the word means a 'setting free'.

The paralytic at Capernaum affords us an example from our Lord's ministry where forgiveness of sins formed an important part in the healing process, although the precise contribution that this, or the faith of his friends made to his healing cannot now be known (Mark 2:1–12).

It is no accident that it is only in the Order for the Visitation of the Sick that the 1662 Prayer Book instructs the person to make a 'special confession of his sins'. A more general confession is frequently made in public services but such an act does not usually help to bring the penitent to a re-appraisal of the direction his life is taking, but merely to a greater awareness of his recent sins. It is possible to spend an apparently sinless week in hospital and yet not be aware that one's sickness is the direct result of a selfish timetable or of wrong priorities.

Formal confession will afford the opportunity for spiritual direction, as is frequently pointed out. But the sick are not simply those who need spiritual direction, but those who often can most *use* it, because of the unfamiliar time and quiet which is now their lot, and which they have had no previous opportunity or encouragement to use.

## HOLY COMMUNION

Come unto me all that travail and are heavy laden, and I will refresh you.

These familiar words come from *the* healing sacrament of the Church, a service which incorporates both means of healing outlined above and unites God's people with the living and healing Christ. It is an occasion where young and old, rich and poor, black and white, and the healthy, kneel together to receive God's healing of the man-made divisions between them. I have had to omit 'the sick' from the list because in practice those who most need healing—the sick and the aged, the shy and the frightened—are the most likely to stay away. The reason for this is that little thought has been given to the practical implications of our theology of the Eucharist as a corporate and healing service. Brief mention might also be made of those whom it excludes because of their fears of coming forward or their physical difficulty in walking, negotiating steps, in kneeling, or in getting up from the kneeling position. What of those whose very devotion and awe frightens them away from holding or drinking from the chalice if they suffer from a slight tremor or shaking? What does this healing service do for the young Christian parents whose fears of going by themselves are greater than their attraction to the Christ who could heal them of such fears?

At a Holy Communion in the home when the house-bound and the bed-ridden are drawn into this central experience of corporate and Christian fellowship, so often the family are allowed respectfully to withdraw; there are no representatives of the local Christian community other than the minister; and such an occasion is frequently called a '*Sick* Communion'. It is a sad fact that, except in hospitals, the cry: 'Tell the Vicar I'll have Communion when I'm feeling a bit better!' is often heard but rarely corrected. In no other context are the parish clergy so immune to the fears and anxieties of the laity—although among those able to attend, such clergy will regularly see hands outstretched to receive the bread of Life, hands wet through nervous tension.

In spite of what I have said above, the Eucharist remains *the* healing sacrament of the Church, but in the majority of churches it has yet to become what it is.

The Body of Christ . . . the Blood of Christ
*preserve thy body and soul* unto everlasting life.

## LAYING-ON OF HANDS

Feeling sorry for him, Jesus stretched out his hand and touched him. (Mark 1:41)

It is not only lepers who are comforted—and healed—by a touch. The normal mother finds this a natural ministry to her children, and there must be few men who can envisage comforting the broken-hearted, supporting the weak or helping the afflicted, while they themselves stand with their hands in their pockets! Jesus' actions in touching people and laying hands on them[1] were obviously dictated more by compassion and love than by consciously resorting to a known means of healing. This is the most personal means of healing which we have so far considered, and that is why it is in this area of healing that misunderstandings and misgivings arise. By association of ideas it is likely that the image of the popular 'healer' will spring to mind more readily in this context than the parish priest, the local minister or the hospital chaplain. The 'healer' would be most likely to place his hands on or near the area of disease or pain. The power at work in the process would be regarded as emanating from him through his hands to restore the Life Force, the healing force, of the sufferer. This ability may or may not be consecrated to God's use and is real—but human.

Experiments with mice and barley seedlings provide clear scientific evidence of the reality of the 'gift of healing'.[2]

Such scientific studies are pursued among parapsychologists and psychic researchers and provide evidence not, as is suggested in the quotation, for '*the* gift of healing', but for '*a* gift of healing'. The Church's healing ministry is, as I have noted above, not dependent on 'healers' with natural, psychic or supranormal abilities. It is the compassionate action of God working through his Church, it is a priestly and a lay ministry,

[1] Mark 1:41; 5:23; 6:5, etc.
[2] Grad, op. cit.

or, ideally, a ministry of the two working together—an increasing practice today being the local minister and Christian doctor together laying on hands. This avoids personality cults and symbolises the scope of God's healing. Doctor Michael Wilson writes:

> . . . when the minister lays his hands upon the head of a sick person, it is as if the hands of all the congregation are with his hands, focusing their love and prayer for the one in need. It is a corporate act of the Church . . . the congregation which has laid its hands upon someone . . . is committed to him in love.[1]

The corporate nature of the act can be made real if it takes place in a corporate setting—the Holy Communion being the obvious one, and this was in fact recommended by the Archbishops' Commission. Some theologians, however, object to this on the grounds that nothing can be added to the benefits received in the sacrament, while others maintain that the Holy Communion is the supreme means of bringing one to a 'state of grace' in which state alone one is completely open to any specific and individual blessings that God has to give. Whatever the theological objections, at the very least a Eucharistic setting ensures that such a ministry is sacramental, unemotional and corporate rather than individualistic, hysterical and public.

If the laying-on of hands is given at such a service, it must not be undertaken without teaching, and should be given only to those who choose to remain kneeling for it. If there are two ministers it is better that they together minister to each person (not alternating), and as it is only the whole who have no need for a physician it is most fitting that they should be seen to minister to each other in this way, just as each needs to receive the sacrament of the Communion. Quite frequently people come on behalf of others (and just as frequently it is they themselves who receive particular blessings—there is a lesson here); when they do, it is natural they should want to tell the minister so. It is suggested that a moment or two of quiet is spent before each person so that if they wish to say anything they may. This will from time to time mean postponing ministry until they are seen privately after the service, where some counselling or confession may be the more appropriate means of healing.

[1] *The Church is Healing* (SCM).

My own practice would be to avoid mentioning physical healing at all at such a service. People are naturally inclined to dwell on their physical aches and pains, on themselves, their past and their present. Just as the funeral service points people away from their present sorrow to God, so a 'healing service' should also point to him, to the future, and to renewed dedication and service. In this way, if physical blessing occurs it has not been created or suggested by words or atmosphere, but has been a by-product of a new God-ward orientation in peoples' lives. The un-comfortable words in Mark 9

> . . . it is better for you to enter into life lame than to have two feet and be thrown into hell . . .

are not inappropriate for a 'healing' service! So often the physical is the *last* area of life to be changed by the Church's Ministry—a reminder that God's ways are not our ways. A reminder that the exhortation at our Baptisms to 'follow the example of our Saviour Christ and be made like unto him' (1662 Prayer Book) is not automatically achieved by the healthy.

The Church today follows the Biblical pattern by making the laying-on of hands a means of blessing, ordination, confirmation, healing and commissioning. Jesus blessed children by the laying-on of hands (Matthew 19:13–15) and many feel that it is an appropriate way to give individual rather than corporate blessing, and not simply in the case of the blind.

Healing and commissioning should not be separated. There are those who prefer the attention of being sick to the responsibility of using their health for God. 'Saved to serve' is a useful corrective for any who might be inclined to make a self-indulgent cult of such a ministry.

While 'healers' generally place their hands on or near the area of physical discomfort, in the ordinary way a minister would lay his hands on the person's head (as is done in Confirmation or Ordination). The advantages are obvious. It visually emphasises the commissioning aspect and at the same time that the ministry is not to bring cure to a part, but wholeness to a person.[1]

---

[1] A short account of 'what is actually taking place' in the ministry of laying-on of hands can be found in 'The Laying on of Hands . . . An Investigation', Rev. George Gage, *The Way of Life*, May–June, 1971.

## ANOINTING WITH OIL (Unction)

If any one of you is ill, he should send for the elders of the
Church, and they must anoint him with oil in the name of the
Lord and pray over him. The prayer of faith will save the sick
man and the Lord will raise him up again; and if he has committed any sins, he will be forgiven. So confess your sins to one
another, and pray for one another, and this will cure you. (James
5:14–16)

This century has seen the revival of this sacrament of healing
within the Anglican Church due, in no small measure, to the
work of the Guild of St Raphael, founded in 1915, to give
teaching on and to forward the Church's ministry of healing
both by prayer and sacramental means. Their publication
*Holy Unction—a Practical Guide to its Administration*, by Prebendary Henry Cooper, is a useful short introduction to those
who are unfamiliar with this particular ministry. The service
is likely to include all the foregoing means of healing—prayer,
confession, communion and laying-on of hands—if it is taken
along the lines authorised by the Convocations of Canterbury
and York.

Unlike the laying-on of hands which is frequently repeated,
Unction is used much more sparingly—usually no more than
once during an illness. One reason for this is that (except in an
emergency) it is ministered only after a very thorough preparation on the part of the person concerned. Often the healing
begins *during* the preparation, as the one to be anointed is
guided to review his relationship with God and with others.
Formal or informal confession will play an important part, as
the object of the preparation is simply to clear away anything
and everything that might come between the sufferers and
God, to rekindle their love for him and renew their relationship
with Christ.

Holy Unction, together with all other means of healing within
the Church's ministry, is essentially a corporate action, as the
late Dr Lambourne and Dr Michael Wilson both point out.[1]
Compared with the laying-on of hands, Anointing with Oil is
a more impersonal means of grace. While this has the advantage
of decreasing the importance of the ministrant as an individual,

[1] Wilson, op. cit. and *Community, Church and Healing*, Dr R. A. Lambourne
(Darton, Longman and Todd).

it has the disadvantage of leading some to think that the oil has magical properties. The time of preparation would correct any such errors, and some feel that the consecrating of the oil is best done as a corporate activity within the situation in which it is going to be used, either in place of, or as well as, previous consecration by the Bishop. Such apparently double consecration need not be meaningless repetition if the Bishop's intention is to hallow it for a priest's ministry in *general* and the intention at the home or the church is to consecrate it for God's use in a *particular* situation. It is the custom to remove the oil from the person's forehead before the end of the service. As such a small quantity of oil is used this is not a practical necessity, and I remain convinced that to remove it cuts right across any intelligent use of symbolism.

I remember a Non-Conformist minister giving me a lift, and my noticing inside the car a small phial of oil. Although I thought I knew the answer, I nevertheless asked him what it was. 'For anointing people,' he said. 'I didn't think your Church did that,' I said, to which he replied 'No, I don't think they do, but they did in New Testament times, and I can't wait for my church to catch up!'

## Exorcism

The Rev. George Bennett begins his chapter on exorcism in his book *The Heart of Healing* (A. James) with these words:

> One cannot go very far in the healing ministry without being confronted by the need for yet another ministration—exorcism, or the casting out of evil.

I have touched on some aspects of the Church's healing ministry of which Confession was perhaps the deepest treatment. Exorcism is definitely spiritual surgery, and, like medical surgery, it cannot be rightly comprehended except by those working within the same healing discipline, and with an understanding of it. Neither can it operate out of context. To stick a knife in someone outside the hospital is murder, to do so within the right context of medicine is to save his life, not take it. Similarly exorcism cannot function or be understood out of its context. Only those familiar with the healing ministry of the

Church—that is with the Healing Christ—will be able to under-stand Christian exorcism. If Christ is not known, nor his victory and authority, understanding exorcism would be like trying to understand—without any knowledge of the law and the authority of those who represent it—how there are some people who can halt a thousand cars by raising one hand!

Exorcism, Christian exorcism that is, is the Church's com-passionate response to people (and places) needing spiritual surgery when, acting with Christ's authority, the Church—through individuals—makes his victory real in a particular situation. Why and how this is achieved will be considered later. First it is important to note those causes for such spiritual ill-health which makes this aspect of the Church's ministry of healing increasingly important.

# CHAPTER TWO

# THE OCCULT EXPLOSION

In Western countries today, the widespread apostasy from the Christian faith, *accompanied by an increasing recourse to black magic and occult practices* [italics mine], is revealing the presence and the power of evil forces ... The need, therefore, for the restoration of the practice of exorcism to its proper place is becoming steadily more urgent and more evident.[1]

IN THIS QUOTATION from his commission's Report on Exorcism, the former Bishop of Exeter states clearly the link between occult practices and evil disturbance. The rapid growth of the Church's ministry of deliverance and exorcism is not a reaction within a materialist Church by those who yearn for the supernatural. It arises as a practical and compassionate response to people or families who are disturbed or troubled. This ought to be obvious but it is not generally understood.

For example, the reviewer of the Exorcism Report in the *Methodist Recorder*, while he showed a commendable lack of interest in the demonic, seemed to imply that the commission was looking at a subject that is of no relevance whatever to those who are 'devotedly busy about our Lord's work' when, he claimed 'devils or demons, real or imaginary, won't dare to trouble us.'[2] To revert for a moment to the medical analogy I have used for exorcism, even to consider the demonic is frequently regarded as the action of a spiritual hypochondriac and not of a surgeon. At a time when Christian ministers and workers are trained and encouraged to learn about all the complex problems of industrial relationships, community welfare, mental illness, marital relationships, addictions, etc., it is strange that they should be discouraged from looking at one aspect of people's *spiritual* illness—a sphere which, until recently, was thought to be the one to which the Christian minister could make a distinctive and worthwhile contribution.

[1] *Exorcism*, ed. Dom Robert Petitpierre, O.S.B. (SPCK).
[2] 'Short shrift for the Devil', Rev. A. R. Vine, May 4th, 1972.

This attitude, as we shall see later, has encouraged the widespread search for spiritual realities *outside* the institutional Churches, a search in mystical and psychic netherworlds for the Way, the Truth and the Life. Such territory is dangerous—judging by the casualties who are turning to Christian ministers for help. Stafford Wright in *Christianity and the Occult* (Scripture Union), speaking of what is popularly called 'demon-possession', writes:

> The occult, with its direct appeal, seems to be the most usual occasion of [demonic] entry.

It is for this reason that those who wish to have some understanding of the ministry of deliverance must be acquainted with the occult scene. In the vital area of diagnosis the inclusion of deliberate or accidental occult activities within the person's life will be a prominent factor in assessing the nature of his distress. It will not, of course, be the only factor or the major one. Doctor Theodor Bovet has rightly criticised the 'unbelievable gullibility' of those who confuse cause and effect because of the high incidence of occult practices among the neurotic, and who proceed to exorcise the moment any occult activity is mentioned,[1] but he insists that a firm stand must be taken where there has been any real commitment to occult practices or ideas. (Those who are in any doubt about the effects of occultism should read Dr Kurt Koch's *Christian Counselling and Occultism*, in which he gives over a hundred cases selected from his vast experience in this area of pastoral care.)[2]

Merrill Unger in his book *The Haunting of Bishop Pike* says:

> Suddenly like a bolt out of the blue, a veritable tempest of occult interest has broken upon the world.

Such opinions are by no means exclusive to Christian commentators on today's scene. In his book *Modern Witchcraft*, published in conjunction with *Man, Myth and Magic*, Frank Smyth describes it in this way:

> Despite the fact that superstition has always been with us, the last few years of the 1960s saw a flowering of interest in occult matters which would have been inexplicable to an earlier

---

[1] *That they may have Life* (Darton, Longman and Todd).
[2] Kregel Publications, Michigan, and also Evangelization Publishers, W. Germany.

generation . . . Now . . . it seems scarcely possible to pick up a newspaper or turn on a television set without some reference being made to ghosts, demons, magicians or witches. The occult, which lay dormant for so many years is once again up and thriving all around us.

What is the 'occult'? Enough has already been said to indicate that in general usage it is a very broad term. It means simply 'hidden' and is used both for such ethically neutral activities as water-divining, and also to describe a whole range of communications with the unseen from astrology to spiritualism, from ouija to black magic.

Interest in occult activities is to be found within the Churches as well as outside them. This may take the form of genuine research into Extra Sensory Perception (ESP) and other phenomena, but as real research is both expensive and time-consuming, the local group which purports to meet for research as often as not degenerates into a club for spiritualist activities for those whose nominal beliefs would otherwise debar them from regular attendance at spiritualist meetings. One even hears of clergymen who are alleged to hold séances, of university chaplains who encourage sessions with the ouija board, while the astrologer still has a place at church fêtes, and one writer begins his apologia for witchcraft with the words—'When Christians touch wood . . .' Magic is nothing new in Church practices. Keith Thomas in *Religion and the Decline of Magic* has a chapter on 'The Magic of the Medieval Church', and in practice many Church members in this century are still bedevilled by magical concepts of sacraments, prayer and priesthood.

In spite of this, there is—or should be—a basic incompatibility between Christian and occult view-points. It is clear that many of those who attend church do not see this division, and succumb to what *The Times* has called 'the seductive charms of the occult'.[1] Just as the distinction between vegetarians and meat-eaters is no less because some nominal vegetarians eat meat, so however occult some Christians are, or however Christian some occultists are, there remains a sharp dissimilarity between the two. The occultist searches for truth in the *hidden* areas of life, in contact with the 'Other Side', in

[1] 'Return of the Occult', May 1st, 1971.

attempts to know the future or to manipulate it. The Christian
is likely to say 'You're looking in the wrong place', and it is
not arrogance or intolerance but reason which prompts him
to say this. For the Christian, truth about God and man and the
relationship between them is something which has been
*shown*, *revealed*, and demonstrated in the life, death and resur-
rection of Jesus Christ. No life-saver is going to lose his life in
attempting to rescue somebody by himself jumping off the
wrong side of the ship! The Christian cannot attribute such
folly to God, and must say that 'the best place to find what
you're looking for is the Cross', for if it is not, then God's
initiative in becoming man and the price he had to pay in
dying for us is a cosmic and tragic irrelevancy.

The attraction of occultism is as old as life itself. An important factor in understanding the Old Testament is that God
calls his people to cut themselves off from occult practices.
This call is summarised in Deuteronomy 18:9–14:

> When you come into the land which the LORD your God is
> giving you, do not learn to imitate the abominable customs of
> those other nations. Let no one be found among you who makes
> his son or daughter pass through fire, no augur or soothsayer
> or diviner or sorcerer, no one who casts spells or traffics with
> ghosts and spirits, and no necromancer. Those who do these
> things are abominable to the LORD your God, and it is because
> of these abominable practices that the LORD your God is driving
> them out before you. You shall be wholehearted in your service
> of the LORD your God. These nations whose place you are
> taking listen to soothsayers and augurs, but the LORD your God
> does not permit you to do this.

There is no evidence whatever that the New Israel revoked this
ruling of the Old Israel. The effect of Paul's missionary campaign at Ephesus was that

> Some believers, too, came forward to admit in detail how they
> had used spells and a number of them who had practised magic
> collected their books and made a bonfire of them in public.
> The value of these was calculated to be fifty thousand silver
> pieces. In this impressive way the word of the Lord spread more
> and more widely and successfully. (Acts 19:18–20)

Earlier, at Philippi, Paul's attitude to a girl soothsayer was to
exorcise the spirit of divination from her, although her pro-

nouncements were, it should be noted, *perfectly accurate* (Acts 16:16–18).

Taken in the light of Biblical teaching the appearance of Samuel to Saul, and of Moses and Elijah on the Mount of Transfiguration are, in the most literal sense, 'exceptions to prove the rule' (1 Samuel 28, and Mark 9:2–8). The latter was an unsought event in a unique life, and only the suicidal would be attracted by Saul's experience! Stafford Wright comments, that neither includes any encouragement to secure their repetition.

The promise held out by the occult is to pass beyond the limits of man's normal knowledge and influence, and it bears a remarkable resemblance to what the Biblical writers saw as the hope which prompts man's rebellion against God—'your eyes will be opened and you will be like gods, knowing good and evil' (Genesis 3:5). While there are perverts in occultism, its attractions are for Everyman, and its sin is the sin of Everyman, of Adam. Condemnation is in-built therefore:

> . . . as in Adam all die . . .

It is not indoctrination which urges us to proclaim the rest of the verse:

> . . . so in Christ shall all be made alive . . .

On many issues Christian and occult views will diverge sharply. While the occultist will put great store by visions and psychic or supernatural perceptions, Christian mystical tradition has always regarded such phenomena as the accidents rather than the substance of contemplative life. The author of *The Cloud of Unknowing* for instance says that for those who seek revelations 'the devil feigneth quaint sounds in their ears, quaint lights and shining in their eyes, and wonderful smells in their noses: and all is but falsehood'.

Of great importance to the occultist will be the state of the dead, and this will be assessed primarily by spiritualistic 'communications' from the Other Side, coupled with that depressing doctrine—reincarnation. The reality of 'eternal life' will be assessed merely in terms of continued personal existence after death. The Christian view of eternal life is far greater than simply a short-term visa to return to darkened séance rooms and haunted castles, although some Christians are drawn by their interest in psychic research to view death in this unbiblical way. Canon John Pearce-Higgins of the Churches' Fellowship for Psychical and Spiritual Studies enthusiastically holds this duller view. In an interview transcribed in Beverley Nichol's book *Powers That Be* he said:

> Look at the Bishop of Woolwich, John Robinson, if I understand him rightly, won't have anything to do with psychic phenomena as evidence for survival. He doesn't seem interested . . . John Robinson . . . merely says: 'What *we* are interested in is eternal life.'

Precisely! While the disagreement among Christians about praying for the dead is well known, the reluctance of some to do so is because of their misgivings about *any* contact with the dead. What *is* clear is that if a Christian takes steps at all to influence the state of the departed, it will be that they should experience God, not that we should experience them. Having prayed that 'light perpetual shine upon them', it would seem an act of selfishness, not of love to attempt to draw them back to the gloom of the séance room.

The occultist takes the very reasonable view that security lies in knowing or in manipulating the future, since it is the future which is our main source of insecurity. In spite of its reasonableness the Christian is called to have a very different attitude.

> So do not worry; do not say 'What are we to eat? What are we to drink? How are we to be clothed?' It is the pagans who set their hearts on all these things. Your heavenly Father knows you need them all. Set your hearts on his kingdom first, and on his righteousness, and all these other things will be given you as well. So do not worry about tomorrow . . . (Matthew 6:31-4)

To be master of one's own destiny is a pre-Christian ambition, it has missed the distinctively Christian paradox that there is greater security in committing one's future to a heavenly Father than there is in trying to manipulate it oneself.

In touching on the three subjects—visions, the departed, and the future—we have seen that the tension between the Christian and the occult approach lies much more deeply than simply the Biblical prohibitions. It is not out of religious intolerance or personal animosity that Christians disagree with occult practices and beliefs; it is a spiritual search of completely opposite orientation.

The Old Testament's uncompromising attitude to the occult reminds us that it is nothing new. Prebendary Cooper in a paper 'Deliverance and Healing' (*Chrism*) writes of occult practices today:

> Looked at historically they bear a striking, and surely not accidental resemblance to the things which went on in the first century of our era when the Light of the Gospel broke upon the heathen world . . . The early Church met the *gnostic* world with demonstrations of the power of Christ to heal. Read St Irenaeus versus heretics to see that plainly. They also met it with demonstration of the power of Christ to cast out evil when it appeared.

Is it a coincidence that the revival of pre-Christian† gnosticism today is simultaneous with a rediscovery of the Church's ministry of healing and deliverance?

The present situation not only in Britain but in America and Europe might well be described in the following words:

> The country was riddled with all kinds of psychic currents. Though there were certain 'occult' activities of a serious and scientific kind, the majority of them were spurious, if not positively dangerous . . .
> . . . patriotism, social respectability, economic security . . . even science had shown their feet of clay. There seemed little within the established order of things that held any promise. A strong religious sense might have pointed a road to salvation. But Christian beliefs, such as they were, were held purely emotionally or intellectually and did not pervade life as a whole . . . The antidote to the precariousness of the present and the hopelessness of the future was sought . . . in experimenting with unending sensual thrills—from drink and drugs to every form of sexual excess . . . [The country] abounded with ['psychic'] lectures, magazines, study groups, fortune-tellers, astrologers . . . hypnotists and mediums. Communication with the 'other side' was almost as common as that with the friend next door.
> Though some of these experiments may have brought solace to those indulging in them, their bulk seemed to express the longing of minds that were unbalanced if not actually diseased.

† I use *pre-Christian* as a theological term rather than an historical one to denote that which has not yet taken into account God's new dispensation.

They would undoubtedly have been treated with disapproval or even have encountered the severity of the law if they had not been protected by a latent tendency in their favour. This tendency may not have been admitted in so many words, but the fact remains that many of the most 'respectable' people worshipped at these spurious shrines.[1]

This passage is not, in fact, a description of London or San Francisco in the 1970s, but of Berlin and Munich. It was written over thirty years ago, and describes Germany between the Wars. History has unforgettably demonstrated that an occult-ridden society is neither perceptive enough nor united enough to restrain the forces of occult leadership. Doctor Rollo May's comments in this situation, while something of a digression, ought not to be missed:

An outstanding example of the self-defeating effects of forgetting the daimonic can be seen in the rise of Hitler. The inability of America and the nations of western Europe to recognize the daimonic made it impossible for us to assess the significance of Hitler and the Nazi movement realistically . . . My fellow liberals and I in America, and in Europe † . . . could not even *see* Hitler or the destructively daimonic reality he represented.[2]

The importance of astrology and the black arts to the Nazi leaders is well known[3] though it is probably an over-simplification and an over-statement to assert that:

Hitler . . . ably supported by satellites such as Hess, Streicher and Goebbels, implemented Satanism to the applause of the German nation.[4]

The mention of Hitler is not to equate occultism and Nazism—the term 'occult' is far too broad to be identified with any one perversion. Indeed many occultists brought variety and contribution to the allied War effort. The then 'King of the Witches', Gerald Gardner, took part in a solemn ritual in the New Forest to prevent the expected invasion and in the latter

---

[1] *We Have Seen Evil*, Rom Landau (Faber & Faber).

† Dr. May was himself in Europe.

[2] *Love and Will* (Souvenir Press).

[3] *The Last Days of Hitler*, Hugh Trevor Roper (Pan) *passim*; 'National Socialism', Ellic Howe, *Man, Myth and Magic*, Vol. 5; *The Devil and all His Works* (Hutchinson), Dennis Wheatley, and his fictional work—*They Used Dark Forces* which is based on the reality of this.

[4] *Death by Enchantment*, Julian Franklyn.

part of 1940, the British Secret Service enlisted the aid of the astrologer Louis de Wohl in an attempt to ascertain what astrological guidance Karl Krafft was giving the Fuehrer, for it was well known that Hitler based his decisions on this.[1]

Nazism serves as a recent and vivid reminder that the occult-ridden society is no new thing, and that such a society, far from becoming powerful, becomes increasingly vulnerable to the destructive powers among those it hopes to manipulate. The main reason for drawing attention to the occult and demonic in the past is to enable us to see the true nature of the present.

To account for the 'occult explosion' is not easy because it covers so wide a range of activities. There are, however, a number of changes in Western civilisation which have com-bined to create societies which readily open their doors to the occult. Some of these factors were noted in Mr Landau's account of pre-war Germany—the weakening of the established order, together with lack of religious commitment in a 'pre-carious present' and facing a hopeless future. Even when a considerable part of the contemporary 'explosion' is seen to be nothing more than the mass media making public what has always been private, there is nevertheless a very real increase in occult practices and pre-Christian beliefs, and, like all historical events, it has arisen for many reasons.

Historically, the loss of so many loved ones in two World Wars gave urgency and meaning to the attempt to make contact with the dead. Spiritualism took on a new relevance and new respectability when what purported to be a few of 'The Few' who had lost their lives, summoned Air Chief Marshal Dowding to a séance of one of the world's most famous mediums, to thank their former chief and ask him to console their relatives.'[2]

The year 1944 saw the death of Aleister Crowley ('the Beast') yet while his name is a legend in certain quarters, and a cult has risen around him, the public at large does not take the occult seriously on account of notorious satanists, but rather because of the influence of the respectable who themselves acknowledge the reality of occult phenomena. In this con-nection Margaret Murray, C. G. Jung and Dennis Wheatley

[1] Howe, op. cit.
[2] Lord Dowding, *Many Mansions* and *Fifty Years a Medium* by Estelle Roberts (Corgi).

have done far more than Crowley, Gerald Gardner or Alex Sanders. Margaret Murray's *The Witch-Cult in Western Europe* did a great deal to establish witchcraft as a subject worthy of the attention of historians and anthropologists; Jung accomplished more than any other twentieth-century thinker to make occult theorising respectable, finding his concepts of the 'collective unconscious' and 'synchronicity' corresponding in many ways with oriental and occult theories;[1] the novels of Dennis Wheatley brought magic ritual from the archives of the British Museum to the local bookstall.

Rationalism, which in metaphysical philosophy and theology sought to explain in a manner agreeable to reason whatever appeared to be supernatural, was a prominent factor in the abolition of witch-hunts and increasing disbelief in magic in the eighteenth century. It is ironic that the 1737 Witchcraft Act was not repealed until 1951 when the decline of rationalistic thinking had contributed to the resurgence of witchcraft once again. Two years later the then King of the Witches, Gerald Gardner, was free to publish a book in which he sought to secure general acceptance of witchcraft as an orthodox religion —a book accurately entitled *Witchcraft Today*.

Scientific thought concerning the nature of matter has also changed. The view parodied in the saying 'Only if you can kick it is it real', is much out of date. In layman's language, the reality of matter is seen not to be in its solidity but primarily in forces and in structures which consist, like the universe, mainly of energy and space. Colin Wilson, author of *The Occult* has said:

> . . . In science a new cycle has begun, a revolt against the old rigid reductionism, a recognition that 'materialism' leaves half the universe unexplained. Biologists, psychologists and even physicists are cautiously trying to feel their way into new worlds. They are acknowledging at last that they are dealing with a *living* universe, a universe full of strange forces. The magic of the past was an intuitive attempt to understand and control these forces: the science of the future will be a fully conscious attempt.[2]

The foundation in 1882 by a group of Cambridge scholars of the Society for Psychical Research attracted the patronage of

---

[1] *The Occult Explosion*, Nat Freedland (Michael Joseph).
[2] *Man, Myth and Magic*,

successive generations of the most distinguished men—Henry Sidgwick, and F. W. H. Myers, being followed by Prof. William James, Sir Oliver Lodge, Prof. Gilbert Murray, Prof. William McDougall, Dr W. F. Prince and many others of equal standing. The seventy years' enquiry recorded in the *Proceedings* and in the *Journal* of the Society affords ample evidence for the validity of psychic research as a genuine science, and Myers' term 'telepathy' has become common usage. It is a great pity that there has been such a delay in accepting the findings of these men because the spiritualistic practices of amateurs have given psychical research a bad name.†

There are a multitude of social factors contributing to the contemporary rise of occultism. The *Sunday Telegraph* has called magic 'one of the boom industries of the last decade'. In installing a dial-a-horoscope service to customers in the Midlands, the Post Office was one of the last big businesses to enlist astrology in an attempt to improve profits, a trend begun in 1930, when R. H. Naylor's astrological features increased the circulation of the *Sunday Express*. This industry covers not only the mass media—films, television, drama, paperbacks—but, as Bryan Breed stated in his report on the occult in the *Methodist Recorder*:

> There is a boom in the occult, parapyschology, astrology, and all the multitude of paraphernalia which surround them. It has become a vast industry with a turnover of millions a year. Whatever occult alley you decide to explore, the industry will accommodate you with the necessary equipment for the journey.

The technological society appears not only to cause people to react towards the mystical and the supernatural, but encourages and equips them to do so.

The promise of the occult is to increase man's status, and when, as Jimmy Reid stressed in his inaugural speech at Glasgow University,

> Everything that is proposed from the establishment seems almost calculated to minimise the role of people, to miniaturise man . . .

it would be strange if such a society did not become occult-ridden.

† *The Society for Psychical Research* is a scientific body, and should not be confused with the *Churches' Fellowship for Psychical and Spiritual Studies.*

Individuals are increasingly acting in groups, because it is in a group that they find identity. The need for identity and purpose, the need to matter as an individual, is driving more and more to occult practices in the hope of having an experience which will distinguish them from their fellow-workers and fellow-commuters, and give them entry to an esoteric group in which they will have status and power. Not only does occultism meet a social need, but a psychological one as well. As was noted above, the neurotic are particularly prone to occult activity, and the schizoid personality, deprived of finding meaning in the natural world, readily turns to the supernatural, finding an affinity more with evil than with good because of his conviction of his own 'badness'.

While historical, scientific and social pressures have encouraged access to the occult, it is to meet his *spiritual*, rather than social or psychological needs that the average individual turns to occultism. The uncertainty of the future drives individuals —whether they are on their death-bed or not—to reconsider their eternal destiny, and the ecologists are driving whole societies to do the same. The churches ought to be full. The front-page headline of the *Church Times* for the week during which these pages were written proclaims: 'Unused Churches could go to other faiths.'

It is doubly sad, because not only are the churches apparently not meeting the current spiritual hunger, but it is their sterility which—more than any other reason that has been mentioned— has driven so many in this post-Christian era to turn to pre-Christian cults. A commentator would be biased indeed if he refrained from stating that *the occult explosion is primarily due to the ineffectiveness of the institutional churches*. This is not to say that the ranks of witchcraft are filled with frustrated church-goers— the problem lies further back than that. What is clear is that many find themselves within occultism because it has never dawned on them that the churches might have the answer to their search; they have never attended a church because to them the church is irrelevant. Others find themselves outside the churches, because as Walker L. Knight points out in his book *The Weird World of the Occult*:

> . . . to many people, today's church seems impotent because it is identified with the problems it should be solving. They see the church as a mere authenticator of the establishment . . . Real

estate is more important than compassion and justice. Spiritual authority is lost in a maze of uncertainty.

The broadcaster and historian Eric Maple concludes his book *The Domain of Devils* with these words:

> There can, alas, be little doubt that in terms of the struggle between ideologies, Satan has emerged indisputably the victor, for Satanic science rules the world . . . while the Churches are everywhere in disarray. There was a time when not to believe in Satan and Hell was absolute heresy, but now the opposite prevails and the clergy fall over one another . . . in attempts to re-define Satan in ways more congenial to the refinements of modern taste.

The re-defining of what are generally called the 'eternal truths of the Gospel' in terms relevant to contemporary society is an important and essential task in each generation. Unfortunately it is, like the law, inevitably always somewhat out of date because of the time it takes for new ideas adequately to be assimilated, thought through, modified, accepted (or rejected) by theologians, and then communicated to the lay person. Re-interpretation has, necessarily, to be behind the times, because it is a process. It is also a specialist-work, which, regrettably, usually means studying in depth at the expense of studying in breadth. The process of demythologising Biblical material for instance was set up to help us distinguish between material which was reporting historical events and that which, like Bunyan's *Pilgrim's Progress*, was profound theological writing but not 'history' in our modern understanding of that word. This second type of writing was designated by the term 'myth'—an unfortunate choice since the average person is likely to attach less rather than more importance to something of that name.

In general, the criteria for judging whether something is 'historical' appears often to rest on the individual theologian's belief regarding what can or cannot happen in history. Except for scholars like Edward Langton, few theologians appear to have taken any great pains to find out what has or has not happened in history, or to have taken account of anthropology, parapsychology, psychic research, comparative religion or spiritualism, before assessing what *needs* to be demythologised. In my own limited reading of these subjects, I have encountered

present-day equivalents of so many New Testament phenomena † that I would strongly discourage scholars and preachers
from too great an enthusiasm for dismissing as unhistorical
what they have not themselves experienced.

This approach not only affects Biblical exegesis, but increases
the gap between the Church and the rest of society. The so-
called 'modern' theologian who glibly dismisses any diabolic
or demonic reality is certainly out of step with modern society,
when in America, sixty-five per cent now believe in a personal
devil, and the Church of England—of all churches—officially
states the need for an exorcist in every diocese!

Re-interpretation and the discarding of certain terminology,
demonic or otherwise, would do little by themselves to create
the feeling of irrelevance that so many have for the Church. It is
far deeper than that, although perhaps indiscriminate 'de-
mythologising' is a symptom of a greater uncertainty.

Canon David Edwards, in a book review in the *Church Times*,
recently bemoaned our theological enthusiasms for

> . . . the death of God, the suicide of the Church, the unknow-
> ability of Jesus, the impossibility of preaching and . . . the un-
> canny ability of so much contemporary church life to avoid
> mentioning matters such as God . . .

Whatever justification for any of the individual items he men-
tions, the overall picture cannot possibly appeal to many today.
Compare Nicolas Stacey's assessment of what is wrong with the
Church:

> It [the Church of England] is hopelessly burdened by its enor-
> mous structure. And I think it is also burdened psychologically
> by the hope that it can eventually get back to running every-
> thing . . . much of its former power was temporal, not spiritual,
> and it's the temporal role that it has lost . . . the Church is
> continuing to decline. The young are more interested in Jesus
> than an institution . . . since its secular powers have declined,
> the answer must lie in a more personal approach to Jesus. If the
> Church is going to rise again, it *must* be spiritual. (*Nova*)

It is not wrong terminology but *a lack of spirituality* which has
been the primary cause for so many making their spiritual

---

† i.e. walking on water; stilling a storm; swallowing poisons unharmed;
raising the dead; water into wine; communicating in other languages; the
'rushing mighty wind', etc.

pilgrimage through occultism. This opinion is frequently expressed by those who are most in touch with the spirituality among young people.

Father Kenneth Leech, in *The Real Jesus Revolution* says:

It seems that religion is on the increase everywhere, perhaps, except *inside* the Church.

Oswald Guinness, lecturing to an international group of students at the L'Abri Fellowship said *'Sadly, in fact, the established Church may be the *last* sector of society to believe in the supernatural.' John Kerr concludes his book *The Mystery and Magic of the Occult* (SCM) with these words:

The Church is becoming profoundly unspiritual, even a little ashamed of religion as such. The occult craze ought to tell the ecclesiastical powers that even though their institutions are in trouble, religion as such is once again in the mainstream. Then the Church can begin to recover its . . . purely spiritual perception of reality without shame and embarrassment . . .
    A number of people are obviously waiting for such a move . . . If Christ is what the Church claims him to be . . . surely he is *the* focal point for man's spiritual quest.

In a recent address on 'New Youth Spirituality, Drugs and the Occult', Fr Leech said that the young turned to Zen, Hare Krishna, Yoga, gnostic mysticism and Satanism rather than to the Church because it did not appear to be concerned with spirituality. The most frequently heard complaint about the clergy, he said, was that they did not talk enough about God! Those, on the other hand, with a clear spiritual tradition, whether Pentecostalists or in monastic orders had considerable influence and respect.

In a *Nova* article, 'The Church and the Jesus Trip', the Rev. Michael Marshall was quoted as saying, 'I believe we are living in an age of genuine spiritual revolution . . . It's crucial that the clergy begin to pray again. That may sound absurd, but they've truly forgotten. Five years ago no youngster would have stopped me on the street and asked why I love Jesus. But it's happening. We *must* preach Jesus.' His reporter adds, 'Marshall's congregation has trebled in three years.'

The Age of Aquarius is, by the grace of God, also the age of *Godspell, Jesus Christ Superstar* and *Amazing Grace*. George

Harrison, unconsciously echoing doubting Thomas, expresses this new yearning:

> My sweet Lord, I really want to feel you
>   I really want to be with you.

The Church is in no position to criticise the theological inadequacy of those who regard Jesus as a radical hero or an oriental guru when it is her own spiritual inadequacy which has driven them to search for the Truth outside orthodox Christian traditions. Those who are called to help people who have been involved in occult practices need constantly to remember how much the Church itself has created the problems it now hopes to solve. As I wrote in *Renewal* Number 40:

> . . . where the Gospel in all its richness is both preached and lived, people need look no further in their search for identity, meaning, purpose, security and reality. Who would renounce Christ and swear allegiance to Satan if *first* they had been attracted to the soldiers and servants of Jesus Christ and invited to join their ranks and follow Him? Who would seek out the destructive powers of the psychic, the magical or the demonic if they had *first* met the transforming power of the Holy Spirit?

To remember the failure of the Church will lead to penitence and compassion. Compassion cannot spring from anger, fear or disbelief which, at a natural level, might be the more likely feeling towards those who in Black Magic or Satanism had deliberately perverted all that Christians hold most dear. Judge not—lest we too are judged, and found guilty. *The Times*' article on 'The Return of the Occult' began with these words:

> The occult is very much part of the contemporary scene. The *'instant religion'* [italics mine] of LSD, the life-style of the underground psychedelic happenings . . . the popularity of the Maharishi and his guru successors . . . —all are manifestations of the . . . occult.

It is no accident that 'religious' and mystical items form so prominent a part. The link is made between the occult and drugs, and LSD seen also as a part of a spiritual search, a means of 'instant religion'. If this is so, then what is popularly called 'the drug scene' has also been given impetus by the failure of the churches to communicate a Christian spirituality. Timothy Leary in *The Politics of Ecstasy* and elsewhere bases his case for the legality of drug-taking on the fact that the use of LSD and similar drugs is part of an individual's religious freedom. The aim, he says, of taking LSD 'is to develop yourself spiritually . . . we are producing religious experiences', and he goes so far as to say that 'drugs are the specific, and almost the only, way that the American is going to have a religious experience'. Unfortunately such religious experiences are little more than a springboard with no indications of which way to jump!

William James himself, half a century earlier, in *The Varieties of Religious Experience* had testified to the 'stimulation of mystical consciousness' by the use of nitrous oxide, and he did not question those who claimed to have a 'genuine mystical revelation' by such means. Of the situation today we read:

> While pleasure, curiosity, the desire to experiment, and even the sense of adventure, are dominant motivations in drug use, there is no doubt that a search for self-knowledge and self-integration and for spiritual meanings are strong motivations with many. We have been profoundly impressed by the natural and unaffected manner in which drug users have responded to the question of religious significance. They are not embarrassed by the mention of God. Indeed, as Paul Goodman has observed, their reactions are in interesting contrast to those of the 'God is dead' theologian . . . there does appear to be a definite revival of interest in the religious or spiritual attitude towards life.[1]

When such comments can occur in a governmental report Christians who are concerned about relevancy and communication should take careful note.

Drugs are not only part of a religious and spiritual search—they have been used since time immemorial to induce states of ecstasy—but they are also, for some, the beginning of it. Anne Leslie in an article on the new Jesus-phenomena (*Nova*, February 1971) commented:

> Ironically, drugs themselves have given young people their first yearnings towards a spiritual reality. As one San Francisco clergyman working among hippie communities put it: 'In the

[1] *Interim Report of the Canadian Government Commission of Inquiry*, 'The Non-Medical Use of Drugs', p. 329 (Penguin).

drug culture many kids develop a spiritual awareness which
the alcoholic culture doesn't have. They believe in a spiritual
reality.'

The clergyman continued with a criticism of the Church which
the Canadian Commission on drugs appears also to have felt.
'They [the kids] have seen visions and demons. Thus a conservative Christianity which hasn't "mythed away" God and
angels appeals to them.' The upsurge of various Jesus-move-
ments since 1971 suggests that he is right, and it has been known
for some time that Pentecostalism is not only the 'third force'
of Christendom but is the only force that is not in retreat. It is
more than coincidence that, using the term in a wide sense,
'Pentecostalism' holds out the promise of a spiritual experience
*and* is generally least ashamed of talking about God. In other
areas of Christendom, it is frequently those with a clear
spirituality, as at Taizé, that appear to be the most relevant,
especially if they combine with this some degree of inde-
pendence from ecclesiastical 'establishment'. Some use the
term 'Jesus-trip' for the spiritual experience that commitment
to him can bring, and while such language is questionable in
that it might suggest that he is no more than an alternative
escape, it at least focuses on him; drug trips are ego-trips, and
are self-orientated.

In *Black Magic Today*, June Johns writing of the use of drugs
in magic rituals says that all too often a religious experience
brought about in this way can convert a dabbler in magic into
an incurable drug addict. 'One of the main dangers', she writes,
'in the practice of magic today is the wholesale use of psyche-
delic drugs.' Dennis Wheatley warns of the same danger in the
conclusion to his historical survey, *The Devil and All His Works*:

> The taking of drugs to create ecstasy at Satanic gatherings has
> long been habitual. Today thousands of young people are being
> hooked in this way and become willing agents in recruiting
> others to become addicts.

Drug-taking, whether apart from occult activities or within
them is part of the same spiritual search, a search which can be
attributed to the Church's spiritual sterility.

Drug addiction is spiritually hazardous and opens the doors
to the demonic, but so does *any* addiction. Addiction is an area
of life over which the individual has insufficient or no control.

There is therefore no such thing as a 'right' addiction—not even to God. 'Puppet on a String' made a good song, but will never be a hymn! A daily prayer of Anglicans asserts that God's service is 'perfect freedom', yet, as Michael Green reminds us, in *Jesus Spells Freedom*, the Church scarcely exhibits freedom as a leading characteristic, and is indeed in 'appalling bondage' especially to tradition.

Addiction to success or to status—or to tradition—is no less *spiritually* dangerous than addiction to drugs. In fact, as society and the Church positively encourage the former, such states may be a greater spiritual hazard because the danger goes unnoticed. 'Deliver us from evil' must first be the prayer of Christian ministers and workers, so that they are free from *their* addictions before seeking to free others.

So if the Son makes you free, You will be free indeed. (John 8:36)

# CHAPTER THREE

# THE OCCULT JOURNEY

*Don't ask a man to drink and drive*

FEW WOULD DISAGREE with the value of that advice—even if they chose to disregard it. Such a warning is clearly based on experience, and given in an attempt to prevent further suffering. Stories about drunken motorists who have managed to drive safely do not make such warnings unnecessary. Indeed, it may be argued that such a warning is more urgent if there appear to be a fair number who give a misleading impression that drinking and driving is not potentially dangerous. No one would assume from such a warning that all drinkers get killed, or that the teetotal are accident-free.

Similarly, warnings about the dangers of occult practices (whether given by Christians or others) are based on experience, and given primarily to prevent unnecessary suffering. Stories illustrating the benefits of occultism cannot invalidate cases which show its dangers. Such warnings emphatically *do not* imply either that all contact with the occult is spiritually fatal, or that everyone who has avoided occult practices is spiritually healthy—my comments about the Church would be very different if the latter were true!

The reason for outlining occult practices, or, more correctly, of practices which writers commonly include under that heading, is to provide some knowledge of the occult as it impinges on, causes, or aggravates the spiritual problems of those in need of help. This outline is not written to encourage readers to study it more deeply, but rather to save them having to look elsewhere. Involvement in helping those who wish to come out of occult or magical practices will furnish the helper with a mass of detail about such activities. What follows will provide no more than the context of such experiences, and will assist the counsellor to assess the sufferer's way of life, for it will be rare that anyone is in some spiritual bondage without something in his own life, or the life of his family, having made them vulnerable.

## THE PSYCHIC

Many of those engaged in occult practices attach great importance to the development and exercise of 'psychic' powers, and to 'hearing' and 'seeing' that which is not normally perceived by the five senses. If such impressions are to be described they have invariably to be clothed in imagery of sight or sound, so 'hearing' and 'seeing' become a necessary although not always literal description. Mention has already been made of Psychical Research and Parapsychology. Those interested in the scientific evidence for Extra Sensory Perception (ESP) and wishing to pursue the matter further will find ample material in the volume of essays, *Science and ESP* (ed. J. R. Smythies) and its Appendix 'A Guide to the Experimental Evidence for ESP'. The non-specialist will find a wealth of material in the popular press, since half the population claims to have experienced the 'I've-been-here-before feeling' (known to psychologists and others as the *déjà vu* phenomenon), and four out of ten claim to have had premonitions; and the rest enjoy reading about it.

To take just one example by way of illustration. It comes from the biography of Wing Commander Stanford Tuck, and has an air of authenticity about it, not least because it is so casually mentioned, and not written to support any particular view-point on these matters.

On June 21st, 1941, a fine, warm day, Joyce [Mrs Tuck] had the afternoon off. At *five minutes past two* [italics mine] she was in her room at home, sitting at her dressing-table brushing her hair. All at once the big, oval mirror seemed to shimmer and ripple like a sheet of water and she reeled forward, sick, faint, breathless. Inside her a voice was screaming: *Something has happened to Robert!* The sensation passed in a moment or two, but the conviction remained. She wanted to run to the 'phone to ring up Coltishall, but somehow she resisted the urge. Throughout the afternoon she fought to reason the thought away—mental telepathy was all bunk, like horoscopes and fortune-telling! She

was over-tired, that was all . . . As she was going into the lounge
at tea-time . . . the newsreader's voice struck at her: 'One of our
pilots is missing. . . .' She . . . looked up and said quite calmly:
'That's Robert. It's Robert that's missing.' And she was right.
(*Fly For Your Life*)

Tuck's Luck as it was commonly called, had indeed run out,
when *he* first looked at his watch it was *eleven minutes past two*—
and he was in his rubber dinghy after baling out of his crashing
Hurricane.

At a more scientific level, as long ago as 1921 Dr Brugmans at
Groningen University set up a soundproof room with a plate-
glass window in the floor which looked down on another room
in which a blindfolded student sat surrounded by curtains as if
in an open-topped box. Those in the upper room picked random
squares on a chess board by drawing numbered slips of paper
from a bag. The student below them, would put his hand
through the curtains and place his finger on the particular
square to which he felt that, by telepathy, they were directing
him. In just under two hundred experiments, the student
placed his finger on *fifteen times* the number of correct squares
that he would have done by *chance*. Fifty years later the same
experiment is conducted by the American Society for Psychical
Research with the refinements of closed-circuit television which
enables the rooms to be at different ends of the building.

Christians need to distinguish between the uninvited psychic
awareness which Mrs Tuck experienced (and which is fairly
common between married people), the truly scientific investigation of which I have given just one example, and the deliberate
development of psychic abilities and telepathic powers.
Christians are divided on the right attitude to such natural
abilities. On the one hand there are those who see them as
potentially dangerous and to be ignored or even renounced,
and on the other, those who feel that any natural gift is a gift
from God, and is not dangerous if used properly. Having
witnessed a number of such discussions I am convinced that
those who speak from pastoral experience are united in wishing
to discourage any deliberate development of psychic powers.
Those who state that such powers are all right if dedicated to
God's use and not to self-advancement, speak more from a
theological view-point, for to them any apparent denial of life
seems to call in question the redeeming work of Christ. While I

agree that the Incarnation calls us to be life-affirming rather than life-denying, as I am writing on the pastoral care and guidance of people there is no alternative but to warn of the dangers of psychic development—human nature, as we say, being what it is. Those who have unsought psychic experiences if they share them at all—and the majority do not for fear of ridicule—do so because they bring as much anxiety as anything else. I remember a priest who worked abroad telling me of the distress he suffered when he would *know* on picking up a baby at baptism whether it would shortly die or not. The same minister 'saw' the fatal car crash of a relation the day before it happened.

In a volume of *Pastoral Psychology* devoted to Parapsychology and Religion, the Rev. Dr Roy Grace wrote:

> There are dangers [in parapsychology] to be sure . . . There are dangerous paths of psychic research and there are safe ones, as Hugh Lynn Cayce, son of the famed Edgar Cayce,† has pointed out. Some would like to possess the powers of fore-sight like Jeanne Dixon, or to hallucinate . . . Some persons have exhibited signs of obsession or possession. Two young women became schizophrenic and began to hear voices. I am not able to determine whether this manifestation came from their subconscious minds, or whether it was genuine possession. Deliverance came with exorcism in the name of Jesus. (Vol. 21, No. 206)

It is not only Christians who warn of the dangers of psychic development. Doctor Harmon H. Bro, writing in America's most successful occult monthly, *Fate*, relates the psychological dangers of psychic development if the motivation is selfish. He warns against cultivating psychic ability 'for motives you cannot disclose to your most respected associates'. (This the American psychologists term 'set', and mean by it the attitudes, intents or purpose with which a person enters a particular experience.) Psychic development opens the aperture between the uncons-cious and the conscious, and is recommended only to those who are 'free from mental and emotional problems' but, as Dr Bro asks, who *is* free from mental and emotional problems? (Certainly not those who would most fervently assert that they were!) When a Christian, like the Rev. George Bennett in a

† A psychic healer of great power. He treated 30,000 patients and died in 1945.

leaflet on *Spiritual, Psychic and Radiesthetic Healing* says that 'the psychic world is fallen and to open the door invites evil powers' he is describing in theological language what is psychologically well known. Doctor Harmon Bro's articles illustrate, albeit in non-demonic language, the dangers of which Christians are so aware:

> Untold numbers of individuals undertake cultivation of psychic ability with a set towards personal or professional notoriety, towards gambling advantage or sexual conquest—and appear to achieve paranormal phenomena with few ill effects. But *far more persons who try the same procedures for these same reasons embark on a course of increasingly distraught behaviour, compulsive actions, alienation from friends and relatives and finally multiple-personality symptoms or suicide.* [Italics mine]

A more accurate catalogue of symptoms of demonic oppression and possession would be hard to imagine, especially when coupled with his comments about twenty-two cases in his own files of individuals whom he has observed for periods ranging from four months to twenty years who engaged themselves in cultivating their psychic ability. Half of them, he writes, 'showed mental and physical illness, divorce, vocational calamity, drug addiction and sexual deviation'. 'I shall not soon forget the power-driven widow who frantically burned incense in her bedroom to rid her of "evil entities" . . . as she withdrew from her friends and family into a hate-supported schizophrenic world.'[1]

The big difference is between the unsought psychic experience and that which is deliberately cultivated. To quote George Bennett again, '*It is when we set out deliberately to experience this kind of thing that the trouble starts.*'

The danger of psychic development is nothing new to the occultists. Dion Fortune (Violet Mary Frith) started her study of analytical psychology and later of occultism because of experiencing a 'psychic attack' from her employer. Among her numerous books and novels on the magical is one entitled *Psychic Self-Defence.*

Perhaps the last word on psychic development should be the Rev. Dom Robert Petitpierre's observation that the psychic is

---

[1] From 'Dangers of Psychic Development', by Dr Harmon H. Bro, in *Fate*, February and March 1971.

*sub*-human, not super-human—it is therefore a retrograde step to develop it; for it is something that man has outgrown—the animals have more of it than we have!

Underlying all practices in the realm of the occult, we find a belief in psychic awareness and psychic power, and the desire to increase and develop them. Psychic powers feature prominently whether in fortune-telling or magic ritual. Magicians and Satanists will almost certainly have undergone intensive training in developing their telepathic powers. In *From Witchcraft to Christ*, Doreen Irvine described one of her powers when Queen of the Witches when she 'could read people's minds easily and know what they would say or do'.

I vividly remember one young man who wished to come out of Satanism telling me, in no uncertain terms, what he thought of the Christian minister who repeatedly sent a message to him on the doorstep to say that he was out, while he himself knew perfectly well that the minister was at home. He persisted in asking for him, until the minister could continue the deception no longer! It certainly adds variety to pastoral counselling sessions to be told what one is thinking—especially if one is fearful, although it can work more positively. The same person on one such occasion very clearly 'picked up' a great sense of joy and peace from myself and my friend in turn, as, more out of desperation than devotion, we turned our minds away from the problem to the person of Christ. 'It's coming from *you* now!' he exclaimed joyfully as he sensed the peace and joy of Christ's presence in each of us.

> The life-story of Jesus is a psychic narrative from beginning to end.

So begins Maurice Elliott's *The Psychic Life of Jesus* in which he substantiates his claim in doubting whether there is a single sign or wonder done by Jesus 'which has not been classified by psychic science'. If, as such spiritualists claim, the 'miracles' and signs of the Gospels are psychic manifestations, how can the Christian distrust the psychic on the one hand, yet rejoice in its apparent manifestations on the other?

Firstly, because of the dangers of psychic development, which, as we have seen, both psychologists and occultists warn about. Secondly, because as Jesus was 'without sin'

(Hebrews 4:15), his 'set' was free from the selfishness which makes psychic development hazardous. Thirdly, there is no indication that Jesus took any steps to develop his psychic ability, or that he deliberately sought 'psychic' experiences. Fourthly, there is a distinction between *psychic* awareness and power and *spiritual* awareness and power. It is to the latter that Christ's miracles of healing and exorcisms seem to belong, judging by the fact that almost without exception those who today have a Christian ministry of healing, or of discernment (1 Corinthians 12:4 ff.), not only insist that it is a spiritual God-given ability but also that such ability is quite different from the psychic insights at a natural level. Spiritual gifts, as Michael Harper points out in *Life in the Holy Spirit*, 'are not permanent endowments, but momentary manifestations' given by God for a particular situation *as needed*. Natural abilities on the other hand operate independently of such times of usefulness. The spiritual flows through the person; the natural, the psychic, flows from the person. This is why spiritualists and others are reluctant to undertake exorcisms because of the heavy demands made on their psychic energy, while those who have disciplined themselves to be nothing more than 'mediatory' healers (see Chapter One) often feel refreshed and even exhilarated after ministering in this way.

The late Fr Gilbert Shaw, an authority on most subjects in this book, wrote (in personal letters in my possession):

actual knowledge [of spirits, demons, etc.] is made known through the ministry of the Holy Spirit and not through the psychic of the Christian being taken charge of by that which is being discerned. The Christian stands within and applies the supernatural—the life of the spirit, which is quite distinct and separate from that of the psychic. The natural—the spiritualist —however much he may claim to use spirit is working within the psychic. It is that we have to make clear in the whole question of healing. . . . Fallen angels and disembodied human souls may, and do, use the psychic, for that is their means of communication; angels and saints only communicate in their own sphere of the timeless, which is spirit. Healing, which originates directly from the transcendental Person of Christ . . . in contrast to natural healing which originates in the Divine Immanence in nature, proceeds to affect the whole man from the sphere of spirit, and not of psychic; hence the pre-requisite of faith.

After pointing out the confusion caused by the theistic language of natural healers who do not know the theology of prayer or understand the difference between natural and Christian prayer, he continues:

> I am afraid that many clergy with their lack of training in ascetical theology and their ignorance of mystical theology, fail to understand this, and their attitude is all too often sub-Christian and their practice nearer the paganism of Aesculapius than the spiritual resources of the Body of Christ.

## SUPERSTITION

The first stage of occult involvement is superstition, which as Jung has shown, is complementary to rationalism for it provides something for those who have starved their spiritual faculties. Superstition has been described as a 'form of personal magic which is used for coming to terms with the unknown'. It is more than wrong beliefs, and both Freud and Jung agree that superstitious practices are rooted deeply in man's unconscious mental processes.[1] This would account in some measure for the persistence of superstition among those whose reason or beliefs deny any reality behind it. One can easily recall such incongruities as Christians touching wood, or having 'lucky' horseshoes at weddings. 'May God bless her and all who sail in her,' is the usual prayer at the launching of a ship, accompanied by the breaking of a bottle of champagne—(originally) to placate the gods!

Enough has already been said of Hitler and superstition. One wonders whether Churchill's penchant for stroking black cats and Eisenhower's gold coin, together with the goats, canaries, lions, donkeys, wolfhounds, geese, dogs, Himalayan bears and rabbits to be found among the mascots of the Allied Forces, even if they did not contribute to the allied victory, created a certain 'balance of power'! Eisenhower, unlike Presidents Lincoln, Garfield, McKinley, Harding, Roosevelt and Kennedy, was not elected to the Presidency at any of the twenty-year intervals following 1840 (i.e. 1860, 1880, 1900, etc.) and, unlike them was not—according to American belief—scheduled to die in office. The extent of superstition based on these six coincidences will be readily apparent at the 1980 election campaign.

[1] *The Psychology of Superstition*, G. Jahoda (Allen Lane/Penguin).

Modern technological man seems more rather than less prone to superstition. Superstition ran riot when Apollo 13, launched at 13.13 hrs. met with near disaster on the 13th. Even at ordinary launchings it is said that there are more crossed fingers, crossed arms and crosssed legs among the NASA personnel than at a contortionists' convention. One of the flight directors insists on wearing first a white, then a red and finally a gold shirt at specific stages of each mission.

Trans-Atlantic air passengers must get small comfort from the fact that at times their lives will be in the hands of pilots who will not entrust themselves to the machine until they have first spat on the wheels. Will the insurance companies soon be encouraging all passengers to use their saliva in this way?

Computers are now used to produce ten-thousand-word personal horoscopes, but superstition goes even further. One American Company which selects all its employees according to their zodiacal sign is unable to use its computer to assist in the selection, because it is biased—it is a Leo! Computer programmers often refuse to feed their machine blue cards because of their belief that it is female. It is interesting to conjecture whether the advance of Women's Lib. will strengthen this conviction, or whether blue cards will once again be used in the belief—or hope—that computers are male after all.

Many superstitions have, or have had, some basis in fact. For example, the reluctance to be the third person to light a cigarette from the same match may be traced to the First World War trenches, when the enemy would have had the opportunity to load and aim during the first two lightings. Most superstitions, however, cannot be definitely traced, or have ambiguous beginnings. 'Touch wood' is, according to one's inclination, a pagan action associated with the oak tree or a nominally 'Christian' action associated with the Cross. It is almost certainly the former which, at a later date, was re-interpreted by the Christian society. The reverse process is now very evident in our post-Christian culture, when our Lord's Cross, the Crucifix and a St Christopher medallion have for many become pagan charms.

In Britain, such 'charms', together with a vast array of pens, key rings, brooches, ornamental pixies and cats, door knockers, replica horse-brasses, semi-precious stones and charms, are labelled 'lucky' and it seems that not even the Trade

Descriptions Act will ever check the increasing use of 'lucky', such is the business which superstition encourages. Ten *million* rabbits' feet are sold every year in the United States . . .

Peoples' commitment is usually a progressive thing—they are drawn further in their knowledge of a subject, or their religious experience. The importance of superstition lies not in the subject itself but as a stepping-stone to other things. Its dangers lie not so much in the actual superstitious actions as in the thinking, or rather not-thinking that lies behind them. The superstitious do not know where they stand, and thus are exposed and vulnerable in a way that the militant atheist, the loyal communist or the committed Christian is not. For superstition is based on half-belief. This not only makes the superstitious so vulnerable, but should exclude superstitious practices from those whose lives are based on total belief and commitment of whatever nature. To the Christian, of course, superstition not only dilutes belief with half-belief, but verges on the blasphemous, for it ascribes to created things, black cats, mirrors, salt, wood, etc., powers which rightly belong only to the Creator. If a Christian commits the happenings of the coming day to God for his fatherly guidance, *then* to feel that the day will go 'better' because one of God's creations, a black cat, walks across his path, is to suggest that God is at the mercy of his creation.

Superstition far from being harmless nonsense then, is a symptom of mental and spiritual weakness, and should be the common enemy of materialists, humanists and Christians alike.

## ASTROLOGY

Foremost among today's superstitions is astrology. According to a National Opinion Poll survey twice as many people read their horoscopes every week as read or hear anything from the Bible. It seems that the woman who told the television interviewer that she read her horoscope 'every day—*religiously!*' was speaking for a large number of the population.

What Martin Luther called 'the shabby art' is thriving once again, having been discouraged by the Reformation and Rationalism. Carl Jung is frequently quoted as saying that astrology 'rising out of the social deeps . . . knocks on the doors of the universities from which it was banished some 300 years ago'. Had he been writing in the 1970s and not the 1930s he would have no longer described it as knocking at the door. With university courses in Astrology and 24-hour Zodiatronic telephone services providing computerised horoscopes on over two thousand American college campuses, such a statement sounds very outdated. In fact later in his life he wrote that the 'heyday of astrology was not the benighted Middle Ages, but is the middle of the twentieth century'.

The basis of astrology is the alleged influence of the planets on our lives, either on their past, present or future. There are certainly indications that there is some truth in this possibility. A great deal of interest has been aroused by the Astra Research Centre for Planned Parenthood in Czechoslovakia where a Dr Eugen Jonas believes that conception is most likely to occur in the same moon-phase as the mother's own birth, and that the position of the moon influences the sex of a child. Absolute nonsense, of course, until one learns that his birth control method based on these and similar beliefs has proved ninety-nine per cent effective in over twenty-thousand cases, and that his work is backed by UNESCO and financed by the Czech government.

Nat Freedland, in *The Occult Explosion*, from which the details of Dr Jonas' work have been taken, writes of other fields of scientific study where the possibility of influences other than the sun and moon are apparent. A factor which does not as yet seem to have been considered is the seasonal variations of diet, fresh air and exercise to which a mother and child are subject. I suspect that the average level of physical and mental health is not the same in Britain at the end of a typical August as it is at the end of a typical February—the cause being little or nothing to do with the stars.

There may be thought to be four types of astrology.

Firstly there is Popular Astrology. By this I mean the generalities which constitute the astrology columns of so many papers and magazines, on which the following story is an apt comment.

A student of psychology at the Sorbonne University in Paris wanted to write his thesis. He put a classified advertisement in a newspaper and passed himself off as an astrologer. For a prepaid fee of 20 francs . . . he would cast a detailed horoscope for each applicant. He received about 400 customers and was thus able to finance his own studies. *He gave the same horoscope to all 400 customers, paying no heed to the signs of the Zodiac* [Italics mine]. His only consideration was the psychological aspect: telling everyone that a good future lay ahead of them, and implying positive character traits in everyone, for people like to believe such things and hence would not regret having paid the fee. He received many letters of appreciation, since the horoscope covered almost everybody's situation. The student then wrote his dissertation and passed his degree with honours. (Dr Kurt Koch, *Between Christ and Satan*)

Another story is told of a newspaper astrologist who fell ill unexpectedly(!). The editor substituted out-of-date horoscopes for many months without detection. Except for the astrologers who actually write such columns, this popular astrology is too general in its application and vague in its content to be taken seriously even by many professional astrologers. Michael Flanders and Donald Swann in their song *My Horoscope* express its triviality nicely:

Jupiter is passed through Orion and coming to conjunction with Mars;
Saturn is wheeling through infinite space to its pre-ordained place in the stars.
And I gaze at the planets in wonder at the trouble and time they spend
All to warn me
*To be careful in dealings involving a friend!*

The second type of astrology might be called Business Astrology. This is the increasing tendency to use astrology to find the propitious moment for starting business transactions, initiating publicity campaigns, planning social events and even elections. It is not only such obviously astrologically orientated ventures as *Hair* that employ the services of a professional astrologer. A growing number of people seek astrological advice for their economic decisions, whether in stocks and shares or in betting. An American has written a book *Astro Economics* in which he relates the apparent planetary influence over two hundred years on the booms and depressions of American economy.

In politics, there seems to be no lack of interest in such things. England can boast George Rogers, and the States, Ronald Reagan. The latter has found the perfect alibi in a standard response to questions from the press, 'I am no more interested in the subject than the average man.' If the *Occult Gazette* is anything to go by—and it probably is not—then Harold Wilson is to be given credit for losing the Premiership in 1970 by refusing to postpone the General Election until October when 'six planets in Scorpio would have swept him in, and the conservatives would have been annihilated'. Maybe such belief in planets with socialist tendencies has arisen to balance the well-established conviction of the allegiance of the Almighty to the conservatives!

The third area of astrology is that of Character Analysis. Jung used astrology in this way as a basis for character assessment among his patients, in the belief that he obtained relevant material for psychoanalysis. This involved no prediction of any kind, and thus was in harmony with his theory of Synchronicity where everything that is born or done in one moment of time has the qualities of that moment of time. This is far removed from the vague generalisations of popular newspaper astrology, and need be nothing more than a purely mathematical calculation based on the exact time, date and place of a person's birth. In 1932, the American astrologer Evangeline Adams was brought to court for her activities, and offered as her defence to do a 'blind' horoscope on any birth data provided by the judge. Her personality sketch of Mister X was so accurate that the judge said that she had 'raised astrology to the dignity of an exact science', and found her not guilty. This decision made New York one of the few states where it is legal to advertise and charge fees for professional horoscoping, a state of affairs not reached in Britain until the repeal of the (1735) Witchcraft Act in 1951.

Before turning to the fourth type of astrology, this is the place to mention that there are two types of astrologer—the mathematical and the 'mantic'. The former, like Britain's professional astrologer Roger Elliot, limit themselves to what can be arrived at mathematically—to personal traits and character. For them astrology is primarily a science.

The second type of astrologer is the 'mantic'. This comes from the Greek 'mantis', a soothsayer or diviner, and means simply 'pertaining to divination'. The introduction of such an unfamiliar word has the advantage of at least half-explaining Chiromancy; Crystallomancy; Demonomancy; Hydromancy;

Lithomancy; Oneiromancy; Sciomancy and the sixty-six other '——mancies' which the occult arts, past and present, have inflicted on our language! The mantic astrologer regards it more as an art than a science, and brings to it a far greater freedom of interpretation, together with insights, and as many means of knowledge as are available to him, mental, psychic or spiritual.

Accurate foretelling may come about through many means, and the following is nothing more than an encouragement to the reader to add to the list. Probability based on rational deduction must account for most accurate predictions, and in everyday life comes into action when boiling an egg or catching a bus. Some prediction is only apparent because the senses are geared to selective attention and interpretation. The sudden appearance of so many cars identical to the model one has so recently purchased is not an objective fact, but our own interest in the model has made us select from, and focus on, certain items in our lives and ignore others. A similar mental process will take place in the life of a person who is living with a mapped-out character or a mapped-out future. This verges on suggestion, which must of course play a prominent part in the credibility of astrology. One does not have to believe in the influence of the planets to realise that it would be highly dangerous to inform many people that they were accident-prone. It must not be thought that astrologers are devoid of either logic or intelligence. To say to a man that he will one day marry, or to a wife that her husband will die before her, logically places them both in the position where (this side of the grave) neither can deny these statements. It takes only a modicum of intelligence to say with genuine conviction to a teenage girl that she will shortly fall madly in love, to a middle-aged woman that she will face times of depression, or to a man in his sixties that he faces a time of change and uncertainty.

The historian will be familiar with the art of prediction by comprehensiveness and ambiguity exercised by the oracle at Delphi. In modern terms this would lead to a 'prediction' that 'either you will make new friends or face a period of loneliness' or to the statement which really says nothing, for example, that 'the best side will win'.

When allowance has been made for the multiplicity of factors which could individually or in some combination make accurate prediction possible, including even a too-ready acceptance of the powers of telepathy and other extra-sensory abilities, there remain cases, and they are not rare, when mantic astrology is not immune to the workings of unknown, and not always beneficial, forces.

The following story illustrates the dangers of dabbling in the 'mantic' aspect of any occult activity.

> A minister who saw his mission as fighting superstition had a horoscope cast for the sake of study. He wanted to prove that horoscope casting was just superstition and deceit. He had to pay a large fee because a detailed horoscope was cast for him. He now waited confidently, believing that the horoscope would not fulfil itself. But he was amazed to see that the prophecies were fulfilled. For eight years he observed that all the predictions came true, even to the smallest details. He grew uneasy at this and reflected on the problem. It had indeed been his preconceived idea that it was all based on suggestion and superstition. Yet he knew that as a Christian he had not been the victim of suggestion. Finally he saw no other way of escape than to repent and to ask God for His protection. The thought came to him that he had sinned through this experiment, and had placed himself under the influence of the powers of darkness. After his repentance he discovered to his surprise that *his horoscope was now no longer correct* [italics mine]. Through this experience the minister clearly understood that demonic powers can be active in astrology. (Dr Kurt Koch, *Between Christ and Satan*)

Professor Robert Carrigan in an important article in *Pastoral Psychiatry* (December 1970) called 'The Revival of Astrology—Its Implications for Pastoral Care' says that astrology is increasingly invading the pastor's counselling sessions. Together with the problems of occult enslavement illustrated by the last story, is the one caused by astrological orientation. He related an angry young woman at a marriage counselling session saying, 'It's no wonder my husband and I can't hit it off, we were born under the wrong signs!'

The dangers are obvious. Doctor Schrank, a medical superintendent writing on the psychology of superstition states 'We can see how dangerous astrology is by the way it produces serious psychic disturbances, a fear of life, despair and other disorders . . . astrology paralyses initiative and powers of judgment.'

Psychologically there are three principal dangers—to project outside oneself the control and destiny of one's life; to retreat from responsibility and personal commitment; and to reinforce weaknesses by conditioning.

Spiritually involvement in one thing leads to another, and Madeleine Montalban, a writer on astrology, is not alone in seeing it as '. . . the basis of all magic'. 'When someone comes to me with a problem,' she says, 'I first read the source of their troubles in their chart, and then help them by casting a favourable spell.' But it is not simply as a starting-point that Christians are wary of mantic astrology. The late Fr Kenneth Ross once summed up the Christian position very clearly (*Church Times*, May 1964):

> In the application of these alleged branches of knowledge there is usually a distinctly irreligious element. The more you believe that things are preordained and inevitable, the less place you can give to human freedom and responsibility and the less room can be found for God.
>
> Magic and religion are mortal enemies, for, whereas magic tries to use the supernatural for its own ends, religion seeks to be used by the supernatural for God's ends. Hence the Church's opposition to spiritualism but not psychical research, to astrology but not astronomy, to fortune-telling but not scientifically controlled character-assessment.

Roman Catholic teaching on the matter is equally plain. Monsignor Cristiani in *Satan in the Modern World* writes:

> To try to foretell the future, except in certain cases of divinely inspired prophecy, is therefore necessarily satanic, in the sense that it is an encroachment on the divine . . . This does not mean that we are suggesting that the thousands of fortune tellers . . . are so many witches and wizards in the pay of Satan. Probably the majority of them have merely adopted what seemed to be a profitable occupation without the least idea that it is immoral and probably diabolic. We are none the less entitled to consider that the Devil is well satisfied with such aberrations, and that prediction, in its contemporary forms, is one of the devices of Satan to ensnare humanity.

The Christian must beware of passing premature judgment on the dependence of people on such irrational things. It may be to meet the need of a *transcendent mythology*, as Dr Carrigan suggests, that people turn to astrology rather than the Christian faith as so frequently expounded. Astrologers are united in saying that the people who come to them are those in need. A widely read amateur astrologer goes so far as to say 'one is dealing most of the time with people in trouble. People only consult an astrologer when they have a problem and when all else—doctors, psychiatrists, clergymen and favourite aunts— have failed to come up with a solution.'

When the responsibility for one's own future has driven the existentialist Sartre to say, 'Man is condemned to be free', it is understandable that so many have found in astrology an alibi for abdicating all responsibility: it is more than the melody that makes 'Whatever will be will be' the most frequently requested song. The Christian's own position, and the attitude he will want to put across to those he counsels lies between these two extremes.

I remember when interviewing a well-known occult writer about exorcism, that she said in passing that I was obviously born in such a month. When I told her that she was five months out, she remarked, 'It must be that by your Christian commitment and disciplined life as a priest that you have substantially changed the real you.' Whatever the truth of her observation from an astrological point of view, she had grasped one essential theological point, that the Christian is no longer dominated by the worldly powers or orders (e.g. Colossians 2), but in Christ he is a 'new creation. The old creation has gone, and now the new one is here' (2 Corinthians 5:17 ff.). Professor C. F. Rogers concludes his study *Astrology and Prediction* with these words:

> What matters in the future is not what is fixed, but how we use our freedom that He has given us to play our part against the fixed background of His laws in Nature.

But let two well-known British astrologers Roger Elliot and Rose Elliot, the former a mathematical, and the latter a 'mantic' astrologer, have the last words, taken from statements they made on television. Firstly Rose Elliot:

> I prefer not to know too much about what is going on in my own chart.

and finally, Roger Elliot, Secretary of the Astrological Association, speaking of the stars, said:

> I would not like to feel that anyone was living their life by them.

## FORTUNE-TELLING

The twenty or so other forms of divination raise the same problems and the same dangers as mantic astrology. The reason lies not in the method used—whether it is palmistry, crystal gazing, card-laying, table-rapping, ouija or automatic writing —but rather in the fact that attempts to look into the future invite unknown intelligent forces and disturb the psychic, mental or spiritual lives of those involved. It is one thing to find in the hands of newborn babies certain heart defects showing in their abnormal palm prints—conditions which do not otherwise become noticeable until it is too late to operate— and quite another to seek a description of the future.

Most divination depends on the various means I touched on in considering mantic astrology; it is only rarely that the intrusion of deep unconscious or external forces become apparent. Crystal gazing depends on the development of clairvoyance—a gift which, a salesman claims, 'seventy to eighty per cent can develop if they follow the guidance we give'. Considering the vast sums spent by the Russian and American Governments on research into ESP it is likely to be so much sales talk. In the same article, 'Flight from Religion' (*Methodist Recorder*, March 18th, 1971) in which this salesman is quoted, comes the story that the Metaphysical Research Society sold a crystal ball to Rolls-Royce as a gift to a retiring director. The dates suggest that it was given *after* the firm's bankruptcy—obviously the donors felt more concern for the director than for the firm!

It is not the place to consider the mechanics of such phenomena as water-divining, but 'dowsing' with a rod or pendulum has the same two aspects as astrology, the present and the future. Occupation with things in the present, except when done at a distance, may employ purely natural powers, and the hazards need be no more than exhaustion at the over-tapping of one's psychic energy. In the 1920s the Bombay Government employed a certain Major Pogson, a water-diviner, in connection with famine relief and finding wells in the chronically drought-stricken areas of India. The *Indian Journal of Engineering* fully acknowledged that his four per cent error made him far more successful than machines specially designed for the purpose. It was, they wrote, a 'bitter pill', but they admitted that it was 'a notable achievement'.[1] Today the military editor of the *New York Times* can write of the 'marked success' that the engineers of the U.S. 1st and 3rd Marine Divisions are having in detecting tunnels, mines and booby-traps of the Viet Cong. Wire coat-hangers now have their place alongside electronic mine detectors.[2]

Of a very different nature is the use of pendulum dowsing to spell out messages from the dead or in a mantic way, where knowledge is gained by the pendulum spelling out words in a way similar to that of ouija. The following are excerpts from a letter from a pendulum manipulator, and quoted from *Christian Counselling and Occultism*.

> I have experimented with a pendulum . . . my deceased grand-mother informed me that a serious danger threatened my son-in-law from a car accident. This recurred several times, until one morning the pendulum moved in a most solemn manner . . . '. . . the crash has just taken place . . . Erich is unconscious . . . he has passed away . . .'
>
> I endured two days of most dreadful anguish . . . I tortured myself with terrible self-accusations. Then when no report came [There was *no* accident at all. Then she thought to herself of the pendulum . . .] 'you old crank, you can say what you will!' But the pendulum!—it raced over the table and I was cursed for my insolence, until I said indignantly, 'If they curse like that in the beyond, they are no better than we human beings . . .'

Her letters continue by outlining the familiar psychological and spiritual disturbances—the hearing of voices, and the inability to think or speak about God, which she described as 'the most serious consequence of the folly'. Although, as Dr Koch points out in his further consideration of the case, such symptoms can appear as signs of depressive or sensitive psychopathic dispositions, compulsion neurosis, schizophrenia and of alcoholic and syphilitic delirium, he concludes that 'not all occult cases which come to the attention of the pastor can be medically diagnosed'.

A frequent means of prediction is card-laying. The Tarot cards are widely used among young people. Sometimes such

---

[1] For further details see *Occult and Supernatural Phenomena*, D. H. Rawcliffe (Dover: New York).

[2] *The Occult Explosion*, Nat Freedland (Michael Joseph).

activities expose those involved to dangers greater than mere psychic or spiritual disturbance. This story is disquieting, however we interpret the powers at work in it.

> A young woman whose husband was missing from the Eastern front went to a card layer to find out whether he was alive . . . The fortune-teller replied, 'Your husband is dead.' The wife waited three months, and again visited a card layer to find out about the uncertain fate of her husband. Again the answer was 'Your husband will not return.' She went home in despair, and turning on the gas killed herself and her two children. The next day the husband returned from a Russian prison camp, and found the dead bodies of his three loved ones.[1]

It is possible that the card layers each had their interpretation overshadowed and influenced by the mother's fears; it may have been unfortunate coincidence; it may have been demonic—it is impossible to tell. It can be said with certainty that such a pattern of events is remarkably similar to the destructive processes which can be discerned when evil forces are at work.

[1] *Christian Counselling and Occultism*, Dr Kurt Koch (Evangelization Publishers, W. Germany).

# CHAPTER FOUR

# THE OCCULT JOURNEY
## —continued

Dennis Wheatley in his encyclopaedic *The Devil and All His Works* concludes by advocating that psychic research should only be undertaken under licence. June Johns in *Black Magic Today* states that the people most at risk of being recruited and initiated into black magic groups are: (i) the young and inexperienced; (ii) the lonely; (iii) the social climber; and (iv) the sexual deviants and mentally disturbed. Leaving aside (iv) it is worth noting that the remainder are socially and legally respectable and ordinary. Psychic researchers only evade the 'ordinary' category because of their scientific and intellectual abilities.

The danger of the occult, as both these writers imply, lies not primarily in the blackmail, sexual depravity, or alleged ritual murder of the black magicians, but in the involvement in scientific projects, groups or party-games of the utmost respectability. The place to begin is, after all, the beginning, and whatever other rules they invert there is no reason to believe that the practising satanist or black magician reverses this one. It sounds melodramatic to hear a speaker say that satanism begins with astrology or ouija-playing, but the truth is clearly illustrated by the warning that Dennis Wheatley has frequently made in press interviews about black magic scouts being sent to spiritualistic circles to pick up those who might be interested in 'something more'. Rollo Ahmed, an authority on the black arts, says, 'Spiritualism, wrongly conducted, forms an excellent channel for the forces of black magic.' It is the thin end of the wedge that is the most dangerous; the top of a steep hill, not the bottom, which causes a vehicle to run away.

Superstition, psychic experimentation and attempts to know or manipulate the future are, as we have seen likely starting-points for the occult journey.

## OUIJA

Perhaps the majority though, start at the ouija † board. This 'game', as some would call it, consists of the letters of the alphabet arranged either on a table or printed on a smooth board, with a free-moving pointer (planchette) or an upturned glass on which those involved lightly place a finger. If conditions are 'right' (or, as you might later prefer to call them—'wrong') the glass or pointer moves around to spell out messages a letter at a time.

The late Dr Carl Wickland, author of the spiritualist classic *Thirty Years Among the Dead*, and a famous psychic investigator, wrote in his book:

> The serious problem of alienation and mental derangement attending ignorant psychic experiments was first brought to my attention by the cases of several persons whose seemingly harmless experiences with automatic writing and the Ouija Board resulted in such wild insanity that commitment to asylums was necessitated . . . Many other disastrous results which followed the use of the supposedly innocent Ouija Board came to my notice and my observations led me into research in psychic phenomena for a possible explanation of these strange occurrences.

Jon Simons, Secretary of the Bureau for the Investigation of Psychic Phenomena, in *The Independent*, January 23rd, 1970, wrote that there can be no doubt 'that these practices have an adverse psychological effect on the inexperienced'. He prefaced this comment incidentally by suggesting that the Church had a vested interest in exposing the dangers of 'dealing with the devil'(!).

Dom Robert Petitpierre, when interviewed by *The Times* about the *Exorcism* Report, mentioned the increasing number of people who were playing ouija, and that sometimes it had produced 'the most frightful consequences with people finishing up in mental hospitals'.

† Usually pronounced 'weejah', not 'weeyah', although it is a hybrid of the French and German for 'yes'.

A minister related to me how he had been speaking at a meeting at which a High Priest of witchcraft was present. When the minister publicly said that it was likely that they could agree about nothing, the High Priest said, 'One thing—the danger of ouija boards!'

The Chairman of an exorcism study-group in this country wrote in his local paper, 'At the requests of priests and head teachers I have talked to teenagers on the verge of breakdown after frightening experiences with the ouija board.' Canon Pearce-Higgins said (*Psychic News*, March 28th, 1970) that he was 'often called in by school teachers for help when they found children were treating the board as a game'. On the ITV programme *Today* he stated that several people had committed suicide as a result, and related this story (taken here from his written account in *Home Words*):

> . . . *all these methods are dangerous* . . . one girl convinced she was in touch with her father ran into difficulties in her first year at college. Her 'father' wrote: *Darling, it is a wonderful world over here. Life does not hold much for you. Come over and join me.* She threw herself under a bus. Mercifully she was not killed . . . after 12 months she is still hearing voices (this very often happens).

The Canon then published *A Letter to a Schoolboy about Ouija Boards, Glass and Alphabet, and Psychic Experiments.*† After a widely publicised ouija-session at a school in Blackpool at which the boys had a 'terrifying' experience, he publicly stated that the dangers the boys were running into were 'quite considerable. It is disgraceful', he concluded, 'that this instrument should be marketed' (*Daily Sketch*, March 17th, 1970) and expressed, I am sure, the opinions of many people, Christian and non-Christian alike. A formal representation was made by the churches at that time (1970) to request that John Waddington's withdraw the game, their reply (January 5th, 1970) was 'We no longer make or sell the item (Ouija). It is now produced in this country by Palitoy Ltd of Leicester.' In the same month a spokesman for Palitoy was quoted by the *Evening Standard* as saying that they considered it 'a harmless novelty . . . We certainly would not market something which proved to

† Available from Churches' Fellowship or Psychical and Spiritual Studies.

be dangerous. As for Ouija the sales have been terrific.' One can certainly believe the last statement. Even a year later, however, the managing director of the firm, Mr R. B. Simpson was alleged (*Manchester Guardian*, January 6th, 1971) to have remarked of ouija

> We do not believe it has any disturbing effects, even for children . . . This is a normal happy fun-type game.[!]

That the sales declined in 1973 in Britain was probably due not so much to the 'life-cycle' of games, but rather because an increasing number of people found an upturned glass and a home-made alphabet more convenient and economical.

The Rev. George Tarleton, who featured prominently in exposing the dangers of ouija, is of the opinion that *'Ouija always effects a person spiritually, *always* without any shadow of doubt.' The scope of the pastoral problem emerges when the findings of the Rev. Peter Anderson's survey of eighty-thousand schoolchildren showed that *eighty per cent* were involved in ouija sessions or playground séances. He has done as much research into ouija as anyone in this country, perhaps more than anyone else, and was involved in a case which happened near Leicester:

> . . . where a vicar has just buried a boy who, it is claimed, committed suicide after playing Ouija. The game was said to have got a grip on his life and made him mentally unstable. One night he rushed out from his home to the fire station, climbed up the firemen's tower and threw himself from the top. Mr Anderson is at present examining the coroner's report, . . . the vicar who gave the address at the boy's funeral preached against Ouija. Later the boy's family who also practised ouija, collapsed. Father left home. The mother entered a mental hospital.

Such things could be a coincidence, but is it accidental that the spiritualist, Dr Carl Wickland, whom I quoted at the beginning of this section, was finding identical results in the 1920s?

The difficulty about dismissing ouija by saying that it is simply someone pushing the glass, only accounts for the smallest and least important aspect of the problems which ouija can create.

Any single case can be interpreted in a variety of ways. The following four illustrations are no exception. Thorough investigation would need to have been carried out before any dogmatic statement about their interpretation could be made. There are, however, items which occur so frequently that cases illustrating them cannot easily be dismissed. Such items include the apparent knowledge of what exists in the present by paranormal means; a similar knowledge of certain events in the future; an apparent contact with a person who has died; and mental and spiritual disturbance.

To illustrate these recurring items:

(i) Bill Johnstone of South Shields lost contact with his father when his father went away to sea. The relations thought that the father had either died or emigrated to Australia. Bill attended a ouija session and, like so many others, 'imagined they were pushing the glass from one letter to another . . . I asked the spirit if he knew where my father was. Back came the message—Dumfries, Scotland.' Enquiries of Dumfries council revealed that a Mr Bryce Johnstone *was* there and living at Alderman Hill Road. When father and son met, father said 'No one in South Shields could have known where I was. Bill was a baby when I last saw him.'

(ii) Mrs June Harding of Basingstoke, together with two other housewives, started to play ouija 'just to amuse ourselves . . . Then it came up with this football forecast [Leeds for the Cup, Derby the League] and after repeating it three weeks running, we got together and laid our bet. We never thought for one moment we should win—we'd never even placed a bet before.' They placed a three pound double with a bookmaker and collected £300. The press at the time said that they intended to try their luck with the Derby and the Oaks. Mrs Harding told me that they got no further guidance of this nature, and, deciding not to push their luck, dropped the practice.

(iii) A choirboy once contacted his departed grandmother in this way. When the boy related the incident to his Vicar, the Vicar said, 'I remember your grandmother as a very devout Christian—ask her what she thinks of Jesus Christ. When, after the next session, the Vicar asked the lad what had happened, the astonished boy said 'She swore!'

'Do you think it was grandma?' the Vicar asked.

'No I don't!' said the choirboy.

'Neither do I,' replied the Vicar, 'and I suggest you leave it alone.'

Similar stories in which the 'spirit of the glass' has been asked questions about Jesus, whether he is Lord, whether he has come in the flesh (1 John 4:1–3) have told of offensive replies— 'that son of a bitch' being among those more printable.

(iv) Maureen went in 1966 as a fourth former to her first ouija session in the hope of contacting the spirits themselves in order to gain power and popularity. Soon followed a period of visions, 'voices', 'footsteps' in her home, and a paralysing fear which led her twice to attempt suicide. Following an exorcism she was quite well, but refused to give up such practices so that (in the words of the minister involved in the case) 'the spirit returned'. There followed a period of increased depression, and she entered hospital for a course of electroconvulsive therapy (ECT) during which she again tried to commit suicide.

The pastoral care of such people does not depend upon understanding how such activities work, and therefore the question is only of secondary importance to those engaged in helping them, and I shall deal with it accordingly. But before I outline some of the possible factors in the working of ouija, mention must be made of 'automatic writing' which operates in the same way, and is generally classed (with ouija) as an 'automatism' because the hand or finger is supposed to work without the conscious control of the user.

Not only will its mechanism be similar to that of ouija, but its results bear the stamp of occult activities:

At a clergy gathering, a minister asked for help because something was 'blocking' his spiritual life. He told me of a close relationship he had with someone who was very dependent on letters written to him in this way. These letters appeared to have included messages from a dead relation (although in retrospect some seemed notably out of character), and they also gave him advice about the future and even indications of what would happen. Having pointed this out as an obvious source of his spiritual bondage, I left him to exorcise the letters and to break off the relationship—which he did. Not only did his ministry enter a new phase of freedom and joy, but the other person concerned stopped the automatic writing and became a Christian.

It is a help to have some idea of the possible influences at

work, and possible interpretations. There are two sides to the
question it raises—the source of the power, and the source of
the information. Firstly the power. Although J. B. Rhine's
famous experiments have proved that, for instance, the fall
of dice can be influenced by thought—even dice thrown
mechanically—it seems that generally ouija and automatic
writing tap an energy which is dependent on direct human
contact, and which is variously described as psychic fluid, Odic
force or psychic force.

The other side of the question is the source of the information,
and with this go the various interpretations of what happens.
Briefly these might be considered together under seven headings.

1. *Chance.* This might account for the success of Mrs Harding
and her friends in their betting on football results.

2. *Conscious fraud.* This might be true of a few cases, but could
not explain the majority. The difficulties of maintaining conscious fraud have been memorably demonstrated in the classic
escape-story of the First World War *The Road to Endor* (Pan) in
which Lt E. H. Jones relates how he convinced the Turks and
the Camp Commandant of Yozgad of the reality of 'the
Spook's' messages through ouija in his bid to escape. Without
ever excluding the possibility of conscious fraud it is certainly
the most difficult of the 'simple' solutions.

3. *Telepathic powers.* With the increasing acceptance of the
findings of parapsychology, such a theory can be scientifically
held, and might be used to explain the reuniting of Bill Johnstone and his father.

4. *Subconscious.* In his *A Letter to a Schoolboy about Ouija . . .*,
Canon J. Pearce-Higgins writes:

I was recently told of an interesting instance where an ouija
board was being used. There was a Freudian psychoanalyst
present, and she finally decided to 'have a go'. As soon as she
put her hand on the pointer, it started to spell out pious
uplift, mildly religious sort of material. She was disgusted at
what was coming out—soppy stuff—and presently gave it up.
Next day, after reflection, she admitted that the religious
aspect of her life was one that she had resolutely suppressed
from her conscious thinking, and that it was highly probable
that the material represented subconscious emotional and religious attitudes in herself.

The Rev. Dom Robert Petitpierre (in the *Yorkshire Post*, November 17th, 1970) was quoted as saying:

> Introducing youngsters to psychic, non-rational forces is producing nervous breakdowns. I spend a lot of my time dealing with people who cannot cope with the result of this sort of thing. It wakes up the subconscious, which then links up with other subconscious . . . There are thousands of ouija boards in existence and I believe they open doors to evil influence . . . people who open themselves to evil influences of this kind are liable to be jostled inside by the pressure of another will.

Modern understanding of the subconscious, and the collective unconscious goes a long way towards explaining the acquisition of knowledge as well as the violent and destructive aspects of what Dr Rollo May calls the 'daimonic'.

Rudolf Tischner, a parapsychologist, points out[1] the danger of such 'motoric automatisms', and admits that they can enslave persons and break up their integrated psychic structure with ensuing peril to mental and psychical health—an identical warning to that given by Dr Bro to those embarking on psychic development (Chapter Three).

5. *An external intelligence.* It would seem necessary in many cases to postulate the influence of some intelligence 'external' to those taking part. When, for instance, an intelligent message is still received although the alphabet cards have been shuffled and placed face down, the presence of some other form of intelligence is certainly as probable as the presence either of a first-rate conjurer, or that a glass table-top was used with some telepathic individual underneath it!

6. *Departed Spirit.* Ouija is a mediumistic device to contact the dead. Without taking all the messages at their face value, the influence of the departed cannot be excluded, although my story of the choirboy contacting his 'grandmother' has an all-too-familiar twist to it.

Canon Pearce-Higgins has some interesting comments about two girls' alleged contact with their 'father' who, as I quoted above, urged one to come over and join him, and led her to attempted suicide.

---

[1] Quoted extensively in Dr Kurt Koch's *Christian Counselling and Occultism*, but here from Merrill Unger's *Demons in the World Today*, a book available only in German, *Ergebnisse okkulter Forschung*, Stuttgart.

They *thought* they were contacting the spirit [of their dead father] but in fact what was emerging was the product of a longing for a lost father . . . the information about father was obviously already in their own shared memory of life with him. In this way a subconscious death wish had surfaced, as though it did not belong to the owner at all.

The Canon then continues to outline another possible cause:

7. *Evil Spirits.*

BUT, I added, if by any chance they had really contacted some discarnate spirit, then clearly such a spirit was NOT their father but one masquerading, drawing the information from the girls' own minds and seeking to destroy them.

Such a theory would best fit those occasions when the board has shown a violent reaction to questions about Jesus Christ, and when the ouija-session marks the beginning of demonic oppression (or even 'possession') in one or more of its players. The Rev. George Tarleton in his tract *Ouija* relates the following story:

It was nearly midnight when the 'phone rang. 'We've a boy here in hospital who has been in a trance state for three whole days. Can you help?' said the policeman. A few minutes later I was bombing up the road in a police car. The boy [aged 17] was lying on a bed in the casualty ward with his hands crossed and his eyes staring vacantly at the ceiling. I asked where the father was and was told he wouldn't come near his son because he had been so violent. This happened when they brought him to the hospital and tried to keep him there by force. 'He went berserk and clawed his brother to the ground and ran off into the night,' said the bewildered father . . . I asked the man when it had all begun and he said, 'When my son and some of his friends in the technical college were playing ouija.' This was becoming a familiar story. I commanded the spirit of the glass to leave him, in Jesus' Name. Within five minutes he had returned to normal, much to the amazement of all. [The Medical Officer of Health had already signed the boy in for a mental institution.]

## SPIRITISM

The editor of a school magazine who wrote that he was always eager to hear news from old boys, particularly any who had *died,* unintentionally expressed something of the hopes of the world's seventy million spiritualists. David Edwards in *Religion and Change* writes:

> ... it is symptomatic of the religious need of our time that with few external aids Spiritualism has established itself as, in some sense, an underground church ... Here ordinary mortals have found reassurance about their places in the universe, and a fellowship with the living as well as the departed. Their grief for a dead God, as well as for husbands or children or friends, has been calmed if not cured.

Among the reasons for the tremendous growth of Spiritualism Canon Edwards mentions its 'warmly compassionate approach to the griefs of individuals mourning the loss of loved ones'. It is no coincidence that two people who in their generation have each given a great impetus to the Spiritualist movement— Conan Doyle and Bishop Pike—were driven to spiritist practices by their grief at the death of their sons. It is an unhappy task to expose the dangers in practices to which so many turn for comfort, especially as the Christian Churches' teaching—or rather lack of it—has given them no discouragement from it. John Betjeman's poem *House of Rest* neatly expresses the neglected teaching of the 'Communion of Saints' as opposed to 'communication with the departed'.

> Now all the world she knew is dead
> In this small room she lives her days
> The wash-hand stand and single bed
> Screened from the public gaze.
>
> . . .
>
> Now when the bells for Eucharist
> Sound in the Market Square,
> With sunshine struggling through the mist
> And Sunday in the air,
>
> The veil between her and her dead
> Dissolves and shows them clear,
> The Consecration Prayer is said
> And all of them are near.

C. B. Moss has put it this way:

Modern necromancy, or 'spiritualism', with its apparatus of mediums, 'controls', table turning, ouija-boards, séances, etc., however tempting to the bereaved, is a dangerous error which no Christian should approach even in jest. Our fellowship with the departed is spiritual not psychic; our point of contact with them is not in the séance-room, but at the altar. (*The Christian Faith*)

A variety of terms will already be apparent, and this is partly due to the Spiritualist preferring (for obvious reasons) to talk of 'sensitives at the Spiritualist Church contacting those on the Other Side' rather than 'mediums in spiritist groups practising necromancy'! In Hasting's *Encyclopaedia of Religion and Ethics* it states that 'Spiritualism is a popular term for what is more correctly called "spiritism".' The logic of such a statement is clear. Spiritism is clearly to do with *spirits*, and the doctrines and practices of the 'Spiritualists' centre very much on the spirit world—our apparent ability to contact them, and their alleged influence and interest in our affairs. It is not out of discourtesy but for clarity that I shall use the term 'Spiritist' for activities which deliberately involve spirits, whether those spirits are thought to be 'departed', 'earth-bound' or 'evil'. The main issues which spiritist activities raise have already been discussed in dealing with 'the spirit of the glass'—ouija.

As well as such automatisms as ouija and 'automatic writing' a whole range of phenomena emerge when considering spiritist actions: trances; apparitions; hallucinations; clairvoyance and clairaudience (seeing and hearing by means other than through the five senses); telekinesis (TK, the moving of an object by a non-material force); levitation (the similar lifting of objects); apports (transporting of objects); and materialisation (the creating of objects). (It was this last item of spiritualist terminology which caused the *Daily Express* to be so amused when a spokesman for the Bishop of Exeter had said that the Bishop had been unable to appoint an exorcist because 'the person he had had in mind didn't *materialise*'!)

There is not space here to consider these alleged abilities and manifestations, nor is it important. As we have seen, for pastoral purposes it matters little whether a suicidal suggestion comes via a written message or a spelt-out one. This also applies to the precise manner in which the departed apparently make themselves known—we may leave the assessment to the parapsychologists. In general a medium, usually now called a 'sensitive', is the important link between the spirits and the seeker. The group activities sometimes resemble those of a Church although there is disagreement among Spiritualists about it being a 'religion'. To attract benign spirits they often commence with a prayer, or their specially re-written hymns—sung to the tunes of the Methodist Hymn Book.

The 'sensitive', or 'medium' (I shall use the latter term as this is not only clearer, but is used by spiritualists themselves, e.g. in the late Estelle Robert's autobiography *Fifty Years a Medium*) is then used to communicate the messages from what is termed the 'Other Side'. The simplest means which is least unintelligible to the outsider is by 'direct voice', that is to say, when the medium goes into a deep trance and speaks or acts without the slightest awareness of what he or she does. In this state the medium talks with the voice of the 'departed spirit' or 'trance personality' as William McDougall would call it.[1]

Considering the apparent status of the departed spirits who are alleged to communicate, from Plato to St Paul, the contents of spirit-messages should rate among the greatest and most inspiring works ever written. This is far from the case, and the messages received are usually trivial, and (an interesting feature from the Christian view-point) are specifically non-Christian. In *Many Mansions* the late Lord Dowding sums up the theology of these communications:

> The first thing which the orthodox Christian has to face is that the doctrines of the Trinity seem to have no adherents in . . . the spirit world. The Divinity of Christ as a co-equal partner with the Father is universally denied. Jesus Christ was indeed the Son of God as we are all sons of God.

He continues to tell how one of the 'advanced spirits' vigorously combats the doctrines of Christ's sacrifice and atonement. Such doctrines are changed in their Hymnal where 'God in Three Persons, Blessed Trinity!' becomes 'who wert, and art, and evermore shall be', and 'O Lamb of God' becomes 'O God of Love'.

When Bishop Pike (see below) asked his dead son through a medium if he had heard anything about Jesus Christ, the message received was, according to the Bishop's own account (*The Other Side*, Allen) 'a rather lengthy dissertation on the nature of spiritual development, something like the following:

[1] *An Outline of Abnormal Psychology*, Chap. xxxii (Methuen).

"I haven't heard anything personally about Jesus. Nobody around me seems to talk about him".' When in the Archbishops' Commission Report *Prayer and the Departed*, the evidence of psychical research was considered, a conclusion in harmony with the Bishop's experience was made.

> It is . . . significant that the mention of Jesus often seems embarrassing to sensitives [i.e. mediums] who claim to be in contact with the departed. This may perhaps indicate that we ought not to expect to learn much by this method about the future life of those within the Body of Christ.

The Roman Catholic Church takes a much clearer position. Father Joseph Crehan, S.J. in the Catholic Truth Society's booklet *Spiritualism* describes Spiritualism as 'vague allegiance to what is little more than a variety of Unitarian beliefs with some psychic novelty thrown in'.

Montague Summers in his classic work *The History of Witchcraft and Demonology* stated the position of the Roman Church clearly:

> Spiritism has been a sweet solace to many in most poignant hours of bitter sorrow and loss; therefore it is hallowed in their eyes by tenderest memories. They are woefully deceived. Hard as it may seem, we must get down to the bed-rock of fact. Spiritualism has been specifically condemned on no less than four occasions by the Holy Office, whose decree, 30 March, 1898, utterly forbids all Spiritualistic practices although intercourse with demons be strictly excluded, and communication sought with good spirits only. Modern Spiritism is merely witchcraft revived. The Second Plenary Council of Baltimore (1866), whilst making ample allowance for . . . trickery of every kind, warns the faithful against lending any support whatever to Spiritism, and forbids them to attend séances even out of idle curiosity, for some, at least, of the manifestations must necessarily be ascribed to Satanic intervention since in no other manner can they be understood or explained.

No other Church has, to my knowledge, had the courage to give such positive guidance in these matters, although many members share the same convictions. The situation in Britain can be illustrated by the fact that when the Rev. Michael Harper, in correspondence in the *Church Times* (January 22nd, 1971), asked the President of the Churches' Fellowship for Psychical and Spiritual Studies for an assurance that members of that organisation shared the belief that Spiritualism should not in any form be practised by Christians as it was extremely dangerous, Chancellor Garth Moore was unable to give it.†

In a personal letter to me Michael Harper wrote, 'We have found that the vast majority of those people who need exorcism have been involved in spiritism.' This is, of course, saying nothing more surprising than that a number of those who had set out to contact spirits appear to have done so!

The Rev. Trevor Dearling of Essex was reported in the press for an exorcism he had to undertake. Apparently five schoolboys held a séance in one of their homes after they had talked about Spiritualism. During the séance one boy 'saw his grandfather, who told him to do violent things, like attacking his friends', said Mr Dearling. The boy later attacked two others, and the headmaster called in the Vicar to hold an exorcism in their classroom, after which their 'nightmare' ended.

It is not merely for its theological inadequacies that the Christian warns of the dangers of spiritism; it is a warning which non-Christians also give.

Rollo Ahmed, an authority on the black arts, in a chapter entitled 'Necromancy and Spiritualism' (*The Black Art*, Arrow) writes:

> Many circles and séances only attract the most undesirable elements of the astral world. The result is the moral degeneration of those who attend, accompanied by ill-health and mental troubles which they seek to have cured by 'Healers' . . . Not long ago I was consulted by a lady who had become obsessed by an entity . . . which had attached itself to her at a 'Healing' meeting.
>
> I do not dispute the fact that spirit communication has brought comfort and conviction of survival to thousands of people, but I do contend that many methods in connection with it should be abolished.

Spirit-healing is on the increase, and it raises acute pastoral problems. If the unreliability of messages from the 'Other Side', and the danger of exposure to evil forces is true, what can be said of seeking healing by contacting the dead? The Christian

† The late Fr Kenneth Ross concludes his booklet, *Spiritualism* (SPCK), with a paragraph on the Churches' Fellowship for Psychical and Spiritual Study (CFPSS) by stating that in spite of their admirable aims, 'its exponents tend to swallow the Spiritualist position hook, line and sinker'. See below, Canon Pearce-Higgins' advice to Bishop Pike.

acknowledges the reality of neutral and natural gifts among people now living, and the present-day work of the healing Christ in and through his Church, but cannot put aside the Biblical ban on necromancy, even though the Churches' lack of interest in its own commission to heal has turned so many away from the Great Physician. There is a strong tendency to feel that if anything *appears* to be 'good', it comes from God, or that all which is supernatural is spiritual. Unfortunately, this is not true, and at a theological level shows a misunderstanding of evil. The New Testament writings indicate that a characteristic of the demonic is counterfeit and distortion. St Paul writes:

> These people are counterfeit apostles, they are dishonest workmen disguised as apostles of Christ. There is nothing unexpected about that; if Satan himself goes disguised as an angel of light, there is no need to be surprised when his servants, too, disguise themselves as the servants of righteousness. (2 Corinthians 11:13 ff.)

a theme taken up again in 1 Timothy 4:1:

> . . . there will be some who will desert the faith and choose to listen to deceitful spirits and doctrines that come from devils; (Greek: *daimoniōn*)

The Johannine writings, too, witness to this:

> It is not every spirit, my dear people, that you can trust; test them, to see if they come from God . . .   You can tell the spirits that come from God by this: every spirit which acknowledges that Jesus the Christ has come in the flesh is from God; but any spirit which will not say this of Jesus is not from God, but is the spirit of Antichrist . . . (1 John 4:1 ff.)

The character of *anti*-Christ is not only that which is against him, but is also that which 'assumes the guise' of Christ.[1]

Although the New Testament teaching would encourage us to treat spirit-revelations with extreme caution, it is well to note that such teaching was written for the situation within, not outside the Christian Church. Whatever counterfeit of Christ is to be found outside the Church, it would be logical to expect the counterfeit more among the real than away from it. Helmut Thielicke, in a paper entitled 'The Reality of the Demonic',

---

[1] Abbott-Smith, *Greek Lexicon of the New Testament*, quoting B. F. Westcott.

stated that 'Anyone who would understand history must be in possession of the category of the demonic,' and I suspect that this is no less true of Church history than it is of the history of Spiritualism. Within the Church the reality of the demonic counterfeit is nowadays largely ignored, and it is easy to understand how those who find Christ unreal and unknowable will find little to interest them in his counterfeit!

St John of the Cross warns of manifestations which are not of God:

> They [spiritual men] sometimes see the forms and figures of those of another life, saints, or angels good and evil, or certain extraordinary lights and brightness. They hear strange words, sometimes seeing those who utter them, sometimes not . . .
> . . . Still, though all these may happen to the bodily senses in the way of God, we must never rely on them, nor encourage them; yea, rather we must fly from them, without examining whether they be good or evil . . . He who makes much of them mistakes his way, and exposes himself to the greater danger of delusion; and, at least, places a great obstacle on his road to true spirituality. (*The Ascent of Mount Carmel*, Book II, xi)

Spirit-healings can be such a manifestation, and while genuine at one level, frequently 'place a great obstacle to . . . true spirituality' to use St John of the Cross's phrase. Doctor Kurt Koch, whose experience in counselling those engaged in occult activities is second to none, writes:

> Every person healed through the influence of mediumistic forces, though, suffers a deathlike blow to his faith. He falls victim to a kind of spiritistic ban.

After mentioning a well-known medium healer in the West Country he continues:

> Thousands upon thousands of people have been burdened through the work of this prophet of spiritistic spirits. And yet the Christians of England remain silent.[1]

An anxious father once told me of the violent epileptiform fits his seven-year-old daughter suffered several times a day, and how on one occasion when he was trying to constrain her wild thrashing he shouted, 'Stop it!' The child in the middle of this violent episode replied, 'I'm sorry Daddy, I can't!' The child

[1] *Occult Bondage and Deliverance* (Evangelization Publishers, Germany).

had undergone intensive medical and psychiatric care, and no cause could be found. The parents, many years previously had gone to the medium healer to whom Dr Koch refers, and the child's trouble was due entirely to this contact. When the parents repented of their action, and destroyed the accumulated literature and correspondence from this spirit-healer, and when they had turned their lives over to the healing of the Spirit of Jesus, rather than of Pasteur and Lister,† a true ministry of the Spirit began. Both the house and the child were exorcised, and the girl's appearance and behaviour at school on her return were so different that her teacher called her out to the front of the class and said, 'Look, we have a *new* Mary!'

The Rev. George Bennett of the Divine Healing Mission writes:

> I have known folk go to spiritist healers to receive what seems to be an almost immediate healing of some infirmity or another. The self-styled 'healer' has told them, or given them the impression, that departed spirits on the other side are benevolently working through them for the good of mankind. But, after a little while, the apparent healing has gone and they are now worse off than before. They have the added burden of mental and spiritual distress. They are sometimes in a frightful mess. I sometimes think that the devil would only too gladly cure a man's bad leg so long as he could get his soul in exchange! (*Spiritual, Psychic and Radiesthetic Healing*)

Passing reference has already been made to Bishop James Pike, and no study of Spiritualism in the Age of Aquarius would be adequate without mention of one who has done more than any other to establish it. That he has accomplished this was in no small measure due to his learning and integrity, and his reluctance to interpret strange phenomena as 'proofs' of anything without the most rigorous scientific investigation. Much of his own story can be found in his book *The Other Side* (W. H. Allen), and since his writing it, there has been a spate of books either adding to or interpreting his story.[1]

The story is usually taken to 'begin' when psychic phenomena started in the Bishop's Cambridge (England) flat, following the suicide of his son, although this is really more of the

† See Chapter One.

[1] e.g. *The Haunting of Bishop Pike*, Merrill Unger (Tyndale House, Illinois). *The Psychic World of Bishop Pike*, H. Holtzer (Crown, New York).

'occasion' of his involvement with spiritism. Earlier he had faced a charge of heresy, and the debate which followed showed that many agreed that a bishop should

> not be so immature, careless and unbalanced in his theological teaching . . .[1]

He had denied the divinity of Christ, and in so doing had placed himself theologically among the spiritists before he became haunted by spiritist phenomena. He was trapped by the alleged communication of his dead son through disturbances in his rooms. He contacted Canon John Pearce-Higgins of the Churches' Fellowship for Psychical and Spiritual Studies, who suggested that the evidence pointed to the fact that his son, Jim, was trying to contact him. The Canon first suggested he used a home-made ouija-board and, together with his secretary and chaplain, see if Jim contacted them. He did not, so the Bishop decided to go to a medium (suggested by Canon Pearce-Higgins), Mrs Ena Twigg, his secretary Maren Bergrud and the Canon being witnesses of the séance. He learned there that Jim's suicide followed a bad LSD trip. The Bishop went to Mrs Twigg a second time before his return to the States, so that he could find out how to contact Jim there if he needed to.

At this séance Mrs Twigg went into a trance and the Bishop was convinced that it was with Jim that he was speaking when another voice spoke through her. 'Jim' told him that he would shortly leave his Diocesan post—an act which the Bishop's resignation fulfilled later, although he had no thought of such an idea at the time. Needless to say his dependence on mediums increased, and the characters taking part in the rest of the story (whether from the 'Other Side' or this) read like a Spiritualist *Who's Who?*—including séances with George Daisley (a well-known mediumistic healer), and the most outstanding medium in the States, Arthur Ford. It was in the middle of a series of séances with Mr Daisley that the Bishop's secretary (who had attended all previous séances with him) committed suicide, thus giving the Bishop yet another reason to contact the 'Other Side'. Before her death the world-famous Edgar Cayce put in a guest-appearance and his 'message' was that she should develop her gift of healing—a sad irony.

One séance with Arthur Ford took place unplanned at the

[1] *Religion and Change*, David L. Edwards.

They got a Bishop how about Elisabeth

Canadian Broadcasting Corporation studio in Toronto. It was filmed and later shown (in part) on the major U.S. and Canadian Television networks, and, as Merrill Unger points out 'dramatically publicised to the world both the Bishop's heresies and his involvement with spiritualism, introducing mental mediumship into the living rooms of homes that scarcely knew such phenomena existed'.

The Bishop's tragic death is well known. He rented a mini-car for a trip in the Israeli desert, and when it stuck, he set out to walk cross-country in the 130° heat. Meanwhile Diane Kennedy Pike, the Bishop's third wife, had a forty-five minute vision of the Bishop dying, which included not only an accurate awareness of the unusual position in which her husband's body was lying, but the sight of his body, as a 'filmy cloudlike substance' ascending heavenwards to a joyous crowd! Needless to say she is still resorting to mediums; the only message of significance which she has received from him being, 'I had an unusual headache about three days before the desert incident'—information which she already knew, but which she is taking as a clue that the Bishop is trying to speak through mediums 'with such telling detail that his presence *can't* be disproved'.[1]

The disturbance caused by spiritist activities affects places as well as people.

Dom Robert Petitpierre, an authority on the Christian ministry involving places, was quoted in *The Times* (April 26th, 1972) as saying:

> I have found a number of cases where council houses, for instance, have something wrong, and people can't live in them. Then I very often find that there have been Spiritualist Groups or Spiritualist functions in them or in the house next door, and although Spiritualists are very well intentioned, they can let in all sorts of undesirable things.

There is an interaction between persons and places, just as a peaceful 'happy' church has been 'touched' by the prayers and presence of Christ and his people, so the same is true of negative influences. The following story certainly brings home the Christian's distress at spiritist practices, and is taken from Michael Harper's *Spiritual Warfare*.

---

*The Occult Explosion*, Nat Freedland.

In conversation one night with a minister and his wife it was discovered that they had problems with their children. One displayed the most peculiar and irrational behaviour at times, behaving more like an animal than a child. He also displayed healing powers, something unusual in such a young person. Their other son was unable to speak, although well past the normal age when children begin to talk. The parents naturally were very worried about this. After questioning it was discovered that in a previous church appointment they had occupied a house which had for many years been the home of a minister who had practised spiritualism openly and unashamedly.

One of these sons had been born there, and the other had been living there during his most impressionable years. The evil influence of the house had been felt by the villagers as well as the family.

After these facts had been established, the boys were prayed over while they were still sleeping, and the power of Satan cut off from them. Within a few days the younger son was speaking, and the first word he spoke was 'Jesus', while with the other son there was never again a recurrence of the peculiar behaviour which had caused the parents such anxiety.

The healing of the boys depended (humanly speaking) on the counsellor having a realistic assessment of the dangers of spiritism, and thus accurately diagnosing the source of their trouble. How long before the entire Church shares Dennis Wheatley's convictions, which he expressed in an interview for *Man, Myth and Magic*?

I do not approve of mediums attempting to contact the dead . . . mediums who get in touch with occult forces are laying themselves open to serious danger. The powers that mediums contact are not the dead, but evil entities, and they are very dangerous indeed.

How ironic that such authorities on the occult are more Biblical in their approach than some authorities in the Church.

## WITCHCRAFT

Witchcraft is widespread. The German Medical Information Service states that ten thousand people are engaged in witchcraft in Germany. In a BBC television programme *The Power of the Witch*, the estimate for Britain was three times as many.

It involves all social classes. While Doreen Irvine's autobiography *From Witchcraft to Christ* (Concordia) tells the story of witchcraft met via poverty and prostitution, *The Times* on the other hand once included this plea for help:

> A WITCH of full powers is urgently sought to lift a 73-year-old curse and help restore the family fortunes of an afflicted nobleman. Employment genuinely offered.

Over one hundred and seventy people offered help (including a cousin of the Earl Marshal of England) almost all of whom must have been among *The Times* readership—an interesting sociological fact in view of the general impression that witchcraft is the prerogative of gipsies. The respectability of individual witches ('witches' is generally used nowadays for both men and women) is shown by their appearances in the past on television with David Frost, Joan Bakewell and Simon Dee. While the television company expected a large number of complaints at the appearance of Alex Sanders 'The King of the Witches', their switchboards were jammed by people not complaining, but wanting his *help*. Herein lies a major attraction of witchcraft—power, power to heal in white witchcraft, power to destroy in black, although the two categories frequently merge, as witches themselves have admitted.

Just as the Church's lack of conviction and teaching on eternal life has led so many to Spiritualism, so the centuries in which the ministry of healing has been in abeyance has led to the reasonable assumption that 'spiritual healing' can only be found elsewhere. Thus one High Priestess in an article 'The Rise of Modern Witchcraft' in *Man, Myth and Magic* tells us:

> Witchcraft, despite its trappings, is just another way of life. The Horned God and Mother Goddess whom we worship symbolise the creative forces which made the universe, and which our ancestors worshipped long ago. Our religion has the same purpose as other religions *except that we believe that the creative forces can lend us power to heal and do good generally*. [Italics mine]

Many publications about witchcraft are of the soft-sell variety, and indicate only the healing and teaching tradition of witchcraft. June John's book *King of the Witches* has a photo of four naked couples having an outdoor picnic, and on it the caption:

> The notorious black mass—nothing more than a feast in the circle which witches believe is shared with their god.[1]

Even occult writers of integrity acknowledge these distortions. Arthur Lyons in his book *Satan Wants You* (a title borrowed from the Kitchener-type posters of the Church of Satan) writes:

> Researchers in the area [of witchcraft] such as Hans Holzer and Gerald Gardner,[2] being sympathetic and trying to erase the stigma from the traditional public image of witchcraft, have done a whitewash job on the entire field, proclaiming solemnly that if there are any 'bad' witches dealing in the darker aspects of the craft they certainly do not know of any. All I can say is that if they are not aware of such goings-on then they have either not dug very far or they are suffering from an acute sense of selective inattention. I have been in the black groups and such practices do exist and on a large scale.

The occult historian Eric Maple has written:

> It is a sorry comment on the religious life of Britain today that membership of the witch cult steadily advances while that of the Church declines.

Colin Wilson in his mammoth work *The Occult* says that modern witchcraft displays much more variety than its earlier counterpart and that 'It would probably be safe to say that there are now more witches in England and America than at any time since the Reformation.' Pastoral experience bears this out. In Birmingham the Suffragan Bishop is chairman of a group that has had to be formed to take into account the occult and devil-worship, and Captain Barry Irons of the Church Army is 'organising the Church Army's counselling service for those who wish to break away from the covens' (*Daily Telegraph*, December 11th, 1972). At the time of my interview with him in 1971, Captain Irons was counselling on average two people a day who wished to come out of such groups, and he has more recently reported that there are twenty-four known witches'

---

[1] A statement very different from one which the same author made in her book *Black Magic Today*: '. . . the Black Mass . . . in Britain today is a deliberate debasement of all that Christians hold dear'.

[2] Authors, respectively, of *The Truth about Witchcraft* and *Witchcraft Today*.

covens in the Birmingham district (*Church Times*, December 8th, 1972).

While I was studying in Birmingham, I heard how another member of the theological college had been helping a person break away from one of these very groups. The story went that the coven-leader met him one day outside the college, and spent some time and energy cursing him. His reply, nicely devoid of theological jargon, was: 'You'd better try harder than that, my Boss is bigger than yours!' (cf. St Augustine 'This dog is chained!').

## SATANISM AND BLACK MAGIC

The categories throughout this outline of the occult tend to merge. This is true not only of ouija and spiritism, but between the darker sides of the occult—the 'left hand path' as the occultists themselves euphemistically call it. In theory such activities as Satanism and Black Magic are separate, but one would be going against popular usage to make rigid distinctions. The prevalence of the press to use 'Black Magic' as an eye-catching headline—even to describing playground ouija-sessions as 'Black Magic Games'—has done a great deal further to blur any divisions there might have been. An example of the flexibility of terms can be judged from the fact that Douglas Hunt's *Exploring the Occult* has sections ranging from Spiritualism to Black Magic, but no section, as such, on witchcraft; Frank Smyth's *Modern Witchcraft* has a chapter on 'Modern Satanists'.

'Black Magic' might be regarded as magical practices used for selfish or destructive ends; 'Satanists', those whose particular brand of magical practices and perversions includes a deliberate act of allegiance to Satan, and of course, the corresponding renunciation of Jesus Christ and the Church, and commitment to a way of life which is not merely pre-Christian (as much witchcraft claims to be) but specifically anti-Christian. It is well known that there are those who would steal consecrated wafers either by breaking into church tabernacles or by taking them away at the time of Communion.[1] Such anti-Christian trends may not continue for long—unless there is a revival in the Church. Anton LaVey, leader of the Church of Satan in

[1] Mentioned, for example, in *Modern Witchcraft*, Frank Smyth.

America, attaches little importance to anti-Christian activities. Arthur Lyons in *Satan Wants You* explains the modern approach:

> Since Christianity recently has become irrelevant to man's current needs, it would be senseless, the Satanists feel, to embody anti-Christian elements into any ritualised form such as the Black Mass; it would be like whipping a dead horse . . . . . . The end of the Black Mass has . . . arrived, for as the authority of the Church as a disseminator of truth has declined, the use of the Mass as an inverted magical ritual has declined. If it did not work frontwards, why should it work backwards?

He quotes LaVey as visualising the day when:

> tridents and pentagrams are thrust into the sky from church roofs instead of crosses.

and as saying:

> The Satanic Age started . . . when God was proclaimed dead . . .

Oswald Guinness at a lecture on 'The Rise of Demonology' recounted LaVey saying, 'We don't break crucifixes now— Christianity is *dead*.' It is not, of course. His error, to use St John's metaphor, is to assess the life of the Vine, by the visible health of the branches, but there are certainly signs of deadness at levels.

In 1971, the Church of England for the first time had fewer than four hundred new deacons. In the same year, four hundred and fifty 'Ministers of Satan' were 'ordained' in one week in a small city in the northwest of the United States. Billy Graham, from whose book *The Jesus Generation* these last details are taken, continues:

> Satan worship is now a world-wide phenomenon. Recently a Presbyterian minister in Britain informed me that the occult and witchcraft are even more pronounced there than in America.

A Christian worker at the L'Abri Fellowship in Switzerland wrote to me: 'I feel the drug scene in western Europe will pale into insignificance once Satan worship gets under way . . . We have young people here who have reached the ultimate Satan worship. Come and see for yourself what havoc—*and what healing*—can take place in their lives!' In the following chapters we shall turn to the healing, meanwhile some further points need to be clarified. Many argue that their allegiance to Satan is not anti-Christian at all. This is far from the truth, as their oaths of allegiance make quite clear, and which I have printed at the bottom of the page should any reader wish to check this statement.† I pass swiftly over this promise, yet have made reference to it because unless the reality of Satanic commitment is understood it is unlikely that the Christian counsellor will see that the only road of salvation from such a point is in the other direction from the one to which the Satanist is committed. Nothing less than a literal *conversion*, a turning around, with, ideally, a taking or a renewal of Baptismal vows will begin to set the person right—and even that is only a beginning.

What causes this perverted commitment? Drug dependence and sexual adventures only partly explain it. There is a theological reason (strange as it may seem!), Arthur Lyons writes:

> The Devil is seldom seen by Satanists as more powerful than God: he is merely more immediate, more of a personal ally to man . . . than God . . .

Archbishop Anthony Bloom was making a similar point when he quipped that our tendency to talk of the Devil as 'Old Nick' reflected the truth that he is essentially 'one of us'. The 'immediacy' of Satan comes out also in the contrasting images of the roaring lion (1 Peter 5:8) and the patient visitor, of Revelation 3:20, who stands and knocks and says: '*If* anyone hears my voice. . . .'

The Satanists and devil-worshippers are not the only ones to heed the *loudest* voice. When Arthur Lyons writes that 'Satan has become the big friend of the little guy', he is not only making a comment about contemporary trends, but about basic traits in man, as the story of Eve symbolises. Too bad that the 'big friend' turns out to be our greatest foe, by holding out false promises of hope and happiness (Genesis 3:1 ff.).

---

† Quoted from a letter lent me by a minister: 'My Lord and master Satan, I acknowledge you as my God and Prince and promise to serve and obey you while I live. And I renounce the other god and Jesus Christ, the saints and the Church and its sacraments, and I promise to do whatever evil I can and I renounce all the merits of Jesus Christ, and if I fail to serve and adore you, paying homage to you daily, I give you my life as your own. This pact was made the —th day of ——, 19—, signed ——.'

The *New York Times* (August 6th, 1972) reported the findings of Morris Cerullo's $30,000 six-month study: that while ten million Americans dabble in the occult, a further hundred thousand worship the Devil. There is little point in elaborating the complex relationships between the Satanist 'Black Pope' LaVey; *Rosemary's Baby*; Sharon Tate; Manson; and Jayne Mansfield, for they are quoted by almost every writer on the American occult scene. In Britain the situation is less publicised because it lacks such spectacular leadership, but the indications are there all the same.

Captain Barry Irons of the Church Army, when talking of the Birmingham covens, said that, 'The biggest threat . . . lies in the Satanist groups composed mostly of teenagers and involving drug addiction, hallucinations, and suicide threats' (*Daily Telegraph*, December 11th, 1972). *The Times* of April 26th, 1972, quoted Dom Robert Petitpierre as saying that 'there are about 400 black magic groups in England and at least one in every university'. In 1970 the Annual Report of a very well-known Christian Youth Camp stated that a particular problem had been

> . . . the prevalence of interest in Black Magic and spiritualism among those attending the camps—young Christians who would one day be the leaders of parish churches, many of whom found it impossible to pray. With this came a warning that all parish priests should prepare to cope with the problem.

The only reason to consider Black Magic at all is to help Christians and others 'cope with the problem'.

Any investigation of magic is dangerous, and of Black Magic *extremely* dangerous. Douglas Hunt in his book *Exploring the Occult* spends over two hundred pages introducing the reader to spiritualism, astrology, astral projection, etc. He has a whole chapter on Black Magic. It begins:

> There seems to be something of a revival of Black Magic. Obscene and horrible happenings have been reported in the Press and more widely in certain private circles.
>
> No warning against any participation in real or alleged Black Magic can be strong enough. Have nothing to do with it, do not inquire into it, and shun like the plague anyone whom you know to be involved in it. Where it is an imitation of the genuine article—as in most cases—it is dirty, childish and

bestial. It can lead to nothing but a contemptible depravity. Where real power is involved the consequences to the operators are disastrous beyond the imagination.

In a lesser degree this is also true of the use of any paranormal powers solely for one's own advantage.

And so his chapter on Black Magic ends! The Christian is in complete agreement in dealing with the subject so summarily, and thankful to those like the Rt Rev. Cyril Eastaugh who have given similar warnings to the Church. The only reason it is necessary to stray a little into the subject is because the parish priest and Christian worker are not in a position to shun *anyone* 'like the plague' even if they have been involved in such things. It is necessary, however, to mention some related problems, and the first one which has already arisen is the problem of studying it at all.

I remember addressing a group of about eighty people— Christians and non-Christians—all of whom were full-time in the 'helping professions'. After I had shared my misgivings about the increasing tendency for teachers to suggest witch-craft and magic as topics for projects, special studies and theses, I asked for a show of hands of those who had come up against this problem. About ninety per cent indicated that they had come across this. A number of well-intentioned adults, clergy included, have studied the subject and as a result made themselves *less*, not more, able to help others.

While many aspects of Black Magic are best avoided—the initiation rites, the alleged ritual murders and political roles— it is necessary briefly to touch on the following:

(*a*) the way people are drawn into it;

(*b*) the problem of ill-wishing;

(*c*) one way in which Christian ministers can be trapped into working *for* such groups;

(*d*) distinguishing between vandalism and Black Magic in their use of churches, etc.;

(*e*) Black Magic and blackmail.

Rollo Ahmed is an authority on the black arts, and in his book *The Black Art* (Arrow) has a chapter on 'Modern Black Magic'. His work is scholarly and objective, and I have drawn considerably from his writing.

(*a*) On the way people are drawn into Black Magic, Mr Ahmed writes:

> There are a few sects today practising black magic who more or less openly announce their perverted religious views, but most of these societies exist ostensibly for astrology, mystic development, and so on, while a few of them call themselves private spiritualist groups . . .

He says that the first line of procedure is an insidious undermining of moral standards by the teaching that evil is only a relative term, that sin has no reality, and that one should give way to one's impulses. (Doctrines no longer expounded simply in secret societies!) At the beginning of the chapter we mentioned June John's observation, in *Black Magic Today*, that the young and inexperienced, the lonely and the social climber were among the more vulnerable groups of society open to the influence of such groups.

(*b*) The problem of ill-wishing, cursing, or, as it is sometimes called, 'death-wishing', is not a problem for many, because they simply do not believe it. Those who do believe in the reality of it, will either themselves have been on the receiving end of such things, or have had the pastoral care of someone so afflicted. Even if the 'mechanics' of it can be described as 'autosuggestion', the symptoms are as real as any other psychosomatic disorder, and present something to be healed whatever our personal views about the ultimate causes. The Christian minister is not committed to any particular theory of the cause, but he is committed to bringing the resources of the healing Church, the healing Christ, to the situation.

In Dr Hugh Trowell's comprehensive review of the literature of psychosomatic disorders up to 1970, *Diseases of Strain and Stress* (Institute of Religion and Medicine), due place is given to being 'scared to death'. 'This', writes Dr Trowell 'is a scientific fact . . . demonstrated by 13 letters from various doctors reported in the *British Medical Journal* in the last five years.' He continues:

> Doctor C. A. Wiggins, known personally to the present writer, gave an example . . . 'I had a note from the Superintendent of Police saying that the man . . . had been bewitched . . . and was convinced that he would die that night, at midnight, and would I examine him. I did so and found nothing wrong and

sent him back to duty . . . I saw him on my evening round, sitting on the bed dejectedly . . . The Assistant told me that he watched him from the other end of the ward, that he never moved until the first stroke of twelve, when he had fallen back (dead) on his bed.'

Further evidence has been gathered by the psychiatrist Dr J. C. Barker in his book *Scared to Death*, in which he discusses at some length the results of fortune-telling in Britain today— reputable fortune-tellers apparently never foretell death, even when they believe it will occur. What about the less reputable?

Some cases are not so easy to explain away as 'autosuggestion'. Take this case, for instance, from a private manuscript in my possession:

My friend, whom I will call Mrs Blank . . . invited a girl to spend a few days with her as she [the girl] seemed mentally and physically upset. But on Sunday she refused to go to church with Mrs Blank, so the latter went off alone. As the morning turned out sunny and warm, she and a mutual friend decided to walk to Hyde Park corner, and there waited until the traffic ceased and only a taxi was rapidly approaching, when Mrs Blank suddenly rushed into its path, was flung down and rolled over and over. The taxi stopped, a policeman appeared and said to my friend 'I *saw* you throw yourself under this taxi!' To which she replied 'Yes, but I don't know why I did it, for I don't want to die.' So he said, 'Well you had better get into the taxi and go straight home', which Mrs Blank thankfully did.

When she opened the gate of her little garden she saw the girl strolling around the house, who suddenly seeing her exclaimed, 'So you *weren't* killed after all!'

'Did you *expect* me to be killed?' countered Mrs Blank.

'Oh no,' stammered the girl, 'I was only startled at your coming home so soon!'

There is a little more to the story:

When the maid came to help my friend take off her disordered clothing she said, 'That young lady told me this morning that she belongs to a Society where the members meet from time to time and decide what they will do to the people they dislike, "and now", she said, "I am so good at it that I can kill anyone I like, even without the help of the circle." And then she added, "I don't think you will see your mistress alive again." '

Had Dr Wiggins' patient in the first example been truly *in Christ*, many other Christians share my conviction that he would not have died—and many *magicians* share it as well. A one-time Queen of the Witches writes (in *From Witchcraft to Christ*), 'people have been known to die because of the curse or spell of a black witch'. But 'the Lord certainly did not permit His servant to be harmed—I tried to put curses on the preacher but they did not work . . . I was puzzled. My powers had never before failed.' She might have added the habit such curses have of being returned to sender! St Patrick's Breastplate was written when the reality of such things was more widely accepted, and the prayer for Christ to be—and continue to be—with us, before us, behind us, in us, below us and above us, etc., is particularly relevant in such circumstances. But Christ does not only protect his own from *external* evil, he gives that 'peace of God which is so much greater than we can understand . . . [to] . . . *guard your hearts and thoughts, in Christ Jesus* (Philippians 4:7, see also verses 4–9). His love and power are as relevant whether such evil is real or imaginary, objective or subjective, external or internal.

(*c*) Sometimes such ill-wishing takes place between rival groups. Thus in *Black Magic Today* June Johns writes:

> The exorcism practised by British and European witches is more often directed against spells and curses which they believe have been uttered against them by other magic groups . . . in extreme cases [i.e. when the magicians cannot clear the situation themselves—even with the use of holy water stolen from churches!] *it has been known for them to ask a clergyman . . . to perform the exorcism for them. Naturally he will not have been told of the curse which is to be lifted. He will have been informed that the house is haunted, or that a poltergeist is troubling the occupants* [italics mine].

I recall reading this to a group of clergy experienced in this aspect of the Church's ministry—'Oh *no*!' murmured a clergyman in a loud stage whisper, and his embarrassment was not lessened by the laughter of his colleagues, whose attitude would have pleased the late Fr Gilbert Shaw, one of whose dicta was that when considering the occult it was essential to maintain one's sense of humour.

(*d*) Even a cursory glance at press cuttings on Black Magic reveal that activities have taken place in or around a great number of churches—at or near Alfriston, Bramber, Carnforth,

Clacton, Clophill, Clinton, Edmonton, Eltham and so on, not to mention the macabre episodes in various woods, or the 'crucifixion' on Hampstead Heath.

The difference between vandalism (so often such goings-on are described as the act of 'vandals') and Black Magic activities is that the latter are purposeful—either a deliberate anti-Christian desecration of something, or the using or stealing of items hallowed by Christian usage. In the absence of a defrocked priest to lead their ceremonies, the use of Christian objects—chalices, candles, crucifixes, etc.—seems to them to be the next best thing. One vicar wisely remarked that, 'The things they stole are about the hardest in the world to dispose of, which makes me think the men wanted them for devil worship.'

Vandals, on the other hand, as someone once dryly noted, would be afraid to go through a churchyard at night!

There was an upsurge of grave-robbing in the early 1960s, and such activities have not altogether ceased. It is interesting to conjecture what that arch-enemy of superstition, Karl Marx, might think at the grave-robbing, voodoo desecrations, ghost and vampire legends centred in his own burial ground, High-gate Cemetery. In 1970, for instance, a burnt and decapitated corpse was found: the police worked 'on the theory that the body had been used for Black Magic'. Earlier two skulls believed to have come from the same cemetery were found as bookends in a drawing room. . . .

The Rev. Donald Omand has some anecdotes of a less grisly nature in his *Experiences of a Present Day Exorcist* (Kimber), as well, as its title suggests, as insights into many other facets of this ministry.

(e) The main power operating in Black Magic requires no belief in the supernatural whatever—the power of blackmail. At one time it was only the groups themselves, some police and some clergy who knew about this; now any local bookstall will readily supply the public with vivid illustrations of it whether as candid exposés, or as fiction. Frank Smyth in *Man, Myth and Magic*'s publication *Modern Witchcraft* writes:

So called Black Magic groups persuade newcomers [secretly drugged of course] . . . to indulge in all kinds of grotesque sexual activities, secretly photograph them, and then use the photographs for blackmail.

June Johns independently confirms this:

> What is not generally known is that a concealed camera . . .
> records the activities and identities of the participants. (*Black
> Magic Today*)

Some writers indicate that there are no bounds to the steps
which a group will take to prevent an initiate withdrawing and
thereby undermining their secrecy. Mr Ahmed indicates that
the danger is spiritual as well as material:

> Once membership of a society of this kind is undertaken, it is a
> very hard matter to get out of the clutches of such people and
> their cult; both materially (as ex-members open themselves
> to guarded blackmail) and spiritually. The evil vibrations
> caused . . . leave impressions on the mind and soul that are
> tremendously difficult . . . to shake off. Melancholia, loss of
> vitality, delusions, suicide and positive insanity are some of the
> consequences of having dabbled in the black art.

Cases fall into two sorts, those that are the outcome of deliberate magic practices, and those arising from amateur
dabbling.

An example of the first comes from Arthur Lyons *Satan Wants
You* in which he recounts the case he witnessed at a magic ritual
designed to conjure up a demon into a young girl. 'As might be
expected the results were disastrous, and the magicians unable
to induce the demon to relinquish control of the girl's body.'
The girl ran away and was never traced.

The following is much more 'usual' in that it has a 'playing-
around' or experimental attitude to magic, an attitude which
can be no less dangerous. It comes from the files of a senior
welfare worker, and is quoted with the boy's permission:

> He talked about a group who read in the press of a vicar in
> Devon who had dabbled in black magic [!] and explained
> his technique of trying to call up the devil. One of the boys
> attempted to copy him by saying the Lord's Prayer backwards,
> holding an inverted crucifix whilst looking at a mirror illu-
> minated by two candles. He then tried to summon the Angel
> of Death in the form of a goat. Apparently the lad went into a
> trance and became so aggressive that he had to be tied down
> with bandages from which he had no difficulty in breaking
> loose. When he recovered the next morning, he had no know-
> ledge of the events but received a telegram informing him

that his grandmother had died the previous evening. [He] . . .
had been afraid to talk about this to people [including his vicar]
for fear of being laughed at.

In 1971 there was a court case in which three youngsters
admitted taking a woman's skull from a grave in St Matthew's
churchyard, Walsall. One of them apologised to the vicar, the
Rev. John Jackson for what he had done. 'It was', the vicar
said, 'one of the wonderful things that happens in the course of
one's ministry. The boy realised how stupid he had been in
getting involved with witchcraft and he asked the forgiveness
of our church and congregation, of which I gladly assured him'
(*Church of England Newspaper*, March 5th, 1971).

In this brief review of some of the main trends in occultism
it might be thought that both the trends and the actual situation are entirely negative. Not so. Although I have stressed the
failure of the Church as a contributory factor to the 'occult
explosion', it has been so that Christians may approach the
situation with *penitence* rather than arrogance. Penitence and
hope are not mutually exclusive, in fact they hang together. The
principalities and powers have been disarmed (Colossians
2:15), it is with bare fists or broken swords that they thus rush
around, while we are given the armour of God, and (so long as
we put it on—a point which some Christians forget!) we shall
stand our ground (Ephesians 6:10–20). The hope is not merely
of avoiding defeat, not even simply of winning a victory, but of
*advancing* victorious.

Prebendary Henry Cooper after his church in Bloomsbury
had been desecrated by Satanists said:

> . . . a seeking after the spiritual and the supernatural—even if
> it can be very evil and very perverted—is certainly not so hard
> and impenetrable a thing as the complacent, affluent, material-
> ist society which is all around it. These people I think are quite
> possibly *more* capable of conversion than many others. If you
> turn a crucifix upside-down, you can, in fact, turn it the right
> way up again.

*Laus Deo.*

# CHAPTER FIVE

# THE PROBLEM OF POSSESSION

'POSSESSION' TO THE majority of people, solicitors and policemen excepted, means '*demon*-possession'. Unfortunately, in general usage both 'possession' and 'exorcism' have so many wrong associations that it is only with misgivings that I use them at all. It is generally thought that there is *one* state only of demonic assault on human lives—a state enthusiastically pictured in the past in which the victim is busily tearing his (but more usually her) hair out, eyes out and clothes off, and accomplishing this metamorphosis in a stance that would make the most accomplished yogi green with envy.

There is in fact a whole range of demonic influences, of which the description above is the most extreme—and, fortunately, the most rare. Writers on the subject have a vast array of terms for the more usual, and ordinary states. Among Catholic terminology 'temptation' to 'infestation' are common (L. Cristiani), while among Pentecostalists 'oppression' and 'obsession' occur as less acute states (H. Maxwell Whyte). Others use terms such as 'bondage', and 'vexed', while there are a number who feel that to be true to the Scriptures one must use 'demonised' as it is a literal translation of the Greek. I shall further consider terms when dealing with demonic states and their relation to mental illness. Meanwhile I shall use three terms—for the mild, the more serious and the acute demonic states—demonic *influence*; demonic *oppression;* demonic *attack.*†

† *Influence* is not so limited as 'temptation'.
*Oppression* is a word naturally used by the people themselves to describe their state, and it avoids the psychiatric term 'obsession'.
*Attack* avoids 'possession'; and has the advantage of suggesting that the state is not permanent, and has no moral stigma.

When considering the apparent take-over of a person by an alien personality or intelligence, I shall use the phraseology of *mediumship* or '*possession*'.

When I read in the Report of the American Presbyterian Church *The Work of the Holy Spirit*, the advice given to laity who had had a neo-Pentecostal experience that 'It is not necessary to carry all the Pentecostal baggage', I immediately thought that such advice was equally relevant to those who were experiencing or studying facets of the spiritual which are not of the *Holy* Spirit. One fear among many about using 'demonic' language or thinking in terms of 'possession', is that to do so means aligning oneself utterly with those who have long been familiar, even enthusiastic, about such things. Most of the 'baggage', whether apocalyptic, medieval, Roman or Pentecostal, can and should be left behind.

Belief in the demonic or in demons (the two are not the same) does not mean turning one's back on the findings and insights of the twentieth century and becoming a spiritual or psychological flat-earther. To accept more literally one New Testament term in the light of present-day experience does *not* mean that the theological work of decades is thrown out of the window or that Biblical truth is regarded once again as residing in the *literal* interpretation of every word. To put it another way, just because in the first century people believed in the demonic and a three-tier universe, it does not follow that in the twentieth century belief in one must entail belief in the other. Some readers may be asking themselves which is the more ridiculous to be asked to believe in—an outdated spiritual system, or an outdated cosmological one?

Is there any room in twentieth-century thinking for the possibility of 'possession'? Is it an *impossible* concept or merely an *unfashionable* one?

Before discussing the concept in relation to mental illness and to theology, firstly a very brief outline of some of the ways in which, in various fields of thought, twentieth-century man is by no means closed to such a possibility.

Historically, the mediumistic state has been known in practically every age and culture. Doctor P. M. Yap, in his article 'The Possession Syndrome' in the *Journal of Mental Science* (January 1960), begins his paper by saying:

The phenomena of 'spirit-communication' in mediumistic trance, of 'spirit-possession', and of 'demonopathy' are closely related, and known to both east and west . . . These conditions do present themselves in many countries and it is misconceived to think that they are to be found only in outlandish cultures . . . This paper examines the possession syndrome as it is manifested in patients coming to the Mental Hospital in Hong Kong† and compares the findings with those described in the literature of the French Catholic patients.

It is not unreasonable to believe that it could exist in the present time; the onus rests with those who disbelieve it to prove that it has suddenly ceased.

Anthropological studies have, in this century, increased our understanding of the phenomenon, its scope and something of its meaning. There is an open debate about it. P. J. Wilson, for instance, writes in *Man*, Vol. 11, No. 3, on 'Status Ambiguity and Spirit Possession' to challenge some of the theories of I. M. Lewis, Professor of Anthropology at London University, whose paperback *Ecstatic Religion—An Anthropological Survey of Spirit Possession and Shamanism* (Penguin) not only brought the subject to the attention of a wide public, but also provided a useful bibliography. Professor Obeyesekere, formerly Professor of Anthropology at Washington, writes in *Social Science and Medicine*, Vol. IV, on 'The Idiom of Demonic Possession—A Case Study'. In this he gives a detailed case-history of a woman —Alice Nona—in Ceylon who is 'possessed' by the spirit of her dead father-in-law.

We read 'During her attacks her father-in-law speaks through Alice Nona and demands certain things.' One was toddy— which Alice 'greedily gulped'—but, the professor writes, 'she showed no sign of intoxication for it was not the woman but the spirit who consumed it'. Here is an excerpt from the case-history (*mala yakā* = dead ancestor):

The monk asked X to speak to the patient.
*X*: What is the relationship of the *mala yakā* to me?
*Alice Nona*: No relationship.
X explained that this was true because X was related to Alice Nona only . . .
*X*: Remember what I told the demon when we were at home.
*Alice Nona* (spirit speaking): You asked me to come to the

† Doctor Yap is Psychiatric Adviser to the Hong Kong Government.

temple. I said I could not. Then you cheated me and brought me here.

*X*: By command (*ana*) of the monk I asked you to leave.

*Alice Nona* (spirit speaking): Yes, I remember, I opened the car door to throw you out and break your throat (*botuva*) but I didn't succeed.

The séance was now over. The monk sprayed some 'charmed' water on Alice Nona and she got up smiling vaguely.

The foregoing is exactly as originally printed; the distinction between that which is said by Alice and that which is said by the spirit within her being not mine, but Professor Obeyesekere's. Christians will immediately recall the way in which the Evangelist relates the story of the Gerasene demoniac (Mark 5) and distinguishes between words said by the man and those spoken by the demons within him.†

The existence of alternating, co-existing, or trance personalities has been intensively studied by parapsychologists and others and is closely linked with the testimony of Spiritualism. The reason is obvious. The Spiritualist Maurice Elliot writes:

> Whenever a medium is 'controlled' by a discarnate human being, he is 'possessed' by a spirit. In his case the 'control' is usually a good spirit. He resists control by discarnate spirits just as he resists the evil influence of incarnate evil persons. But where for any reason, there is little or no resistance, evil spirits gain an entry.[1]

If a Spiritualist can use the reality of mediumistic trances to argue for the reality of demonic possession—Mr Elliot uses this to preface his remarks on the reality of the Gerasene demoniac—a Christian may in clear conscience do the same!

Doctor Carl Wickland started to study the subject because (as I mentioned above) of the casualties of ouija-playing. His wife was a medium, and by 'exorcising' the possessing spirit from the sufferers temporarily into his wife, he was able to converse with them. (It is interesting in passing to note that his means of 'exorcising' them was by applying static electricity to the spine and head of the patient for about ten minutes.) These conversations have been written out in detail. The results

---

† Compare verse 9 *legei* (Gk sing) and verse 12 *legontes* (Gk plural).

[1] *The Psychic Life of Jesus* (Spiritualist Press).

of such 'possession' are, according to Dr Wickland, murder, suicide, addiction, and a host of lesser evils. No summary of the book can do it justice, and his evidence should certainly not be dismissed before it is read. Suffice it here to quote Canon J. Pearce-Higgins' review of the book when it was recently reprinted:

> As far as clergy are concerned the case-histories appear to validate the New Testament account of Jesus casting out evil spirits, and show that there is no need on scientific grounds to 'demythologise' them.

For those who are not eager to accept the evidence of a Spiritualist, even though a doctor and a psychiatrist, the well-documented studies in psychical research may be an easier testimony. Sally Beauchamp's three trance-personalities have been described in detail in Dr Morton Prince's six-hundred-page *Dissociation of Personality*, and in numerous articles in the *Journal of Abnormal Psychology*. Fortunately for the busy reader summaries of such cases are frequently made. Professor William McDougall's *An Outline of Abnormal Psychology* (Methuen) has a number of useful summaries, and most Christian writers on 'possession' allude to them: Leslie Weatherhead and Canon Stafford Wright in *Psychology, Religion and Healing* and *Mind, Man and the Spirits* respectively.

F. W. H. Myers in his two-volume work *Human Personality and its Survival of Bodily Death* also summarises the case of Sally Beauchamp and concludes that:

> The fact of possession has now been firmly established.

Various volumes of the *Journal of Abnormal Psychology* with its articles on 'The Divided Self' and the 'Psychogenesis of Multiple-Personality' (Vol. XIV) show the degree to which the subject has been studied, but none more so than the case of Mrs Piper.

Mrs Piper was the object of the most prolonged investigation in the history of psychical research. The records ran to three thousand pages, and were based on some eighty-eight sittings before members of the British Society for Psychical Research. Professor William James's comments at the conclusion of his review of the case in *The Proceedings of the American Society for*

*Psychical Research* have been frequently quoted, but will bear being quoted again:

> . . . other intelligences than our own appear on an enormous scale in the historic mass of material which Myers first brought together under the title Automatisms. The refusal of modern 'enlightenment' to treat possession as an hypothesis to be spoken of as even possible, in spite of the mass of human tradition based on concrete experience in its favor, has always seemed to me to be a curious example of the power of fashion in things scientific. That the demon-theory will have its innings again is to my mind absolutely certain. One has to be 'scientific' indeed to be blind and ignorant enough to suspect no such possibility. (Vol. III, 1909)

A contemporary authority on schizophrenia, Dr R. D. Laing, who has contributed greatly to an understanding of the social factors at work (e.g. *Sanity, Madness and the Family*) writes in *The Divided Self*:

> A most curious phenomenon of the personality, one which has been observed for centuries, but [italics mine] *which has not yet received its full explanation*, is that in which the individual seems to be the vehicle of a personality that is not his own. Someone else's personality seems to 'possess' him and be finding expression through his words and actions, whereas the individual's own personality is temporarily 'lost' or 'gone'. This happens with all degrees of malignancy.

On more than one occasion such a state has been recognised by the law. In 1970 a man was freed by the Court of Appeal on the grounds of his being a 'split personality'. In concluding the case, the Lord Chief Justice said, 'This man is, or was, a shy isolated person . . . but has built up a personality endowed with all the opposite traits, and it is in the name of this personality that this offence was committed' (*Daily Telegraph*, November 17th, 1970). A year later, a schoolboy caused £70,000 worth of damage by setting fire to a school. The line of defence taken was 'possession by an evil spirit which so overwrought the mind of the boy that he did the deed not with his own mind but a mind wholly possessed by the spirit'. There have been cases where such a line of defence has given the impression of a demonic alibi, but in this case the boy's house had had poltergeist disturbances, the father had tried a magical exorcism, and after the fire the boy was exorcised by the Rev. Christopher Neil-Smith, who was asked to testify in the case.

There are clear indications, therefore, that it is not only Pentecostalists who recognise the possibility of a person's being 'possessed' by a personality or intelligence other than his own, but anthropologists, Spiritualists, supported by the findings of parapsychology and abnormal psychology, and the law.

The next question is how the concept of being the vehicle of an alien 'spirit'—which was crucial in the two legal cases just mentioned—relates to the findings of medicine, psychology and theology.

## MEDICINE

The growing recognition in medical thinking of the psychosomatic factors in many bodily ailments is beginning to dissolve the false barriers that have isolated the bodily, mental and spiritual aspects of the person, and, one hopes, the barriers between doctors, psychiatrists and priests, whose jobs have tended each to be linked with one of the 'parts'. Such a trend must be welcomed by Christians as a move towards thinking of people as *people*, and not exclusively as bodies, brains or Baptism-statistics. The Church though, must not jeopardise its position as a healing agency by abdicating its traditional responsibilities. When an increasing number of GPs are now saying in effect, 'I could dismiss many of my patients if only I could deal with their *guilt*,' it is obviously not the time to depreciate the traditional means of confession and absolution, whether in private or within worship, still less to describe such depreciation as the result of 'modern' thinking.

An indication of the breaking down of these false barriers between the medical, the psychological and the spiritual can be seen in a statement which the Rev. J. C. Neil-Smith made in the *Yorkshire Post* that *ten* doctors had sent patients to him for exorcism—a number which will no doubt have substantially increased since it was reported in 1970.

Prebendary Henry Cooper in a talk given at St Anne's, Soho, said:

*I have been told on more than one occasion by a psychiatrist at a mental hospital that the patient's trouble was not really within his competence, and that it could only be dealt with by the Church because it was a spiritual matter, and that there was some objective evil there.

The Exeter Commission Report *Exorcism* (SPCK) safeguards any misuse that the Christian minister might be tempted to make of the more fluid situation which exists now between the healing disciplines.

> In the first place it should be assumed that the patient's illness has a physical or mental cause, and the case may thus be referred by his general practitioner to a competent physician in psychological medicine. The exorcism of a person must not be performed until possible mental or physical illness has been excluded in this way. (p. 23)

It continues by stressing that failure at a medical or psychological level to bring healing should 'not necessarily be taken as evidence that the illness is spiritual', nor, conversely, does relative success of such treatment exclude a 'residual spiritual problem'.

The Church's approach to the problem must avoid on the one hand minimising our Lord's work through medicine and psychiatry, and on the other an excessive timidity which frustrates his work through the Church. Charcot himself (who taught both Janet and Freud and was an outstanding researcher of hysteria) in an article on 'Faith Healing' wrote:

> The goal of medicine . . .[is] the cure of patients without distinction of what curative process is used.[1]

Within the complex interplay of body, mind and spirit, one medical disorder, or group of disorders as some term it, is of particular relevance.

## EPILEPSY

Epilepsy is an ill-defined group of disorders characterised by fits or seizures. Of the most well known, the *grand mal* state, seven stages of the fit can be discerned.[2]

    (i) *Premonitory stage*, in which many patients are aware of the impending attack.

---

[1] Quoted in Dr Ilza Veith's *Hysteria* (University of Chicago Press).
[2] For the general reader I have thought it clearer to depart from the more usual five stages and thereby avoid subdivisions. I have also avoided medical terminology.

(ii) *A collapse into unconsciousness*, often with a cry.
(iii) *Muscular rigidity* and contortion.
(iv) *Muscular jerking* in which the tongue may be bitten.
(v) *A state of limp unconsciousness.*
(vi) *A gradual return to consciousness.*
(vii) *A period of great inactivity* (sleep), *or great activity* (violence).

The emotional stability and security which the victim may or may not experience, influence in some degree the frequency of such fits. Furthermore the social stigma still attached to epilepsy, due partly to the strange appearance of such fits and to the patient's inability to do some kinds of work, means that for many the psychological and social aspects cause them more suffering than the attacks. The care and acceptance by the Christian community of the epileptic, of all sufferers, may be considered among the most valuable. Medically, the increasing use of anti-convulsive drugs (phenytoin, primidone, etc.) is making it possible for eighty per cent of all patients to gain either complete or partial control of their seizures, and thus to live as normal and useful lives as society will let them. When, for example, an estimated twenty-four million Americans oppose the employment of epileptics in any occupation whatever, and in England public schools often refuse admission to epileptic children, the repercussions of their illness and the extent of their emotional problems begin to emerge.

The cause of some epilepsy can be detected, and among the most common causes are brain damage; pressure on the brain through blood clotting; tumour; infection; fluid excess (oedema); coma caused by diabetes and liver or kidney disorders; severe fever; asphyxia; electric shock; and various drugs. When such a cause can be traced the condition is termed *symptomatic epilepsy.* All forms of epilepsy register abnormal brain-wave patterns on an electroencephalogram (EEG). Epilepsy in which these abnormal brain-wave patterns *cannot* be traced to any known physical cause is generally termed *idiopathic epilepsy.* In *symptomatic epilepsy* not only can the symptoms be treated, but also the causes, for they are known. In *idiopathic epilepsy* as nothing is known of the causes, only the symptoms can be treated, and apart from the fits the individual can remain in perfect health.

It is of more than passing interest to note that *two out of three epileptics (i.e. 1,600,000 in Britain and the States) suffer from epilepsy of no known cause (idiopathic) and one in five receive no benefit from existing drugs.*[1]

The premonitory stage which one in two patients experiences is termed an *aura*, and the nature of the subjective feelings which announce the onset of an attack also gives food for thought:

> pains in a particular part of the body, strange sensations, tremor, a mysterious [usually foul] smell or vision unrelated to anything in the surrounding environment, a feeling of panic. (*Pears Medical Encyclopaedia*)

The third item of particular relevance to this study is what is sometimes called the 'automatism' or *epileptic equivalent* which not only has obvious medico-legal importance but, I suspect, spiritual importance as well. It describes the last state (vii) when it takes a turn not to inactivity but to over-activity. It takes the form of

> extreme violence whilst in an altered state of consciousness . . . and may take the place of a fit or follow one so that the individual may carry out murderous attacks which are quite pointless without knowing what he is doing.

The story of the epileptic boy in Mark 9:14–27 is of particular interest and is, fortunately, among the most detailed yet primitive stories we have. The Evangelists between them give us no less than six descriptions of the boy's illness—three from the boy's father:

1  . . . there is a spirit of dumbness in him, and when it takes hold of him it throws him to the ground, and he foams at the mouth and grinds his teeth and goes rigid. (Mark 9:17–18)
2  All at once a spirit will take hold of him, and give a sudden cry and throw the boy into convulsions with foaming at the mouth; it is slow to leave him, but when it does it leaves the boy worn out. (Luke 9:39)
3  . . . he is a lunatic and in a wretched state; he is always falling into the fire or into the water. (Matthew 17:15)

---

[1] This sentence is based on figures and percentages given in *Epilepsy*, Pryse-Phillips; 'Counseling and Epilepsy', B. Graymont in *Pastoral Psychology*, Vol. 22; and those supplied by the British Epileptic Association.

and three from the eye-witness:

> 4 . . . as soon as the spirit saw Jesus it threw the boy into convulsions, and he fell to the ground and lay writhing there, foaming at the mouth. (Mark 9:20)
>
> 5 . . . the devil threw him to the ground in convulsions. (Luke 9:42)
>
> 6 Then throwing the boy into violent convulsions it came out shouting, and the boy lay there so like a corpse that most of them said, 'He is dead'. (Mark 9:26)

It is possible to discern the different stages of the *grand mal* attack which I outlined at the beginning of this section.

(i) *The premonitory stage* is probably referred to by the description of dumbness (see 1) because of the unresponsive state which overcomes the victim. Jesus described the lad as deaf also (Mark 9:25).

(ii) *The collapse into unconsciousness* is described as 'throws him to the ground' (see 1), 'always falling . . .' (see 3), 'fell to the ground' (see 4) etc.

(iii) *The stage of muscular rigidity* is of so short duration that it is not surprising that it is not explicitly mentioned, although the sudden expulsion of air through the narrowed vocal chords which muscular spasm creates is noted in the 'sudden cry' of Luke 9:39 (see 2 above).

(iv) *The stage of muscular jerking* is apparent in all descriptions above except 3, and causes writhing, grinding of teeth and foaming at the mouth.

(v) *The state of limp, or 'flaccid', consciousness* is indicated by his lying so like a corpse that the bystanders thought he was dead (6 above), and may also be indicated by the father's description of him as *xērainetai* (Mark 9:18) if translated 'become exhausted' rather than 'rigid', as C. E. B. Cranfield suggests as an alternative.[1]

(vi) *Gradual Return to Consciousness* followed (vii) by a *period of great (in-)activity* is suggested by the father's description of the demon being 'slow to leave him, but when it does it leaves the boy worn out' (see 2 above). It was during this stage that Jesus

> . . . took him by the hand and helped him up, and he was able to stand. (Mark 9:27)

[1] *Cambridge Greek Testament Commentary* (CUP).

Doctor W. Pryse-Phillips in his book *Epilepsy* (Wright, Bristol), describes this passage as the occasion when 'a despairing father brought his epileptic son to be cured', and since the Revised Version most translators and commentators have not hesitated to make or imply the same diagnosis.

Doctor John Wilkinson writing on 'The Case of the Epileptic Boy' in the *Expository Times*, Vol. LXXIX, No. 2 draws an important conclusion:

> It is clear from our comparison of the details of the gospel records with modern medical description of the disease, that the boy suffered from the major form of epilepsy. This, however, is not a final diagnosis, for epilepsy is a symptom not a disease. It is due to a sudden disturbance of nerve cells in the brain and may have many causes ... *Therefore to arrive at a diagnosis does not automatically exclude demon possession as the cause of this disease* [italics mine] as some commentators maintain.

After distinguishing between symptomatic and idiopathic epilepsy, he writes:

> If demon possession is a fact there seems no reason why it could not be the cause of some cases of epilepsy. We do not know enough about the spirit world to disprove demon possession, nor enough about epilepsy to deny that it may be caused by such possession.

If the nature of the Gospel narratives is here sufficiently reliable and accurate in its description of the *symptoms* that both doctors and theologians feel justified in diagnosing the illness as *grand mal* epilepsy, it would not be fanciful to submit that the Evangelists are no less accurate in their descriptions of the *cure*.[1]

The disciples had tried unsuccessfully to heal the lad. Jesus enquires about the history of the illness, and learns from the father something of its duration—'from childhood'—and its nature—'it often throws him into the fire and into the water, in order to destroy him' (Mark 9:21-2). Then Jesus heals him by commanding the spirit to come out of the boy 'and never enter him again'—a far cry from the charms and incantations of his contemporaries.

---

[1] Even if, following Bultmann, the episode is regarded as two separate miracle-stories, there is considerable evidence for an epileptic diagnosis even within the verses 21-7 passage.

Then throwing the boy into violent convulsions it [the demon] came out shouting, and the boy lay there so like a corpse that most of them said, 'He is dead'. [Matthew adds 'the boy was cured from that moment'.] But Jesus took him by the hand and helped him up, and he was able to stand.

While Luke concludes:

... and gave him back to his father, and everyone was awestruck by the greatness of God. (Luke 9:42)

Doctor Wilkinson, whom I quoted above, writes:

Modern medicine knows no cure for idiopathic epilepsy ... there is no method of treatment which will cure an epileptic immediately and permanently. Fits may cease with the passage of time but of no patient can we say with confidence that they will never have another fit. That is why the instantaneous cure of this boy by Jesus is so striking from a medical point of view ... modern medicine cannot cure epilepsy like that.

Doctor Lechler when writing on epilepsy and demonic possession (in *Occult Bondage and Deliverance*), gives an important warning. 'It is inexcusable and sometimes quite disastrous', he writes, 'to find certain Christian workers labelling almost all cases of epilepsy, unconsciousness and fits as symptoms of demonic subjection.' Nevertheless it would seem quite justified to say that *some* cases of *idiopathic* epilepsy and epileptiform behaviour may be caused by spiritual malady. Also that since an act of exorcism can have no results whatever if the illness is not in some way demonic, if in retrospect a case of idiopathic epilepsy is cured by exorcism it must have been a case of demonic oppression in some degree. Had the lad in the Gospel story suffered from symptomatic epilepsy our Lord could only have cured him by an act of healing rather than exorcism, just as he healed the man with an impediment in his speech (Mark 7:32–7) and a blind man (Mark 8:22–5) by the laying-on of hands, but a dumb and a blind *demoniac* by exorcism (Matthew 12:22 ff.).

F. J. Perryman in *Whom Resist* draws on his experience in the ministry of deliverance, and writes:

What about epilepsy? I have known cases which appear to have been caused and/or aggravated by Satanic interference with the person. The deliverance of one woman happened in our home ...

After an outline of her past history, he continues:

> Sitting in an armchair talking one day she suddenly slipped off
> to the floor, foaming a bit at the mouth and apparently helpless.
> Without stopping to think I stood over her and, commanding
> the devil to leave her, I added, '——(using her name). In the
> name of the Lord, get up, and sit down, you are free.' She
> did so and was free and normal. She . . . visited us often, she
> never had another fit . . . I am inclined to think that some
> of the cases dealt with by our Lord were of this nature . . .

One of the most striking parallels to the Gospel narrative which
I have come across is in Peter Scothern's leaflet *Prayer and
Fasting*, the value of which is in no way lessened by the textual
omission of the words 'and fasting' from Mark 9:29 in modern
texts, and greatly increased by the humility and honesty with
which he recounts an experience early in his ministry.

> The daughter was an epileptic and suffered greatly. She
> was constantly tormented by evil powers. These strange
> influences would cast her to the ground, she would foam at the
> mouth and cry . . . twitch and twist in terrifying contortions.
> The first time I saw her in this dreadful condition I was much
> afraid. I returned [home] . . . challenged by this great need.
> Only a powerful authoritative ministry would deliver her. I
> recognised my weakness and lack of power, so I spent two days
> in prayer and fasting . . . Every sense of fear and weakness left
> me. I returned, and hardly had I entered the room when she
> threw another serious fit. The devil tore her and suddenly
> screamed out of her. She was miraculously released, and I left
> rejoicing in the Lord. What an amazing deliverance. I praised
> God for the lesson I had learned . . . 'This kind can come
> forth by nothing, but by prayer and fasting.'

The neurologist, Jean Lhermitte, an authority on 'possession' concludes his study *Diabolical Possession, True and False*[1]
with the question:

> . . . when the doctor recognises in a patient all the elements
> of a definite disease, has he the right to see in it *only* the effects
> of a natural process, even when a scientific treatment is able to
> cure it?

He would surely have agreed with the *Jerusalem Bible*'s heading
for the Markan story of the suffering boy as an *epileptic demoniac*,

[1] Burns and Oates. See also Dr Lhermitte's, 'Pseudo-Possession' in *Satan*
(Sheed and Ward).

and not glibly have dismissed it as a contradiction in terms as some commentators without medical qualifications might do.

Those who equate heartiness with spiritual health need to be particularly careful in diagnosing 'spiritual' ill-health, because of the multiplicity of purely medical factors which can create depression and listlessness in the most ardent Christian. Here Leslie Weatherhead's analogy of the lantern is useful. The light, he says, may be dim not only because the flame is burning low (spiritual life), but because the glass around it (one's physical body) is not allowing the light to come through.

Just as so much medical health and healing is encouraged by a healthy mental and spiritual outlook, so, conversely, any spiritual burden, 'demonic' or otherwise, is going to work against wholeness and healing.

The interaction of spirit, mind and body makes diagnosis no easy task, as is illustrated by the case of Mrs A. Mrs A complained of 'the hordes of little black demons' which periodically whizzed around her head. A less spiritually imaginative patient would have described the symptoms as 'spots before the eyes'. I have no doubt that her doctor success-fully 'exorcised' these 'demons' by a suitable dosage of liver extract and vitamin $B_{12}$, and that our Lord was well pleased. (Incidentally, had she been treated with exorcism, such a mistaken diagnosis would *not* have been fatal. It would have had no effect whatever on her condition, and she would have been handed back to her doctor with the message that as exorcism made no difference whatever, the symptom must be arising from a mental or physical cause rather than a spiritual one. In spite of popular belief I have never come across a case where exorcism produced any ill-effects.)

## MENTAL HEALTH

A great number of people assume that psychology has made a successful take-over of any religious understanding of man; prayer and conversion, guilt and forgiveness can not only be described as so many mental processes but this is the only adequate way of describing them. When Albert Einstein was once asked whether everything could be described scientifically he answered that it *could*, but that it would make no sense because 'it would be description without meaning, as if you described a Beethoven symphony as variations of wave-pressure'. There is always a tendency to confuse the mere description of a thing with a statement of its meaning or its cause. In medicine I have suggested that the label 'epileptic' and the label 'demonic' need not be mutually exclusive. It may similarly be said of psychological and psychiatric labels, that they, also, are more descriptions of *symptoms* than of causes. Victor White in *God and the Unconscious* deals with this question:

> Finally, the question must be asked, has not modern psycho-pathology disposed of the whole conception of diabolic posses-sion? Has not science made it plain that what more credulous ages considered to be the signs of an indwelling devil are now all taped and docketed as manic-depression, schizophrenia, epi-lepsy, hysteria, paranoia and the rest? Do we now not know that what were then thought to be devils are 'really' unas-similated unconscious complexes? . . .
> . . . We need to beware of assuming too readily that a new name necessarily involves a new explanation which refutes the old.

On the subject of such 'labels' he concludes:

> This writer's limited acquaintance [Fr White was a foundation member and lecturer at the Jung Institute of Analytical Psychol-ogy!] with psychiatric literature, confirmed by discussions with psychiatrist friends, strongly suggests that the names by which mental diseases are classified are [italics mine] *purely descriptive, and in no sense at all cover etiological explanations: that is to say they are no more than labels for certain syndromes or symptoms which are commonly associated together.* To the extent that their respective psychosomatic 'causes' are understood (which would not seem, in most cases, to be to any great extent), this would seem in no way to invalidate such conceptions of their diabolic origin . . .

Certainly the terms *hystero-demonopathy, hysteria-demoniacal phase, demonosis, demonomania, demonopathy* or *demoniacal somnambulism,* in spite of their 'demonic' theme are not generally used to describe a demonic cause, but to describe bizarre behaviour. If such terms are used merely to describe certain syndromes or symptoms, then it would be logical to accept Victor White's contention that the terms manic-depression, schizophrenia, epilepsy, hysteria and so on are, similarly, mainly descriptive of *symptoms* not of causes. The ultimate cause, therefore, al-though sometimes within the sphere of medicine or psychiatry

—as for example when schizophrenia is caused by a chemical imbalance—is not always so, and in the body/mind/spirit unity it would be logical to expect the causes of some suffering if not traceable to bodily or mental factors to be due to spiritual ones.

While psychology may not be always equipped to state the cause of mind-disturbance, its contribution is very considerable in assessing states of pseudo-possession.

The Rev. Alan Harrison of the Guild of Health in an address to the William Temple Society of Bournemouth told this story:

> *I remember one of my psychiatrist friends saying that he had a very elderly spinster in hospital with hallucinatory voices, and that there was a particular voice called Harry. She found him rather distressing because he would make sexy suggestions to her. He did feel—although this was not a case of casting out evil spirits but a case of internal projection—that laying-on of hands might help. She became much better; Harry of course was still there, but he's no longer making sexy suggestions, he's singing hymns!

More often the alleged entity, whether a Harry or a demon, is not something the patient wishes to be rid of, but is a convenient projection of a lower side of their nature, which gives them the perfect alibi to behave as they really wish, while at the same time abdicating responsibility for such behaviour. This is reflected in the common expressions:

> I don't know what got into/possessed me, I really don't!
> I wasn't really myself!

Pseudo-possession may be a state reached by autosuggestion. Alternatively the demonic can be projected either as an alibi, as above, or just as often as an hysteric device on the part of the patient to attract and keep attention, as in Elizabeth's story below. Furthermore the 'unassimilated unconscious complexes' may be deliberately externalised and objectified by psychotherapy in order that, as the familiar phrase puts it, the person may come 'face to face with himself'.

Elizabeth was a teenage girl whose doctor had decided to certify her that evening at six o'clock if her erratic behaviour did not cease. The doctor told the parents that he did not mind *who* they called in.

The message eventually reached me that she was 'possessed',

and could I find someone to call on her. I could not, and had to go myself. I took with me two mature Christian lay-folk (one a woman) and another Christian minister, with whom I had previously worked.

With the knowledge and permission of her GP and her parish priest we duly arrived no more than three hours before the doctor's deadline for committing her to a mental hospital. She was in bed and somewhat distraught, though not so much as her parents. She talked of the demons whizzing around inside her head, but other than her own choice of language, showed no symptoms of true demonic oppression or of demonic attack. Any exorcism would have been inappropriate, as there was nothing there of a truly demonic nature to cast out. She was certainly in need of healing. After informal confession on her part, we asked her whether she believed that Jesus Christ could heal her so that she would be rid of these 'demons', and whether she wished him to do so.

She answered 'yes' to both questions and with a quiet gentle prayer, with laying-on of hands, we asked our Lord for his healing, and left. She was not certified, and was not only healed sufficiently to make such a drastic step unnecessary, but started to take an active and healthy part in her church life, and when last I heard of her, she was a Sunday-school teacher.

I have quoted that story at some length to allay any fears there might be that this ministry of the Church involves any inevitable clash with psychiatric thinking. The parents of Elizabeth had recently undergone an exciting spiritual experience of the Holy Spirit; this had probably widened the gap between them and their daughter who had had no such experience. By talking in terms of 'demons' she thereby regained their attention, and became the focus of their love and concern. Much of her talk was of demons, which is quite uncharacteristic of the truly demonically afflicted, but it happened to be something which was particularly effective in gaining attention—as many an hysteric has similarly found in maintaining the interest, and taking the time, of the clergy. Psychological and psychiatric studies are not only invaluable in discerning pseudo-demonic states, but also leave room among their description of symptoms for 'possession'.

Thus Dr P. M. Yap, whom I have already quoted, in a paper read to the Yale University Department of Psychiatry entitled

'The Possession Syndrome' (*Journal of Mental Science*, Vol. 106), distinguishes between the acute and less acute degrees of possession by the depth of consciousness. His three-fold classification being (i) Histrionic, (ii) Partial and (iii) Complete. The Complete state is marked by 'clouding of consciousness, skin anaesthesia to pain, a changed demeanour and tone of voice, the impossibility of recalling the patient to reality, and subsequent amnesia'. Half of his cases were diagnosed as *hysteria*, and almost a quarter of them as *schizophrenic*. Half of the cases were treated by electroconvulsive therapy (ECT), and all cases diagnosed as hysteria were freed from the 'possession syndrome'† while seventy per cent of those diagnosed as schizophrenia were similarly well and able to return to work. (He gives a detailed bibliography of relevant psychiatric literature up to the date of his writing, 1960.)

In the *International Journal of Social Psychiatry* (Vol. XVII, 2.) Dr R. K. McAll discusses and re-formulates Dr Yap's classification and makes, by implication, the distinction between 'infestation' by evil forces, and that caused by people, either dead or alive. This is an important distinction, to which I shall have to return, and one which he made 'from the experience of over thirty cases' (written in 1970).

When lecturing at the Texas Medical School of Psychiatry, Dr McAll was interrupted in his lecture by a student saying, 'Say, Prof., Mrs So-and-so—we said she was a schizophrenic, but *this* is what's the matter with her!' Her notes were brought in immediately, and on reading them the professor said, 'She's a Roman Catholic; go and phone her priest.' This was done there and then, and the priest's response was, 'That's OK, it's all written in my book, I'll come and do it anytime you like!' Dr McAll then continued with his lecture! The day has not yet arrived when such a thing could happen among a group of theologians. Dr Frank Lake in a talk on the demonic recalled the occasion when 'Hans Rudi Weber was giving a talk on Christ's Victory over the Demonic Powers to this large gathering of psychiatrists and theologians. It was quite amusing to see how uncomfortable the theologians were at this strange exhibition of what I think they regarded as Medievalism from a distinguished member of their own theological group. It was as if they were apologising to the scientific psychiatrists present

† 'Syndrome' = a complex of symptoms.

that a theologian had returned to the era of demons and evil possession. By contrast the psychiatrists were in fact leaning forward eagerly recognising that the collective demonic is something with which they are continually dealing. As they said afterwards, "Why didn't some theologian tell us about this before? We know what he's talking about, we live with it." '

In *Suicide and Attempted Suicide*, Professor Stengel notes that both Durkheim and Freud's theories of human behaviour (one finding origins in society and the other in the unconscious) 'have one important aspect in common; both see the individual's actions as the result of *powerful forces over which he has only limited control*' [italics mine]. It is of such forces in individuals that Dr Rollo May uses the word *daimonic* ('... any natural function which has the power to take over the whole person')[1] while such forces in society have prompted theologians like Thielicke to talk of the 'demonisation' of the world.[2]

A foremost writer on the subject was the late Professor Jean Lhermitte. In his article, 'Les possédés sont-ils des fous?' (translated here by E. Langrish, and from *Ecclesia 67*) he concludes:

> There are many genuinely possessed people. The critical and scientific approach has dispelled many clouds and broken down many myths, but even so, the number of people demonically possessed in our modern world is considerable. This statement is based on lengthy personal experience.

## SCHIZOPHRENIA

The symptoms of schizophrenia are the disordering of perception, of thought, of emotion, and of actions. They are classified into four groups according to the area of major disorder, e.g. a schizophrenic whose problem is dominated by delusions and hallucinations, the hearing of voices, etc., is said to be suffering from paranoid schizophrenia (or 'paraphrenia' for short) because his perception is disordered. Schizophrenia is the commonest reason for long-term psychiatric hospitalisation. Many suggestions have been put forward as to its cause, but there is no unanimous opinion. Among the most important is

---

[1] *Love and Will* (Souvenir Press); Dr May takes the concept of the demonic which includes positive and negative possibilities, and hence bases his spelling on the Greek.

[2] *Theological Ethics*, Vol. 1, *Foundations* (Black).

the theory that it is a constitutional fault leading to a bio-chemical imbalance, but others stress the psychological influences while Drs R. D. Laing and A. Esterson, in *Sanity, Madness and the Family* (Penguin), for instance, have stressed the social factors. It seems likely that no agreement will ever be reached over its cause while it is regarded as one illness having so wide a range of symptoms. Rather, I suspect, it may be due to a multiplicity of causes. Peter Hay (after reviewing all suggested 'causes' of schizophrenia in *New Horizons in Psychiatry*) sums up simply, that 'Its cause is unknown.'

The following story illustrates both bio-chemical and spiritual 'causes'.

*'Philip' had for *twenty years* been in and out of mental hospitals, and been tormented by 'beings' and 'voices' which forced him to smoke and walk endlessly, or to scream and shout to drive them away. It appeared to be a case of schizophrenia plus demonic influence. His Vicar would not co-operate with a suggested exorcism, so he had to be taken elsewhere. At the church his ranting and raving stopped, and since exorcism the disgusting 'voices' stopped and have never plagued him since. From formerly living a selfish and indulgent life, he is now living as a free and disciplined Christian, with regular times of quiet, prayer and communion, and a great love and care for others. He remains a schizophrenic but is now able to assess himself and to regulate his daily small drug dosage.

There is no error whatever in diagnosing his original behaviour as schizophrenic, nor in describing his present bio-chemical state as schizophrenic. The doctors and psychiatrists are not *inaccurate* in diagnosing epilepsy or schizophrenia; it would be arrogant to suggest that they might be. It is obvious enough that the accurate diagnosis and treatment at any one level, whether spiritual, mental or physical, remains only *at one level*. and is therefore merely a *part*-diagnosis and *part*-cure of the body/mind/spirit unity which we term a person. Error is not usually by wrong diagnosis but by a *too limited* diagnosis.

In 1965, Mavis was sent by her general practitioner to see her *seventeenth* psychiatrist because of 'blackouts' lasting up to three days . . . At the commencement of the second interview she said . . . 'I disappear to bed because the voices have been mocking me again . . .' She could recall four hospital admissions. In the first she had eight months of deep insulin coma and ECT . . . In the second she was again thought of as a schizophrenic on account of the hallucinations, withdrawal from reality, and inappropriate effect . . . In another hospital she underwent air studies and an angiogram, thinking she might have a pre-frontal tumour. At the fourth hospital they regarded her as an hysterical psychopath. One admission had been on certificate, she had been discussing her purchases in a shop with 'the voices' and was unable to be recalled to reality . . . (*International Journal of Social Psychiatry*, XVII, 2)

She was cured by an exorcism, as the article later points out (and I shall draw on the account of this exorcism by the priest concerned when considering demonic 'manifestations').

The diagnosis of the fourth hospital that Mavis was an 'hysterical psychopath' links her condition with what has historically been known as '*hysteria*'—an ailment closely allied to the subject of this study.

## HYSTERIA

The famous French neurologist, Jean Martin Charcot, defined four phases of hysteria: the epileptoid phase, the phase of large movements, the hallucinatory phase and the phase of terminal delirium, and even such medical terms convey something of its symptoms.

In the standard history of hysteria, Dr Ilza Veith[1] considers the 'possessed' states of history to come within the scope of her work. Indeed, as if to emphasise the fact, the cover of her book is adorned by a grotesque face sketched by Rubens for his painting *St Ignatius of Loyola exorcising the possessed*, and, according to her, illustrative of Hysteria: Demoniacal Phase.

She prefaces her work by saying:

In recording this history I have endeavoured to present the disease as the various authors, and other people of the periods in which they lived, understood it, with little or no intent to reconcile their concepts with those of today . . .

She says that the manifestations of disordered minds have displayed an amazing resemblance in all cultures and throughout the span of observed human conduct, and furthermore that no modern textbook of psychiatry would be complete without a

[1] *Hysteria: The History of a Disease* (University of Chicago Press).

lengthy chapter on this ailment. And yet, in both America and Britain the term 'hysteria' has now been dropped. The reason is not that the illness suddenly ceased, but that 'hysteria' became a 'blanket-term' and covered too wide a range of symptoms to be useful.[1]

The American Psychiatric Association have replaced 'hysteria' with the term 'conversion symptom', while British usage includes 'conversion hysteria'.

'Conversion' here, is used in a psychoanalytical sense and not a religious one. A clergyman who is suffering from 'conversion hysteria' is one who if he feels he is in the wrong job, unconsciously creates a mental or physical symptom (e.g. loss of memory or voice) to resolve the conflict, and is not one who has uncontrollable emotion at an evangelistic rally!

The diagnosis of Mavis, in the case above, as an *hysterical psychopath*, would not seem to give us much information about her, even in psychiatric terms, which is a pity, because it is known that she was cured by exorcism. *Psychopath* has been described as a 'term that embraces anyone whose behaviour is unacceptable to the society in which he lives', while *hysterical*, as we have seen, denotes merely that the mental or physical symptoms have been unconsciously motivated.

Doctor Theodore Bovet, in *That They May Have Life*, writes:

> It is generally recognised that the vast majority of the classic phenomena of possession are observed in the mentally ill or neurotic, and can both be explained in natural terms, and also in certain cases cured by natural methods. The subjective feeling of being possessed by an alien spirit which thinks within the affected person, speaks through him in a strange voice, and even in a foreign tongue, and forces him into actions which he would never otherwise perform is a well-known phenomenon of psychopathology . . .
>
> Hysteria may in fact be defined as an illness in which whole sectors of the personality . . . become split off and forced into the unconscious, where in certain circumstances they may form a kind of 'second personality' which can give the impression of being a 'possessing spirit'.

After saying that when it became possible to describe these conditions, psychiatrists came to the conclusion that 'all cases

[1] e.g. 'the malady so signified lacks definition, pathology, pathogenesis, unitary symptom structure, unitary course or outcome'. (*Clinical Psychiatry*, Mayer-Gross *et al.*)

of possession were to be interpreted as hysteria', he concludes:

> . . . anything which apparently did not fit into this framework
> was to be regarded as the result of inaccurate observation.
>
> In practice they were very largely right; but there remains
> none the less a sufficient irreducible hard core of material to
> make clear that the question is still essentially unsolved.

The hysterical personality is particularly open to suggestion whether from itself (autosuggestion) or from others. Hence any outward act of healing would be particularly beneficial. Pseudo-possession by autosuggestion or suggestion will not be uncommon, and this may be relieved by what I would term pseudo- or quasi-exorcism. In *Miracles of Healing*, Lewis Maclachlan describes exorcism which is akin to this:

> Several cases of obsession in recent years could be recalled in
> which Christian ministers have used an act of exorcism to give
> relief to patients who so intensely believed themselves to be
> possessed by evil spirits that other treatments had proved un-
> availing. This kind of prayer was used not so much because the
> ministers who did so believed in demonic possession but because
> the patients did, and seems to be justified by its results.

Theologically this is a contemporary version of the theory of 'accommodation' by which our Lord is said to have used demonic terms solely to 'accommodate' himself to the beliefs of those around him; a sound enough practice in psychotherapy. If Mavis' symptoms were cleared by the 'suggestion' of a pseudo-exorcism, the sixteen psychiatrists whom she had previously visited had failed in an elementary technique of psychotherapy.

## THEOLOGY

After reviewing the concept of 'possession' in history, anthropology, Spiritualism, parapsychology, abnormal psychology and the law, and having briefly outlined some relevant aspects of medical and mental illness, I come finally to theology. The reason for considering the theological implications last is because I hold the view that the work of the theologian is to comment on and interpret Christian experience, and to hold doctrines of God and of man, and of God's creation into which all that is *real* can have a place. If there has been *one*, just one *real* case of demonic possession in history, then the theologian must have an understanding of God's world in which such a thing is possible. Neither he, the scientist or the doctor can select from reality only those things which harmonise most easily with current thought and terminology.

The importance of the theological interpretation cannot be over-emphasised, because it is best suited to give cause, meaning and purpose, where other disciplines are concerned mainly with secondary causes and symptoms.

A school-teacher recently brought a teenage lad to me who had become involved in various occult practices and was an increasingly disruptive influence in his school. The teacher related to me how the psychiatrist not only approved of the boy coming to see me, but had said, 'If X could incorporate his experiences [visions, healings, voices, etc.] into the framework of a religious faith, he would be all right.' In other words, the boy needed a *theological view-point* to give context and meaning to the realities to which he had exposed himself.

The theological difficulties are clear enough, although I think we can dismiss any charge of dualism, or even 'interim dualism'. Few, if any, Christian ministers would engage themselves in an exorcism with only a fifty-fifty chance of success, and the ministers whose exorcisms run in hundreds make any dualism of two equal-and-opposite forces statistically impossible.

In 1935, Edward Langton wrote an article in the *Hibbert Journal*, 'The Reality of Demonic Powers Further Considered', in which he stressed the urgency of reconsidering the demonic as a valid category, and of studying it in the light of modern findings. He wrote:

> After years of studying the subject † we are convinced, first, that the ground ... upon which the traditional belief in demons has been condemned as obsolete, is not conclusive or altogether valid. And, secondly, that no theory so far proposed as a substitute for the traditional doctrine of evil spirits or demons has proved itself capable of explaining *all* the facts so well as the traditional theory does. We share to the full the desire to explain the facts of nature, however mysterious ... by means of naturalistic interpretations, when that is possible.

† Author of *Good and Evil Spirits* (SPCK), *Essentials of Demonology* (Epworth), *Satan–A Portrait* (Skeffington), *Supernatural* (Ryder), etc.

Ironically, any theological speculation about the nature of the demonic was curtailed by the all-out effort to fight its realities within Nazism, a conflict which led some German theologians to re-introduce the 'demonic' as a theological expression of the depth and mystery of the world's evil.

Among those who did not see the belief in evil spirits incompatible with a twentieth-century world view was Archbishop William Temple, who, in *Nature, Man and God*, expressed his belief in the Devil and that a large share of the responsibility for the evil in the world 'belongs to him and to subordinate evil spirits'.

Professor James Stewart, in 1951 (*Scottish Journal of Theology*, Vol. IV), wrote an article, 'On a Neglected Emphasis in New Testament Theology', and argued that while the New Testament clearly rejects dualism, that a theology which rejected the demonic was 'milk-and-water' and 'passionless' and ill-equipped to combat the evil forces which are at work in the world.

The 1960s witnessed the beginning of the occult explosion, and the deliverance explosion which had, pastorally, to accompany it, and not surprisingly more attention was paid to the 'powers'. 1960 saw the publication of Ling's *The Significance of Satan* (SPCK), and the following year Heinrich Schlier's *Principalities and Powers in the New Testament* (Burns & Oates) and Albert H. van den Heuval's *These Rebellious Powers* (SCM), and in 1962 Gerald Bonner's *The Warfare of Christ* (Faith Press), books whose importance is quite disproportionate to their size. They make an interesting contrast to the publications which heralded the 1970s, for these were not primarily theological studies, but books written by those who were caught up in the demanding pastoral work which was being thrust upon them— Michael Harper's *Spiritual Warfare* (Hodder) and Donald Omand's *Experiences of a Present Day Exorcist* (Kimber) symbolically ushered in the new decade. Both the Scripture Union and the occultists turned their attention to the new situation, as can be seen in J. Stafford Wright's, *Christianity and the Occult*, and Françoise Strachan's *Casting Out the Devils*, which appeared in 1971 and 1972 respectively. Miss Strachan's book was the first to draw on the experiences of Christian ministers who were established in this area of Christian healing—the Rev. J. C. Neil-Smith, Rev. Dennis Peterson, Rev. George Tarleton,

Fr Simon Tugwell, and Dom Robert Petitpierre, who edited a booklet '*Exorcism*', which included the Bishop of Exeter's Commission Report, and was published in the same year.

The recommendation of the Commission that each diocese should have someone specially trained in this ministry had already been acted on by a number of Bishops in the eight years following their receipt of the original report and before its publication in 1972. The original report was not intended for publication but the changing scene made it more widely relevant and hence its publication after a time-lapse which unfortunately 'dated' the Report by its obvious unawareness of the interdenominational, charismatic and lay factors in the Church's ministry of the 1970s. Some indication of the change can be illustrated by the fact that when as a Senior Research Fellow at the Queen's College, Birmingham, studying exorcism I wished to borrow a copy from my Diocesan Bishop, he felt unable to lend it to me, until I had first obtained the permission of the Archbishop. Two years later, the Report—with additions rather than omissions—was being sold, and being sold out, in this country and wider afield.

The Report had, as one would expect, a mixed reception. Professor Peter Baeltz in an article 'Old Wine in New Bottles' (*Theology*, March 1973) expressed, in passing, both the theological difficulties and theological dangers raised by the Report. 'I confess myself puzzled', he writes,

> by the recent recommendation† that every diocese in the Church of England should have its trained exorcist. I do not doubt that phenomena occur for which exorcism has traditionally been considered appropriate . . . It is the presupposed conceptual structure which I find difficult to share. It is part and parcel of a way of understanding the world as a scene of conflict between good and bad spirits which is certainly characteristic of the New Testament, but which is not characteristic of our general outlook today.

I hope that my earlier comments about leaving behind most of the apocalyptic, medieval, Roman or Pentecostal baggage,

† In common with many others, Professor Baeltz probably did not realise the time-lapse between the writing and the publication of the Report. See also my letters in *The Times*, July 31st, 1972 and *Church Times*, May 5th, 1972.

and on not becoming a spiritual or psychological flat-earther, although written before the professor's article was published, will go some way towards allaying his fears.

Of the theological hazards he is well aware, and expresses them more clearly than I would dare to do.

> The immediate temptation is for us [theologians] simply to impose upon the Scriptures our own cultural outlook and ignore or reject whatever fails to chime in with it. But then we shall hear only what we are already prepared to believe. We shall cut the gospel down to our own measure . . . the risk of our failure to hear the whole truth of the gospel in its strangeness as well as its aptness, remains.

The adequacy of the theological views is desperately important. If a person is brought to someone like Professor Baeltz, exhibiting the phenomena 'for which exorcism has traditionally been considered appropriate', the healing of the person depends a great deal on whether the theology is adequate, because upon the theology will depend any action (or inaction) which might contribute to the person's wholeness. The terminology is immaterial, the healing of the person is not.

A number of ministers, including one Professor of Theology, have told me how, after witnessing their first exorcism, they have had to modify certain aspects of their theology in the light of the reality which they have seen. The main point at issue has been expressed by Gerald Bonner in *The Warfare of Christ*, and quoted here from Professor E. L. Mascall's *The Christian Universe* (Darton, Longman & Todd):

> He [Mr Bonner] finally refers to a matter which it is difficult to get academic theologians to take seriously but which is more and more troubling those in positions of pastoral responsibility, namely 'the experiences of those who have had to deal with persons or places in some way subject to demonic influences, whether by infestation, obsession or possession', and he urges very sensibly that 'anyone who wishes to discuss the demonology of the New Testament ought to be prepared to consider the experiences of contemporary Christians who are in no way particularly credulous and superstitious, but who have had experiences of supernatural phenomena closely resembling the cases of demonical possession recorded in the New Testament.'

# CHAPTER SIX

# DELIVERANCE

I HAVE ALREADY distinguished between 'deliverance' and 'exorcism'. This distinction is by no means always made[1] but it is nonetheless important that it should be, just as surgery is part of general medical care yet distinct from it. To change the analogy to the one used by our Lord in his parable about the returning spirit (Luke 11:24–6), there are two causes of trouble in a house. Either the trouble may lie in the fabric, or it may lie with the occupants. To renew the former is a comprehensive and lengthy business and may be likened to healing. The expulsion of troublesome lodgers is a simpler and quicker task. Although the trouble caused by woodworm or damp is unlikely to be cured instantly, that caused by lodgers will cease the moment they are non-resident. This analogy explains what to some is unaccountable, namely the instantaneous benefits of exorcism, and its difference from healing and deliverance which are usually processes of which it is merely a part.

*If* the sufferer's trouble is partially or wholly demonic, then it will cease when the demons have been chucked out. My term 'chuck out', although a slang expression, expresses accurately the usual New Testament verb† (Greek, *ek-ballō*) which means literally to *throw out*. It is quite possible, however, to *throw* out as a reluctant duty, treasures of which we are fond and with which somewhat loth to part. On the other hand we '*chuck* out' that which we have no time or use for, and we are glad to be rid of it. We do not spend time re-examining wistfully that which we have 'chucked'—and the same uncommitted detachment is

---

[1] e.g. in Morton Kelsey's *Healing and Christianity* (SCM).

† Used over thirty times in the context of exorcism.

essential where the demonic is concerned, whatever words we use about it.

The importance of the context of exorcism in a programme of deliverance and healing has nowhere found more striking expression than in the parable about it alluded to above:

> When an unclean spirit goes out of a man, it wanders through waterless country looking for a place to rest, and not finding one it says, 'I will go back to the house I came from'. But on arrival finding it swept and tidied [Matthew adds *unoccupied*], it then goes off and brings seven other spirits more wicked than itself, and they go in and set up house there, so that the man ends up by being worse than he was before. (Luke 11:24–6)

Prebendary Henry Cooper in his paper 'Deliverance and Healing'[1] begins:

> Deliverance and healing; it is obvious that this is the right sequence of thought. To be delivered is one thing: to be made whole, set right, rehabilitated, set in a proper context of society, related to fellow men and to God, and so on is to be healed. Merely to be saved from evil, might [italics mine] *be like the man in the parable whose demon left him empty and went and collected seven demonic squatters to end up eight times worse than before.*

This state might be the result of merely being 'saved from evil'. It is difficult to over-emphasise the importance of this. The Church must not concern itself with exorcism until it first concerns itself with total healing; healing of the scope that Prebendary Cooper indicates. The danger of even considering the deliverance ministry is that it may be taken out of the context of the *whole* Gospel and seen as the panacea for all ills. Although the healing ministry of the Church is undoubtedly taking its rightful place in the Church's life and witness, it is by no means sufficiently established to ensure that deliverance and exorcism will invariably, or even usually, be considered in their proper context. Morton Kelsey remarks that 'The "orthodox" Christian whether liberal or conservative has . . . little or no interest in physical or mental healing through religious means,' and relates a recent experience in these words:

> . . . the experience just a few years ago of a friend who is state commissioner of health for one of the large eastern states. At his instance a group of doctors were called together to discuss

[1] Published by The Guild of St Raphael and the Guild of Health.

the whole subject of spiritual healing . . . While the physicians on the whole were deeply involved in the discussion, the clergy who attended hardly treated the subject as a serious one.

The reading of what follows will be premature for those of this type of 'orthodoxy', and they will be ill-equipped either to assess it or practise it, in the same way that I am in no position to assess medical surgery—other than by a simple judgment based on whether the patient gets better or not.

While an exorcism may appear to be undertaken by an individual—although in reality he will be exercising a corporate authority—this wider healing is in practice as well as in essence the work and the gift of the Spirit-filled community, as James 5:14–16 makes clear. The rehabilitation and setting-right in society and with God, is a ministry which draws on all the resources of the Body of Christ and, I suspect, a good many outside it.

The main question therefore is not, 'Where can I find an exorcist?' but rather 'What must *we* do for this suffering person now and in the future to ensure his full deliverance to God?' †

The expulsion of a demon may be temporarily accomplished by submitting the patient to a shock of some sort, and expressed like that, the very small part that 'exorcism' plays in the total salvation of a person is clear. It also indicates that the role of the 'exorcist' could, and perhaps should, be a very minor one. In that case, who plays the major role in the healing of those demonically oppressed or attacked?

The answer is simply their local minister or parish priest, and the local Christian community assisting them and supporting them. The person on the spot, whatever his views of the demonic, is the one who, with others, can contribute most to the all-important case-history.

## CASE-HISTORY

Jesus asked . . . 'How long has this been happening to him?' (Mark 9:22)

The place of an adequate case-history of the person concerned is a vital one, if the full healing of the person is the goal of all endeavours. For the case-history will confirm (or deny)

† It is better to think of deliverance *to* God, rather than from the Devil.

impressions reached by other means; it will indicate main and contributory causes; whether the afflicted state has been invited or not; and important considerations for after-care. Relevant after-care (like appropriate convalescence) will be very much concerned with readjustments in living to *avoid* what had previously caused the person to suffer.

The chapters of this book dealing with the occult and its dangers are most relevant here. Their inclusion was *solely* to assist in seeing in a person's case-history items which may have some relevance to his present state. I hope, for instance, that the mention of 'ouija' would certainly be taken a little more seriously as a result of the evidence I have brought together. Françoise Strachan in *Casting Out the Devils* (Aquarian), summarised this when she wrote:

> Quite a number of Christian priests state that the main causes of possession are by ouija board, Spiritualism, dabbling in black magic, and witchcraft . . . all unanimously agree that involvement with black magic and the ouija board really is playing with demonical fire, and always *does* cause trouble sooner or later.

The (hypothetical) person who spends his weekends 'tripping', his weekday evenings at amateur séances and ouija sessions, and Friday night at his coven, would be helped little even by the most 'successful' exorcism, unless steps were taken to ensure that his life-style changed. It is the case-history which gives knowledge of such a past.

In ascertaining facts it is perhaps useful to note that most people do not have a well-defined notion of what are 'spiritualistic activities', and, as the Rev. George Tarleton advised me, they need to be asked specifically whether they have played with the 'spirit of the glass', indulged in table-tapping, etc. Capt. Barry Irons, from his rich experience in these matters, points out that those in Satanist groups will have their Christian name changed, and that a primary task is to find out their real name.

The scope of the case-history should be as wide as possible. Spiritual bondage is literally the *inheritance* of some—those, for instance, who have been cursed by their mothers at birth. Some psychic disturbance is linked more with the *place* in which the people live. If, for instance, the previous inhabitants moved out after their first week living there, it is an indication that the minister might profitably concern himself with the history of the place, rather than the people (see Chapter Eight).

Cases of disturbance, whether psychic or spiritual are not without *cause*, and the case-history will probably make this clear. As the Pentecostalist pastor Richard Bolt said of demons on one occasion, 'You don't just pick them up like chickenpox!'

How does the importance of the case-history fit in with exorcism at mass meetings? The answer is that it does not; and that the general misgivings about public healing services are even greater when such healings involve exorcism. The danger of others being adversely affected is, as we shall see, not to be underestimated. What is even worse is the isolation of the act of exorcism, away from the care and prayer of the local Christian community.

The scope of the case-history, and the items of particular importance may be deduced in general from my outline of the occult, and may be brought together under eight headings:

(i) *Medical.* The person's medical state and the relation of his doctor to his present distress. As well as such 'obvious' diseases to note as epilepsy, alcoholism and accidents involving shock or concussion should be noted. Asthma and other 'psychosomatic' illnesses may express inner tensions.

(ii) *Psychological.* Their classifications should be noted, especially if accompanied by destructive impulses or addictions or suicidal tendencies. The exact nature of 'voices', if these are claimed, warrant more attention than is usually given them, and the messages are to be assessed.

(iii) *Social.* The patient's relationships at work and with those outside the family.

(iv) *Personal.* The patient's experiences, particularly his resentments, habits and traumas, e.g. deaths in the family.

(v) *Psychic.* Any mediumistic abilities, or 'spiritual' manifestations, and any involvement with non-medical healers or healing.

(vi) *Religious.* Does the person live his life ignoring the 'Other', or with religious commitment in some form? If the latter then does this commitment mean a bondage and a slavery to superstitious ideas?

(vii) *Occult.* All involvement with the occult should be noted.

(viii) *Place.* Any disturbances in the home, or which seem to be associated with the place (see Chapter Eight).

Within the Anglican Church a number of Bishops are not authorising exorcism until they are in possession of the person's case-history. If the parish priest sets out to make such a record it is a good idea to make it in duplicate. The former Bishop of Durham insisted on full case-histories being kept of all cases in his care.

## DIAGNOSIS

How is a diagnosis made of demonic trouble?

An outstanding authority on these matters was the late Fr Gilbert Shaw, who in an important series of articles in the *St Raphael Quarterly*[1] wrote:

> The special gift [of discernment of spirits] is not essential for diagnosis, which should be, even if the exorcist should possess it, by the rational elimination of material causes.

When an increasing number of people are discovering, through a neo-Pentecostal experience of the Spirit, a new 'discernment of spirits' (1 Corinthians 12:10), it is a timely reminder that this is a ministry of the Body of Christ drawing on all the Spirit's gifts. This is not however to minimise or underestimate the importance of such a gift, but to stress that they are the Spirit's gifts to the Body rather than for the encouragement of individuals indiscriminately to embark on 'charismatic' ministries.

Doctor Kurt Koch, whose book *Christian Counselling and Occultism*[2] is indispensable for a serious study of deliverance, comes to a similar conclusion to Fr Shaw's when he asserts that the pastor's equipment must first be 'Technical Knowledge' and secondly what he terms 'Charism'. Using a charismatic gift *without* some technical knowledge he writes, 'can lead to psycho-spiritual mangling of the psychically ill, even when there is no occult subjection present'. He continues to stress the importance of each means of knowledge, and their complementary nature. He also gives a warning about both the dangers of underestimating and overestimating knowledge whether through what one might call 'Reason' or 'Revelation'.

[1] Vol. 4, Nos. 6 and 7, and Vol. 5, No. 1.
[2] Evangelization Publishers, West Germany.

It is not always possible to discern whether the 'evil' is subjective or objective, nor, according to some, is the distinction so very important. Agnes Sanford, for instance, in *Healing Gifts of the Spirit* (James, Evesham) says:

> If the patient himself says, 'I feel I am possessed', then the patient has given him the key. Either he is possessed or he suffers from the fear of possession. In either event, a person may say a simple prayer of faith in the love of Christ, and may dismiss this troubling spirit, whether it is objective or subjective . . .

Similarly Prebendary Cooper in the Guild of St Raphael's leaflet *Exorcism* writes:

> The difficulty of diagnosing as to whether or not the alleged evil is subjective in the minds of the persons concerned or objectively located in the place is not so important as would at first appear, for the form [of service] may be used without attempting to settle the question.

The Rev. Doctor Roy Grace in two cases related in Chapter Three concluded that he was 'not able to determine whether this manifestation [possession symptoms and 'voices'] came from their subconscious minds, or whether it was genuine possession. Deliverance came with exorcism in the name of Jesus.'[1]

Although in some respects the diagnosis is all-important, the witness of these writers reminds us at the outset that Christ in his healing work may use our diagnoses and actions, but is not entirely dependent on them. In this way exorcism is *unlike* surgery, although I have frequently made an analogy between them. The working and possible overruling of God does not absolve us, however, from the responsibility of approaching the subject and making the diagnosis conscientiously.

In its advice on 'the Exorcism of Persons', the *Exorcism* Report states that 'In the first place it should be assumed that the patient's illness has a physical or mental cause, and the case may be referred by his general practitioner to a competent physician in psychological medicine. The exorcism of a person must not be performed until possible mental or physical illness has been excluded in this way . . .' It later realistically points out that 'the apparent failure of medical treatment should not necessarily be taken as evidence that the illness is

[1] *Pastoral Psychology*, Vol. 21, No. 206, September 1970.

spiritual . . . Paradoxically the relative success of medical treatment should not be considered as excluding a residual spiritual problem, requiring spiritual treatment.'[1]

The Christian pastor will be foremost in recognising the importance of medicine and psychiatry within God's purposes of healing, but gratitude and respect for these branches of healing must not lead to an idolatry of them, nor to an abdication of authority where spiritual matters are concerned. The diagnosis that a person is suffering from guilt, or even from demonic attack, is *in addition to* diagnosis of idiopathic epilepsy or atypical schizophrenia, but is not of any less importance. Some have expressed this by the unfortunate phrase 'demonological angle',[2] as distinct from a medical or psychiatric one. What I take this misleading term to mean is *spiritual diagnosis*, for I do not think that anyone can really advocate diagnosing with any such implied 'slant'. I would not happily know that my stomach-ache was diagnosed by a doctor from a 'hernia angle', for he would probably see one where there was not, or miss the real cause of the trouble. In *The Pentecostals*, Hollenweger quotes a Dr Schulte writing about Blumhardt as saying, 'It is not possible to give a diagnosis which distinguishes between sickness and possession . . . They represent two possible aspects of the same event.'

Many authorities would regard this as an overstatement, but such a point of view underlines the unity of man—spirit, mind and body—in which all aspects of the person share in the suffering of any particular part. As St Paul wrote, 'If one part is hurt, all parts are hurt with it' (1 Corinthians 12:26).

Doctor Paul Tournier once wrote,[3] 'Doubtless there are many doctors who in their struggle against disease have had, like me, the feeling that they were confronting, not something passive, but a clever and cunningly resourceful enemy.' In his book *Occult Bondage and Deliverance*, Dr Kurt Koch related the following:

The well known doctor and preacher Dr Martyn Lloyd-Jones had invited me to speak before a group of psychiatrists on the subject of occultism and occult oppression . . . afterwards I was

---

[1] Section 6 (Published by SPCK).
[2] Doctor T. Bovet in *That They May Have Life* (Darton, Longman & Todd) quoting Thurneysen's *Die Lehre von der Seelsorge*.
[3] *A Doctor's Case-Book in the Light of the Bible* (SCM).

attacked by two psychiatrists who claimed that the biblical accounts of possession . . . were merely cases of mental illness . . .

Another man stood up and came to my defence . . . he said . . . from his own practice alone he could quote up to eleven different cases of possession. Another psychiatrist then endorsed what his colleague had just said, adding that he had come across three or four cases of possession himself. I found it unnecessary to defend myself any more.

The last two examples are some indication that the interrelation of body, mind and spirit is beginning to be reflected in a breakdown of the false divisions between doctor, psychiatrist and pastor. Another indication is the growing tendency to acknowledge the 'psychosomatic' causes of ill-health, which, in spite of the term, frequently include the *spiritual* aspects, or pneumasomatic aspects as they might literally be called. These trends should encourage those who might otherwise be reticent in pointing out spiritual factors in a person's suffering.

Since medicine is increasingly recognising the mental and spiritual causes of illness, and psychiatric terms and treatment are (as I indicated in the last chapter) concerned with symptoms rather than causes, it means that neither medicine nor psychology is in any position to deny (or affirm) a suggested cause that lies outside the rightful scope of their study. A doctor may have personal opinions about the alleged influence on bodily health of flying saucers, reincarnation, demons or prayer, but *as a doctor* he is in no position to deny or affirm the influence of such things, as their alleged reality lies outside the sphere of medical investigation. He may as a personal hobby conduct an intensive enquiry into one or other of these and be able to talk with authority on the matter, but until such time as he does this he must remain largely agnostic. Such 'agnosticism' is no different from the suspension of judgment which is expected when a medical diagnosis is given—except, of course, by those qualified in medicine.

A *spiritual* diagnosis has, therefore, as much validity as a medical or psychiatric one, and is certainly of equal importance. If an assessment at the spiritual level is a true one it will in no way clash with an accurate diagnosis from any other discipline, and in so far as it is likely to be concerned with things at the depths of a person's being, rather than on the surface, it may well turn out to be the most important diagnosis of all. Such vital conclusions will not be reached lightly or arbitrarily, and a consideration of the relevant spiritual realities and considerations must now follow.

## SPIRITUAL DIAGNOSIS

Firstly, I shall deal with diagnosis of spiritual things by reason, and then diagnosis of spiritual things by spiritual discernment. For clarity's sake I shall consider the more acute states of demonic oppression and attack, not because they are the most frequent, but because some understanding of the worse states includes an understanding of the lesser—while the reverse is not true.

Who are the people most prone to demonic affliction? Dr Yap's study of the 'Possession Syndrome' in the *Journal of Mental Science* (January 1960), compared patients in France and Hong Kong, and confirmed the popular idea of the affliction being the prerogative of illiterate widowed or divorced women. Perhaps times change, and certainly these findings were published before the 'occult explosion' got under way in the early 1960s. This may account for the very different picture given of the Rev. Christopher Neil-Smith's work in the *Yorkshire Post* (November 16th, 1970):

> Many of the people who ask Mr Smith for help are professional men: architects, surveyors, solicitors, barristers, doctors and so on. 'Although this type of person could easily be cynical [said Fr Neil-Smith] they all recognised evil was there, and felt cleared after exorcism.'

Although since, in an article 'Occultism—The Future'[1], Fr Neil-Smith is quoted as saying, 'In the last two years I have exorcised over 1100 people' the preponderance of illiterate widows might still be true, unless the 'professionals' were flocking in their hundreds! He thinks that highly sensitive, psychic or artistic people are vulnerable, but says that 'demonic forces can enter a person through emotions—hate, suspicion, fear and various forms of perverted sex.'[2] It appears that social status and

[1] Article No. 111 in *Man, Myth and Magic*'s series 'Frontiers of Belief'.
[2] Quoted from 'The Ghost Hunters', Russell Miller, *Mirror Magazine*, January 31st, 1970.

literacy, and even temperament, may have little to do with spiritual vulnerability compared with habits and priorities.

An important question to many is whether a Christian can or cannot be 'possessed'. Much ink has been spilt, and to my mind wasted, over this question. The Overcomer Literature Trust, for instance, when reprinting Jessie Penn-Lewis' *War on the Saints*, felt obliged to abridge her original work because 'first and foremost they felt that they could not endorse the teaching that a born-again, Spirit-filled, Christian can at the same time be demon-possessed'. Michael Harper deals with this question— and a good many others—very wisely in his *Spiritual Warfare*, which I would commend to the reader. He writes:

> In the [New Testament] sense of 'having' an evil spirit, then no Christian is immune.[1]

Unless 'possession' is taken to mean 'ownership', then as Principal Edman of Wheaton College has written:

> Theory says, No, but facts say, Yes.

Most writers on the subject would agree with him.[2]

Although it is difficult to avoid the term 'possession', since it is used by Roman Catholics and Pentecostalists alike, it is, like 'exorcism', unsatisfactory. A replacement is hard to find, and while the Authorised Version of the Bible remains with us, it is unlikely to be ousted from its present position. The New Testament, however, talks mainly of the sufferer being 'demon-ised' (*diamonizomenos*), or 'having demons' (*echōn daimonia*).[3] While demonic 'attack' avoids the implications of 'ownership', it could not really be used of invited 'possession' of, for instance, a medium who voluntarily goes into a trance, not, one imagines, with the hope of being attacked!

The mention of *inviting* such states introduces what must be regarded as the two major classifications of genuine demonic affliction—whether it has been invited, or whether it has arisen accidentally. Professor T. K. Oesterreich, in his classic work *Possession, Demoniacal and Other*,[4] makes this two-fold distinction

---

[1] Published by Hodder and Stoughton.
[2] e.g. H. A. Maxwell Whyte in *Hidden Spirits*.
[3] For an outline of New Testament terms, see *Demonic Possession*, W. Menzies Alexander (T. & T. Clarke, Edinburgh) Appendix B.
[4] Trans. D. Ibberson, and published by Paul, Trench & Trauber, 1930.

by the term 'voluntary' and 'involuntary'. The voluntary aspects probably lie behind the term *'invocation* psychosis' used by the Japanese in cases of possession to which Dr Yap refers.[1]

A vicar in the midlands told me of an acute case that was brought to him of a man who had invited demons to enter him at a ouija session. The invitation was—as one would expect— accepted, and resulted in multiple possession.

The Rev. George Bennett related how a person who had suffered from mental and physical illnesses did not want to see him but had been brought to him by a friend.

> Her first words were, 'You can't help me. Nobody can! I sold myself to the devil two years ago.'[2]

Such Devil subscription was touched on in Chapter Four, and the wording of the pact appended there is enough evidence to indicate that it can be very much a reality. If such a commit- ment to the Devil has been made with a reasonable degree of conscious choice (although the widespread use of drugs at such occasions must limit the times when this is so), it is not for the Church to express her compassion by temporarily removing symptoms on demand—like the mother of a spoilt child. The Gospel—Deliverance—Exorcism is the order of need.

Some voluntary invited possession is not a deliberate liaison with the forces of evil in the way of black magicians, but an opening of doors in ignorance of the spiritual 'gate-crashers'. This has already been made clear in considering the dangers of occult involvement, whether it is psychic development, super- stitious dependence, or the range of 'spirit' activities from ouija to séances. Ouija is alleged not to work without first an *invitation* to the 'Spirit of the Glass', and 'Are you there?' is the key question of séances as well.

The most specific invitation for spirit-possession is by mediums who use trance during which they invite 'possession' by an alien intelligence, which communicates through them by

---

[1] Yap, op. cit., and K. Miyake's article, 'On the Psychoses observed in Japan' in *Trans. 6th Congress Far East Assoc. Trop. Med*, 1925; an article which I have not seen.

[2] *The Heart of Healing* (James, Evesham).

speaking messages, of which the medium has later no recollection whatever. Lhermitte has written:[1]

> In all the numerous examples of demoniacal possession found in the abundant literature devoted to the subject, invasion by the demonic personality is only evident in certain states, called attacks or trances, during which the possessed person no longer controls himself and even loses consciousness of his own natural personality. It cannot therefore be said that a splitting of the personality occurs, but rather as Eschenmayer and Oesterreich maintain, that the loss or lapse of consciousness becomes *an essential characteristic of demon possession* [italics mine]; to this suspension of the functions of the consciousness can be added the subsequent forgetfulness of what has occurred during the attack.

Hence Dr Yap in discussing 'The Possession Syndrome'[2] can say that 'There is no essential psychological difference between spirit-mediumship . . . and the possession phenomena seen in cases sent to hospital; nor is there any between mediumistic phenomena in Hong Kong and that in the West.' Earlier in his paper he notes that Dr Lehmann of Montreal informed him that out of five French-Canadian cases two were precipitated by involvement in séances, while among his own patients he pointed out that 'several . . . were superstitious, believing in fortune-telling and . . . spiritualistic cults. When asked a leading question two of them admitted that they had thought of becoming professional mediums themselves.'

On the all-important question of who are the people most prone to demonic affliction, Fr Gilbert Shaw wrote:[3]

> Personal infestation is most likely to arise in cases of mediums who have laid themselves open, or in those who through the curiosity that prompts an undisciplined search into the realms of the occult have sought extra-sensory experience.

Such states, then, can arise voluntarily by *invitation* either knowingly or unknowingly. Some observations about the *uninvited* states must follow before considering some of the symptoms, because the distinction between a deliberate or accidental involvement with evil forces—even if the symptoms

---

[1] Article 'Pseudo-Possession', in *Satan* (ed.) Bruno, Sheed & Ward, 1951.
[2] *Journal of Mental Science*, Vol. 106, No. 442, January 1960.
[3] See footnote 1, p. 124.

are the same—presents a very different case to the pastor concerned, in the same way that a Casualty Department is only an incidental help to the suicidal.

The overwhelming factor in accidental or 'involuntary' possession is, as has been made clear above, involvement with the occult, for it is basically the worship of what is created. Viewed positively, those who are immune from such suffering are those whose doors are 'shut' to psychic, occult, magical or demonic forces and pressures, who love God (and hence live without fear) and whose lives not only have a spiritual foundation in this way, but a psychological one as well—in that their love for God will show itself in an ordered way of life and service to others. This is not to imply that the Victorian church-man was the least vulnerable in human history. The demonic distorts, and there is just as much distortion in religious pride and hypocrisy as there is in the twisting of human values and order that are so characteristic of our over-reaction to Victorianism. Nevertheless our present uncritical acceptance of thinly disguised doctrines that the abnormal, the immoral, and the wrong are *really* the normal, the moral, and the right, certainly cause Screwtape to chuckle with delight, especially as they are so often propounded with an almost 'religious' intolerance unknown since the Middle Ages.

The apocalyptic state of world affairs appears largely to be due either to 'them' who anonymously rear their ugly heads in each crisis, or to the 'demands' and 'pressures', monetary, political, social, and personal that seem at every turn to be preventing every individual and group from doing what it really knows to be right. The mythology of the 'thems-and-pressures' may be seen by future historians to be the New Testament concept of wrestling '. . . against the Sovereignties and the Powers who originate the darkness in this World . . .' (Ephesians 6:12), but with the terminology changed. Some theologians already feel this. Thielicke, for instance, writes:

With the progress of secularization the world has been able to cease its chafing under the yoke of commandments and the straitjacket of so-called 'Christian' states and customs. It has attempted to organise and constitute itself exclusively on the basis of factors already inherent within itself. As a result, we have been able for the first time to see clearly what the world really is . . . we are beginning to get some idea of the monstrous

nature of its demonic potential, and we have a sneaking
suspicion that the visions in the Johannine apocalypse are
not too far removed from reality. Hence it is not by accident
that there has developed among us a new readiness to take
demonic powers seriously, as is attested in the repeated attention now given to this matter by such serious writers as . . .
Tillich, Schmid-Noerr, and Würtenberg.

His conclusions are important, because although they are not
concerned with individual demonic problems, it is perhaps only
against the theological understanding of the 'powers' that the
realities confronting the individual can be understood.

He continues:

If with increasing secularization we enter more and more the
stage of excessive emancipation—we might call it the stage of
increasing disclosure of the world's most sinister possibilities—
one thing at least is clear: this does not imply the emergence
of any new factor in our understanding of reality. It is not a
question of the old categories having become so inadequate
that we are now forced to shift our co-ordinates quickly . . .
On the contrary, it is altogether possible to set forth our 'new'
knowledge of the reality of the demonic precisely in the name of
the biblical view of reality. The times . . . do not yield anything
new. . . .
    They simply provide us with certain aids by which we may
see biblical reality afresh. And that is all they do. What we have
discovered about demonic reality and about the emancipated
world is wholly along the lines laid down by the Bible.[1]

In continuing the work of Christ, the Church is called to be a
'cultural exorcist', to use Harvey Cox's phrase, and her need
to be the 'individual exorcist' might decrease in proportion to
her effectiveness in the world and in society.

Against the background of what Thielicke terms the 'demonisation of the world', can now be considered the accidental
demonisation of the individual. Since the Biblical terms are
true of today's realities the New Testament's frequent analogy of
warfare is particularly pertinent. Of this St Paul wrote, 'let us
give up all the things we prefer to do under cover of the dark;
let us arm ourselves and appear in the light. Let us live decently
as people do in the daytime: no drunken orgies, no promiscuity
or licentiousness, and no wrangling or jealousy. Let your

[1] *Theological Ethics*, Vol. 1, *Foundations* (Black).

armour be the Lord Jesus Christ; forget about satisfying your
bodies with all their cravings' (Romans 12:11–14).

These distorted ways of living are those which the demonic
can exploit and eventually control. When St Paul wrote in
Ephesians, '. . . never let the sun set on your anger or else you
will give the devil a foothold', he was expressing Jung's 'autonomous complex' which begins by us having the anger and
ends by the anger having us.

Who are the casualties in warfare? The disobedient, the
unarmed, the weak, the undisciplined and those with illusions
about the war being somewhere else! So too are the casualties in
spiritual warfare. The Church has always naturally prayed for
the lonely, the weak and the suffering and in so doing has put
before them the huge shield of faith, and put the spiritual
armour (Ephesians 6:14–17) on those who through no fault
of their own are too weak to equip themselves. The disobedient,
and the undisciplined will not accept such help, and there are
many unarmed because, in spite of their morning paper, they
are so influenced by nineteenth-century rationalism as to be
convinced that the 'thems-and-pressures' are no more than
superstitious myths to describe Mr Brown and Mrs Smith, and
Mr Jones and . . .

The disobedient will include those who have disregarded
God's rules for wholeness and happiness because of a misconceived notion that such measures are central to a Christianity seen as a repressive morality, rather than as offering (to
those who are 'in Christ Jesus') the freedom and liberty of the
children of God (Romans 8).

There is a great difference between the demonic and demons.
The reality of the demonic is obvious to all who are not
blinded by it.[1] Tillich's observation that Jesus' temptation by
the demonic was 'often represented by his own disciples',
accounts for Jesus' rebuke of Satan addressed to Simon Peter
(Mark 8:33), when Simon tempted him with the will of man
rather than the will of God. If we acknowledge the demonic in
the Rock on which Jesus was to build his Church, we shall (as
Christians at any rate) not relegate the demonic solely to the
-isms and -ologies with which we disagree.

Demons are spirit-beings with intelligence and malevolence.

[1] See Tillich's comment, 'The demonic blinds; it does not reveal', in
*Systematic Theology* (Nisbet).

They are not mere forces, or urges. The Bible is not concerned to *reveal* their nature, it is concerned with God's revelation of himself, and such insights as it gives are only 'in passing'. St Paul, for instance, would not have us know anything about them other than Christ's victory over them. When preaching on the petition 'But deliver us from evil', Karl Barth once said:

> I have no intention of preaching to you about the Devil; one cannot preach him . . . But, nevertheless, this is something real, which modern Christians tend to pass over too lightly. There is an enemy possessed of superior power who we cannot resist without God's help. I have no love of demonology nor with the way people concern themselves with it nowadays . . . Do not therefore ask me questions about demons, for I am no expert![1]

While I would not presume to share Barth's knowledge, I am glad to share his ignorance; and should the reader wish to consider demons in more length, he may do so with the help of appropriate books in my bibliography, while the contemporary demon manifestations which must now follow should enable an assessment to be made of them based on fact rather than superstition or prejudice. Whatever conclusions are reached—even if Freud's description of them as 'repressed bad desires', or Jung's 'autonomous complexes', or Rollo May's 'natural functions which have the power to take over the whole person' are seen to be sufficient—the point is not the winning of a battle between psychiatric and theological terminology. It is the victory of Christ already won in the battle with the demonic and with demons—whatever reality they have for us and others, regardless of our belief in them or the terms we use to describe them.

The reality of demonic influence will not always be readily apparent in either a medical or a psychiatric diagnosis because, as we have seen, spiritual malady is almost bound to express itself in mental and/or physical terms, yet these need not be distinguishable from familiar bodily or mental illnesses. At a medical level, drug trials can help in diagnosis for 'these usually produce opposite reactions to the expected use of the drug'.[2] This somewhat amusing phenomenon may be due to the fact that, as Dr Lechler writes in *Occult Bondage and Deliverance*, 'A

[1] *Prayer and Preaching* (SCM).
[2] 'Demonosis or the Possession Syndrome', Dr K. McAll, *International Journal of Social Psychiatry*, Vol. XVII, No. 2, Spring 1971.

mentally ill person is in fact still ill, even when he exhibits certain symptoms characteristic of possession. On the other hand a possessed person is in fact mentally healthy in spite of the fact that at intervals he may exhibit certain symptoms of mental abnormality.'[1]

The demon reaction is likely to be aroused only by being approached at a *spiritual* level, this is why the particular manifestations which are truly 'demonic' occur only at a Christian counselling session or during a time of prayerful ministry, or in the presence of someone in whom the demons are aware of Christ.

What follows is a small selection of cases which appear in print. Hardly any case illustrates only one demonic manifestation. After these illustrations I shall outline the symptoms of possession as stated by various authorities on the subject, and then try to summarise the main aspects of 'possession' and leave the reader to make his own assessment of the New Testament narratives in the light of such contemporary experience.

### Example 1

A vivid and unforgettable illustration of this [Satan revealing his vile nature] occurred one day . . . in Harrisburg. During my stay we ministered deliverance in Jack's home to a young man named Jim. One evil spirit proved most stubborn. Its name was 'insanity' and it screamed and raged and swore. As we gave the repeated commands for the demon to come out, Jim fell on the floor and began to retch. All at once he brought up a quantity of mucouslike material. While Jack Herd's poor wife cleaned up the mess on the rug in one spot, Jim continued to be sick in another. Then to our shock and dismay, Jim lunged free from our grasp, thrust his face directly into the vomit and began to eat it. As we dragged him away the demon within him began to scream: 'Leave me alone! . . .'[2]

From the account of a Texan minister to the account of the Anglican Priest who ministered at the exorcism of Mavis (whose medical attention at four hospitals and under seventeen different psychiatrists was related in Chapter Five under 'schizophrenia').

[1] Kurt Koch is the author of the book. Dr Lechler's essay is Part 11, and is one of the few sources giving guidance to distinguish between the demonic and disease.

[2] *Deliver Us From Evil*, Don Basham.

*Example 2*

A psychiatrist friend of mine telephoned to say that a patient had been referred to him with whom he needed my help. She . . . did not respond to any known hospital treatment. He was convinced that she was possessed. At this time I had jumped on the passing theological band-wagon of the time and had firmly demythologised everything in sight—including the devil and all his minions. I declined the invitation to join in this particular ministration and somewhat presumptuously suggested further medical treatment. This was sufficient to invoke from him the challenge. 'Were you or were you not, in your ordination, given authority to bind and loose? Here is a woman who is bound—loose her!' [During the service] . . . At the word of command that the binding spirit should leave her in the Name of Jesus, there was a great cry which came from her, 'Leave us alone'. All very biblical. She remembered nothing of this afterwards . . .[1]

H. A. Maxwell Whyte, an evangelist in Canada of great experience in the deliverance ministry recalls the first time he heard the demons speak.

*Example 3*

Then we gave the command. To my astonishment, this man shot vertically into the air . . . and came down again with his head shaking to and fro as if he were a toy in a dog's mouth . . . after coughing, vomiting and writhing. Then they [the demons] started to speak. We had read about demons who spoke to Jesus, but we had never heard anyone in our day hearing demons speak. We know different now.[2]

For anyone who thinks that the foregoing ascription to demonic intelligences is the result of inaccurate observation or religious 'colouring' in the retelling, the following observation of the noted psychologist Professor Pierre Janet from his article, 'Un Cas de possession et d'exorcisme moderne' ought to carry some weight.

*Example 4*

It was a very extraordinary spectacle for us who were present to see this wicked spirit speak by the mouth of the poor

[1] From a private ms. in my possession.
[2] *Deliverance over Demons* (Whyte, Canada).

woman, and to hear the sound of a masculine voice, now that of a feminine voice, but so distinct from one another that it was impossible to believe that only the woman was speaking. She murmured blasphemies in a deep and solemn voice: 'Cursed be God,' said he, 'cursed the Trinity, cursed the Virgin.' Then in a higher voice and with eyes full of tears: 'It is not my fault if my mouth says these horrible things, it is not I, I press my lips together so that the words may not come through . . .'[1]

The *Roman Ritual* includes twenty-one rubrics on the Exorcism of the Possessed, and is printed in full in the Appendix at the back of this book. The possibility of the demon(s) speaking is taken for granted, 'He [the exorcist] will bid the unclean spirit keep silence and answer only when asked. Neither ought he to give any credence . . . if the latter maintains that he is the spirit of some saint or of a diseased party, or even claims to be a good angel' (from rubric 14). Verbatim accounts of dialogue between the exorcist and the evil spirit(s) will be found in Mgr Cristiani's *Satan in the Modern World* (Barrie & Rockliff, 1959), a publication carrying the Imprimatur of the Roman Catholic Bishop of Southwark. In the Roman Catholic symposium *Satan*, F. X. Maquart concludes his article, 'Exorcism and Diabolic Manifestation', by saying that, 'In genuine possession the action of the demon doubtless dominates the body, seizes on its organs and uses them as if they were his own, actuates the nervous system and produces movements and gesticulations in the limbs, speaking for example through the patient's mouth—that is precisely the thing that characterizes possession.' Such views are not exclusive to the Roman Church. Mrs Daphne Buckley of the Full Gospel Deliverance Crusade (London), writes in her book *The Ministry of Exorcism*, 'Most of these spirits which scream, can also speak through the patient's vocal chords,' while Pastor Peter Scothern of the Voice of Deliverance can write, '. . . by controlling the vocal chords they [demons] can speak at will. I have often heard the voice of a demon spirit.'[2]

While the 'speaking' manifestation has been common to the situations so far related, other manifestations have been mentioned, including screaming, crying out, falling, shaking,

---

[1] Translated in Oesterreich, op. cit., from *Névroses et idées fixes* (Paris).

[2] *Mastering Demons Today* (leaflet), available from Voice of Deliverance, 8 Buxton Rd, Mansfield, Notts., and Mrs Buckley's *The Ministry of Exorcism*, from Full Gospel Deliverance Crusade, 9 Corbett Rd, London.

writhing, vomiting, blasphemy and lying. I have dealt with the speaking first, because it is to the modern mind one of the most puzzling aspects of the Gospel records. In Mark, for instance, of the four accounts of Christ's healing of demoniacs, the first says of the unclean spirit that 'It shouted, "What do you want with us, Jesus of Nazareth . . . you are the Holy One of God." But Jesus said sharply, "Be quiet! Come out of him!" ' (Mark 1:23-4). In the second we read, 'the unclean spirits begged him, "Send us in to the pigs . . ."' The third occasion involved an exorcism at a distance, so that the state of the woman's daughter at the time of the exorcism is not related. The last occasion (Mark 9:26) 'it came out [of the epileptic demoniac] shouting'. Together with these accounts is the general statement in Mark 3:11-12, that 'unclean spirits, whenever they saw him, would fall down before him and shout, "You are the Son of God!" ' †

It will be clear from the demonic manifestations already mentioned that they fall into two classes: on the one hand what may be called *physical* manifestations, related primarily to the outward bodily appearance, and secondly what might be broadly termed *mental*, by which I have in mind changes of inner nature, thoughts, motives, attitudes, reactions, etc.

Since I began with the physical manifestations of speaking, I shall continue with the physical ones, although the examples will either introduce or confirm other symptoms as well.

*Example 5*

The *Roman Ritual* indicates three specific signs of possession: . . . use or understanding of an unknown tongue.[1]

*Example 6*

Maxwell Whyte writes:

We have already said that speaking in tongues is not absolute proof of the baptism of the Spirit, for a demon-possessed person

† I have deliberately excluded Jesus' healing of Simon's mother-in-law, which although exorcistic, was not the healing of someone rightly described as a demoniac or 'possessed'.

[1] Quoted in *Satan*, in Maquart's article, 'Exorcism and Diabolic Manifestation'.

can speak in tongues. In the deliverance of a demon-possessed girl in Manila . . . the demon spoke perfect English. We are not prepared to believe that tongues once spoken by the Spirit of God may not finally end up by being tongues spoken by a demon power that has taken over because of grievous backsliding.[1]

Doreen Irvine's autobiography, *From Witchcraft to Christ*, related her deliverance at some length, and so provides one of the few accounts written from the sufferer's point of view. She was hailed by over a thousand witches as 'Queen of the black witches' for winning a contest of occult powers, climaxing in her being able to walk through a bonfire of seven-foot flames unharmed.† This she accomplished by calling on her then 'master' Diablos. Her new status brought luxury and travel, and in considering the manifestation of demonic 'tongues', it is interesting to read that:

## Example 7

There was no language barrier, for when I called upon Lucifer to help me, he did, and it was not long before I could understand the various tongues, not long before I could converse with ease.

To turn to other manifestations:

## Example 8

As soon as the boy had to pass a church crucifix . . . he fell unconscious to the earth. At the exorcism in church . . . the possessed uttered a terrible cry. We seemed no longer to hear a human voice but that of a savage animal, and so powerful that the howlings . . . were heard at a distance of several hundred metres from the convent chapel . . . The weak child flung the strong father to earth with such violence that our hearts were in our mouths. At length after a long struggle he was overcome by his father, the men who were witnesses and one lay brother,

---

[1] *Deliverance over Demons* (Whyte, Canada).

† The prohibition about 'walking through fire' may not need to have been amended in the RSV to 'one who burns his son or daughter as an offering' (Deuteronomy 18:10).

and led into the presbytery. By way of precaution we had him bound hand and foot with straps, but he moved his limbs as if nothing of the kind had been done . . . [1]

## Example 9

In very rare cases where the demon is excessively aggressive it can cause a violent physical jolt to the exorcist, and to the onlooker the wrestle can be quite terrifying to see. One exorcist told a lady what to do to get rid of her entity. He knocked the nail on the head with his diagnosis, for the entity became aggressive and strong in her body and knocked him on the head with a sudden and violent blow . . . but luckily did not knock him unconscious. [2]

## Example 10

On one occasion he [Fr Neil-Smith] received a 'phone call at four in the morning . . . She said her husband was going berserk, smashing up the house, and the other occupants were in fear of their lives. Mr Neil-Smith arrived to find the scene of absolute chaos. 'The actor was a big fellow . . . and had smashed a great deal of furniture and was shouting and contorting himself hideously. As I entered, a china vase shattered on the wall by my head. I immediately felt the presence of demonic evil and acted accordingly, making the sign of the cross and praying rapidly for the demon to depart. The actor's eyes glazed over and he fell on the sofa in a dead faint. He was never troubled again.' [3]

These references to violence and paranormal strength compare interestingly with Mark's statement about the Gerasene demoniac, that 'no one could secure him any more, even with a chain [compare especially Example 8] because he had often been secured with fetters and chains but had snapped the chains and broken the fetters, and no one had the strength to control him. All night and all day . . . he would howl and gash himself with stones . . .' Sceva's seven sons who presumed that the Name of Jesus was a magic symbol found that the demoniac

---

[1] Oesterreich, op. cit.

[2] Françoise Strachan, *Casting out the Devils* (Aquarian Press).

[3] *Man, Myth and Magic, Frontiers of Belief*, No. 88. 'The Flesh and the Devil', an article devoted entirely to Fr Neil-Smith's ministry.

'hurled himself at them and overpowered first one and then the other, and handled them so violently that they fled from the house naked and badly mauled'. No wonder other magical dabblers decided to burn their bridges by burning their books (Acts 19:13–20)!

In spite of the importance attached to diagnosis, and preliminary medical and psychiatric care and investigation, Fr Neil-Smith's early morning experience in the last example reaffirms the fact that rubrics and books can never be more than guides. To have obtained the Bishop's explicit permission for the case,† together with a competent medical and psychiatric diagnosis, or to have compiled a detailed case-history, could probably not have been done prior to a suicide or a murder, nor would anyone presume that such things were necessary even if they were available at such an hour. An interesting point which I have heard Fr Neil-Smith mention in public talks which he has given on the subject, is that so often people *know* what is wrong. After all the actor's wife did call her *priest* not her doctor.

That priests are not called out more is I am sure not because the people are convinced that it is wholly physical or mental, but because they are afraid that their minister will not take it seriously and may be unable to help them. At a large conference on Deliverance at which I was speaking a few years ago *every* person there who was active in this ministry indicated that cases had reached them via ministers who were unsympathetic to the needs of such people.

Christopher Woodard tells the following story in *A Doctor's Faith Holds Fast*, which may be in some ways related to my last points.

### Example 11

A young soldier . . . went out of his mind as a result of the strain he had gone through, and he became very violent. He started laying into his fellow soldiers and trying to kill himself, so his mates held him to the ground while they sent for a doctor. A doctor came and examined him, and, seeing this young fellow foaming at the mouth and screaming and throwing

† In Fr Neil-Smith's case this would not be necessary anyway as the same article points out he has 'permission to practise . . . from the Bishop of London'.

himself around, he was reminded of the story of the youth on
the shore of Lake Galilee, the story told in the New Testament.
He looked up and asked, 'Where is the padre?' When the
padre was found, he came and saw the young man lying there
on the ground, pinned down by half a dozen others. The doctor
said to him: 'Surely this a job for you, padre?'

The doctor, like the actor's wife in Example 10, seems also to
support Fr Neil-Smith's conviction that basically people *know*.
The demon, it is clear from the above, was (as we say of some
diseases) 'a killer'. Most stories have an ending and it is the
demon's character which goes a long way towards explaining it.
The story continues:

The padre doubted whether he could do very much, but not
wishing to appear nonplussed, he said: 'In the Name of Jesus
Christ I command this thing to come out of you!' So saying he
made the sign of the Cross. The boy immediately appeared all
right, but the padre dropped dead.

The result is tragic but not really surprising. Those sons of
Sceva who used the Name of Jesus as a magic ritual happened
to get away with their lives—their successor did not. The danger
of demonic transference is a very real one.

*Example 12*

There was the case of a newspaper reporter who watched an
exorcism and was affected to the extent where he vomited and
passed out . . . And then he too had to be exorcised. He
certainly had a story to write, if he could remember it![1]

Françoise Strachan's final comment about his not being able
to remember the incident, is based on the frequent loss of
memory (amnesia) experienced in these and in trance states,
if in fact the two can be distinguished. Thus George Bennett
relates his ministry to a person who had previously sold herself
to the Devil.

*Example 13*

. . . she told me her story and I was able to minister to her. She
swayed as I did so, as if she were about to faint, and then
suddenly collapsed. I helped her to a chair and laid my hands

[1] Strachan, op. cit.

on her, praying the Holy Spirit to flood her whole being . . .
Two or three days later she asked me what had happened as
she could not remember much of our conversation or the
ministration . . . she became a regular member of her church
and was soon preparing for confirmation. It is strange how
such sufferers only vaguely remember the exorcism itself.[1]

### Example 14

I fell to the floor as if dead, [Mr Neil told me afterwards]. When
I came round, I knew nothing of what had gone on. I knew only
that I was free of these demons.[2]

Dr Yap says that 'Complete' possession is marked by '. . . subsequent amnesia', and Dr McAll states that out of thirty cases,
seven 'did not know that any exorcism was taking place'.
Some of this is due to or concomitant with the state of unconsciousness, which was mentioned in Examples 10, 12, 13
and 14. Such a state is very much a manifestation *at the time
of exorcism* as each of these examples illustrate. It can hardly be
used as a pre-exorcism symptom, although as Example 8
indicates, confrontation with holy things can bring a state of
unconsciousness, where the boy, you will recall, 'fell
unconscious' when passing a church or seeing a crucifix. The
mechanism is to my mind not actually demonic *as such*, but a
conversion hysteria (see Chapter Five) to resolve the internal
conflict caused by the demonic reaction against the sacred, and
a personal abhorrence of desecration.

'Demonic reaction against the sacred' is the last and major
non-physical symptom of demonic possession to which I now
turn.

### Example 15

All the priests of the place and from round about came and
spoke to her, but the devil replied to them with a contempt
which exceeded all bounds, and when he was questioned about
Jesus he made a reply of such derision that it cannot be set
down.

[1] Bennett, op. cit.
[2] Doreen Irvine, *From Witchcraft to Christ* (Concordia).

The reticence of the account, together with the fact that a number of priests were concerned with the case indicate that this example from Oesterreich's book is taken from long ago. Three hundred years later, though, the same manifestations are apparent. From the verbatim account of a Roman Catholic exorcism comes the following dialogue:

### Example 16

Then he made Satan [the name which the demon gave in this instance] look at the crucifix, and Satan cried out: 'And that too . . . you bring out that puppet! . . .'
. . . 'In the name of the Virgin Mary . . .'
'Madam! O Madam!'[1]

The following is an incident arising out of a Pentecostal ministry:

### Example 17

One time while bringing deliverance to an obsessed woman, I asked the demons possessing her to speak about the Blood of Jesus. A deep male voice replied, 'We hate the Blood of Jesus.'

### Example 18

Summoning all my courage I tried to speak with assurance and authority . . . the voice came again, sly, dripping with sarcasm. 'She says she loves him.' 'Loves who?' I asked automatically. 'You know who.' The voice was angry and petulant now. 'Him . . . Jesus!' The word was spat out like a curse.[2]

Such reactions to Jesus do not happen according to the exorcist's appointments book. Pastor Williams relates in his booklet *Demonology—A Bible Truth* the occasion when he was walking along in Manchester talking to another Christian. Walking by his side was a young man who, the other Christian informed him, was a Spiritualist, when 'suddenly without prayer, he [the Spiritualist] was thrown flat on his face on the pavement. He looked as if he were dead . . .'

[1] *Satan in the Modern World*, L. Cristiani.
[2] *Deliver Us from Evil*, Don Basham.

*Example 19*

Dennis Bennett in *The Holy Spirit and You* relates the following incident and offers an explanation.

> A young woman from St Luke's Church was going along the street in downtown Seattle one day, minding her own business, when suddenly an elderly lady rushed at her, screaming obscenities and threats, and waving her stick angrily. The Christian girl was startled, but not frightened, as she recognised what was happening. The old woman was demonically possessed and the evil spirit in her detected the presence of the Holy Spirit in the young lady, and immediately was aroused to angry protest . . .
>
> Such incidents are not uncommon . . . If a person has been serving Satan, and gotten himself thoroughly oppressed or possessed by enemy power and influence, he will be repelled by anyone who is walking in the Spirit . . . One of the most striking examples of this is the great resentment shown by spiritualists to those who have received the Baptism in the Holy Spirit.

It is a long way from downtown Seattle to the streets of Manchester—yet the similarity of the two incidents is striking, especially when it is known that Pastor Williams prefaced his story by saying, 'Just a few months after the baptism of the Holy Spirit, I was walking along the Manchester streets . . .' Spirit can only be discerned by spirit—and it works both ways.

Reaction against Christ can take many forms; violent revulsion of Christian symbols (Example 8), Christian places, people, actions—in short against everything that proclaims Christ.

As I have already related, I recall a psychoanalyst telling me that when in training she was taught that if she suspected a patient was involved in Black Magic, she was to produce a crucifix suddenly, whereupon if the patient was 'invisibly hurled to the back of the room', the case should be referred to a priest. There is no psychological explanation of such a thing, and her professor was wise enough to discriminate between what his branch of healing was equipped to deal with and what it was not—a lesson not only for some of his colleagues, but for pastors and clergy. Dr McAll in a talk entitled 'Physical States that might be confused with the Demonic' said that truly demonic cases expressed themselves by 'a violent hatred of Christ' and gave examples of a patient tearing up a Bible. An Anglican vicar once told me of a frail little woman to whom he ministered in his church. During the ministration she underwent a vivid personality change, resulting in the vicar being punched in the face and a Bible being torn up and thrown to the corners of the building. The old lady had no recollection of doing this, and 'came round' to enquire innocently 'Dear me, Vicar, what has happened, your face is bleeding!'

*Example 20*

The following took place in a service at which Maxwell Whyte was speaking, and illustrates not only reaction to Christ, but an example of the authority a discerning minister has in such situations.

'He's lying, I tell you!' I heard him [the demoniac] say. 'Everything he says is a lie!' Suddenly he lunged to his feet and gave a shriek which electrified the audience. 'He's lying . . .!' Maxwell Whyte pointed a finger at him and said evenly, 'Young man, if you can control yourself, sit down . . . if you cannot then go to the prayer room and we'll minister to you later.' I was greatly amazed to see that the incident had in no way shaken the lecturer's composure, even though the audience, including me, was in a state of near shock.[1] Apparently the youth trembled so much his glasses fell off. Mr Whyte, after seeing to it that the boy was taken to the prayer room, said to the audience, 'What you have witnessed is not unusual in a meeting where the deliverance ministry is being introduced. The truth of deliverance often causes evil spirits to react in some such dramatic manner.' This probably answers the question that may have arisen about why there are rarely such reactions in 'normal' Church services because few 'normal' Churches introduce deliverance so specifically . . .

The limited knowledge of the demons is shown by the fact that they would be safer if they kept quiet. Daphne Buckley even tells of an occasion when a demon replied through the person, 'I've come out now!', which is, I suppose, the demon equivalent to the child who answers the door by saying, 'Mummy has just told me to tell you she isn't here!'

[1] Basham, op. cit.

Although these examples are mostly of acute cases, and therefore display the maximum powers of the demonic, the scope and range of their power and intelligence is no more than God allows them; their violence, or their threats and blackmail are insubordination. There is no dualism here—it is only the subordinate who can be insubordinate. The desert fathers regarded Satanic reactions as 'those of an alarmed enemy, not of a confident invader'. As Cullmann has written of the powers:

> they are, so to speak, bound as to a rope which can be more or less lengthened, so that those among them who show tendencies of emancipation can have the illusion that they are releasing themselves . . . while in reality, by this striving which here and there appears, they can only show once more their demonic character; they can not however actually set themselves free. Their power is only an apparent power. The Church has so much more the duty to stand against them, in view of the fact that it knows that *their power is only apparent, and that in reality Christ has conquered all demons*[1] [italics mine].

Some demonic manifestations can best be described as 'animal-manifestations', and present real but perplexing symptoms. I have no doubt that the literature of witchcraft offers some possible explanation, but it is a field of enquiry which may be left to others, though I should indicate that the phenomenon exists, so that pastors confronted with acute states of demonic suffering are not taken too much by surprise.

*Example 21*

> Coming from the same area [Yorkshire] a young man was sent to us. He had a degree and was a brilliant mathematician, but had had a couple of nervous breakdowns. He was taken into our room so that we could talk to him, when suddenly he began to get on his hands and knees and bark like a dog. What a terrible thing to write but how true . . . after prayers he seemed to get better and better . . .[2]

In severe cases, writes Daphne Buckley, the demons will make 'someone wiggle across the floor like a serpent with their tongue darting in and out'. (Perhaps the medieval artists used less artistic licence than we usually imagine!) Her experience at the

---

[1] *Christ and Time*, SCM.
[2] *Demonology—A Bible Truth*, A. Williams.

DELIVERANCE 149

Full Gospel Deliverance Crusade is entirely in keeping with the well-documented anthropological studies of what is termed 'animal possession'.† Dr Yap's study included two cases of such theiromania in which the possessed acted in ways characteristic of a fox and a snake. From time to time I have had enquiries from those involved in this ministry asking whether they are the only people to have come across such phenomena.

### Example 22

When I [Pastor Williams] was in Holland in 1960 . . . a man stood up who appeared to be trying to disturb the meeting. Five or six Dutch brethren rushed over to him and with great difficulty got him out of the hall into the vestry. After calling us in to pray we discovered that the man was of terrific strength, in fact it took six or seven people to hold him down and he was making a noise like a pig. It fact it was so realistic that one would think one were in a pig-sty We had a tremendous time fighting against this evil power. I asked one of the Dutch pastors if any sense could be got out of him, to which they answered, 'O yes—deep sin.' I asked what kind of sin. They said he went with the beasts of the field. I shall never forget that man nor the manifestations of demonic power.[1]

From the hundreds of accounts of contemporary demonic affliction it would have been easy to select less spectacular examples, and to have omitted the vile and the blasphemous, but to have done so would not have been to write about the demonic—because it *is* vile and blasphemous, it *does* seek to destroy and kill. Christ's victory did not make the enemy more congenial, it defeated him; defeated evil is still evil—and frustrated evil at that!

I imagine there are two sorts of readers; those whose spiritual eyes are open to see the demonic, and who will see in the examples of this chapter clear-cut instances of realities already familiar to them. The other readers will be those who for various reasons will find such accounts 'eye-openers' mentally— and I hope spiritually. To the latter I would wish to make clear that, as I stressed at the beginning of the book, I am not interested in or fascinated by the demonic, nor have I investigated

† See for example *Trances*, Wavell *et al.*, including an invoked horse-possession for entertainment, in which a boy ate hay.

[1] Williams, op. cit.

it. All I have done is to draw on the experiences and writings of the increasing number of Christians who this century have obeyed Christ's commission (Luke 9:1-2) not only to preach the Gospel, but also to heal the sick and cast out demons. Although the accounts may seem sensational to those unfamiliar with such things, they are the clearest means of introducing the subject.

As well as preternatural strength there is to be found preternatural knowledge, on the part of demoniacs now, as of old. 'I know thee who thou art', has preceded a discomforting revelation of himself as one or two exorcists have experienced. I shall give just one example, not so much because it is so very important for diagnosis, but it does throw some light on the fact that the girl in Acts 16 who was a fortune-teller, needed to be *exorcised* of evil spirits, and afterwards she was no longer able to earn a living by prediction.

### Example 23

A minister writes:

> Another voice, quite unlike Judy's spoke out through her lips. It said 'I don't want her to live because she wants to serve the Lord. I am not Judy. I want to kill Judy . . . you don't believe in Satan do you?'
> 'I certainly do not!' I replied emphatically.
> 'All right then, I'll prove it to you,' the voice boasted. And it then proceeded to tell me intimate details of my private life.

If that were the only example, it could be dismissed as telepathy, but as the Roman Catholic writer F. X. Maquart cogently points out: thought-reading is a rare occurrence and presupposes a special gift which presumably the person has either had since birth or acquired later in life; both are easily established if true. It is purely gratuitous, therefore, to introduce extraordinary psychic and mental powers to 'explain away' such things. 'If it be established that the patient has never displayed any gift of thought reading, then this gift is not to be relied on to explain his knowledge of foreign languages he has never learnt.' Nor, one might add, his knowledge of the whereabouts and nature of Christian things, or of the past life of the exorcist.

The *Roman Ritual*, in rubric 15 on exorcism, having first discouraged the exorcist to converse with the unclean spirits unnecessarily, says, '. . . necessary questions are, for example: about the number and name of the spirits inhabiting the patient'. I shall deal with the 'name' in the next chapter, meanwhile is it going too far to suggest that *multiple* demonic possession has to be believed? Of my Examples, numbers 2, 3, 14 and 17 implied multiple possession. The Roman Catholic experience implies the same. While Don Basham can say, 'Sometimes a person seems tormented by only one spirit, often there are more', the German authority Kerner is quoted by Oesterreich as saying, 'It often happens that we recognise in a single individual not merely one demon but several at once or in succession; there speak in him two, three or more voices and individualities.' The Rev. Alan Harrison of the Guild of Health in a lecture on the subject, stated 'a plurality of demons seems to be quite a common factor in all this'.

Most Pentecostalist literature on the subject treats multiple possession as the norm. The deeply investigated case of Mrs Piper (see Chapter Five) led Myers, in his monumental *Human Personality and its Survival of Bodily Death* (Volume Two), to conclude that in certain cases two or more spirits may simultaneously control different portions of the same organism. Canon Pearce-Higgins' review of the cases investigated by the Spiritualist Carl Wickland in *Thirty Years Among the Dead*, said of them that 'It was found that in many cases the patient was controlled by several entities,' and, incidentally 'that these could not all be removed by one [mediumistic] treatment.'

It seems that facts are stranger than fiction, and that the state of 'Legion' and the former state of Mary of Magdala (Luke 8:2) might after all belong to the former. Our Lord's teaching about the seven other demons is so extremely relevant as a parable, that any claim to literal accuracy could add no further weight to it.

The lesser demonic manifestations will all of them be distortions of one form or another; false doctrines and perversions of truth in spiritual matters, for instance St John's description of the Devil as 'a murderer from the start' is all too meaningful. When he goes on to say, 'he was never grounded in the truth . . . he is a liar, and the father of lies', the frequent demonic symptoms of doubting one's conversion, or the conviction (or, more accurately, delusion) of having committed the unforgivable sin are to be expected.

To summarise so far, it has been suggested that both reason *and* discernment are necessary for the diagnosis of spiritual illness as distinct from illness of the body or mind. 'Possession' or demonic attack may be *invited* knowingly or unknowingly; but it will mainly be *uninvited*. The former states might be illustrated by Satanists and mediums, while any occult involvement *might* bring about the latter.

Such accidental demonisation may be best understood by a wider understanding of the 'powers' and the demonisation of society. It was then stated that 'demons' were malign intelligences which could make their presence known by physical changes and what might loosely be called 'mental' changes in the patients. Twenty-three 'Examples' were then given illustrating first the physical manifestations especially of speaking (1-4), 'tongues' (5-7), aggression and strength (8-10). Then the dangers of demonic transference (11-12), and the less physical aspects: amnesia (13-14); violent reaction to Christ in various situations (15-20). A digression was then made (to make the picture complete), on 'animalistic' possession (21-2). Preternatural knowledge (23) concluded the manifestations, and then followed some facts to suggest that multiple possession is very frequent. Throughout, sufficient details were given of each case if they introduced new facts, or substantiated those already mentioned.

In the next chapter I shall deal with exorcism and the exorcist, but before that, there are, unfortunately, possible *non*-demonic factors in 'possession' cases. These, I shall not set out in detail, but they do need to be considered for a right diagnosis and an appropriate ministry.

The two main points are (*a*) the possibility of 'possession' by the departed, and (*b*) the possibility of possession by the living.

Possession by the departed is not mentioned in the Bible, and many friends of mine, for example Prebendary Henry Cooper and the Rev. Dennis Peterson, would argue strongly, on quite different grounds for the impossibility of 'earth-bound' spirits. Spiritualists, and those of similar beliefs, on the other hand make the return of departed earth-bound spirits a part of their creed, and do so at the expense of any demonology. Canon Pearce-

Higgins on television dismissed the Exorcism Report on these grounds as 'almost complete nonsense'. I shall deal more fully with the problem in Chapter Eight when dealing with Places.

Most apparent earth-bound spirits are undoubtedly lying spirits, as some of the ouija and other spiritistic cases in Chapter Four make clear. The cultural setting will encourage or discourage the interpretation by observers and patients as possession by departed spirits. Thus Dr Yap's assertion that twenty-two cases out of sixty-six 'were possessed by the spirit of dead relatives' may not be reliable, especially as one was possessed by 'Jesus Christ' and another by 'the Virgin Mary'. This suggests that in this part of his report he was indicating states as generally understood rather than his psychiatric assessment of them. George Bennett, in his leaflet *About Exorcism*, gives a case of a possible discarnate spirit involved with a human personality, and a case in Dr McAll's article[1] although certainly involving the demonic, involved also the dead lesbian partner of the woman concerned.

Father Gilbert Shaw summarised the possibilities thus:

> There must be a careful diagnosis for it is not always a demonic intelligence that is attempting to control—in many cases it is undoubtedly a split within the personality's own being—a self-possession—and in some it may not be demonic but from an earth-bound humanity involving the prayer of reconciliation rather than the judgment of exorcism.[2]

> I live, now not with my own life but with the life of——who lives in me. (Galatians 2:19)

If we insert *demons* into St Paul's quotation we have a picture of possession which is demonic. If we insert the name of some earthbound relative, it describes the rare state that I have just outlined. If we can think of those whose lives could be justly described by the insertion of the word 'mother' (or, less often another relative) we shall be recalling instances of 'possession by the living'. Approached in that sort of way the suggestion, instead of being an absurdity, will for many be the most familiar and the most realistic.

'I live, now not with my own life but with the life of *mother* who lives in me,' describes the most acute state of what is so aptly termed 'smother-love'.

[1] McAll, op. cit.      [2] Shaw, op. cit.

The following is my account of such a case, and it has been read and accepted by the Christian psychiatrist concerned.

A mother, during the course of her counselling, went into church alone one day, and felt that God was making known to her that she had never 'cut the umbilical cord of her youngest son'. Her son was in a town 450 miles away, certified in a mental hospital, where he had been for eighteen months. The mother thereupon prayed that this unnatural link would be cut. *At that exact moment* the son felt himself cured, the mother herself was cured of a heart complaint, and the son's wife at that time in a place for T.B. was also cured. The son resumed his job within two days.

Such cases are outside the scope of this book, but they do make clear that however much credence we give to the power of the demonic, that it is only one of many influences that distorts and destroys, but that none of these is beyond the touch of the Healing Christ. Amid the profusion of possession-states and the bondage they bring, is one state which is never accidentally experienced, but only ever by invitation. Of Christ, Anglicans have regularly prayed, '*Grant that we may evermore dwell in Him, and He in us.*'

# CHAPTER SEVEN

# EXORCISM

FROM THE MANY contemporary accounts of demonic states in the last chapter, the conclusions of authorities on the subject can be better assessed. Rather than quote in full their various diagnostic outlines, I shall make one general summary and indicate which items are supported by which author by appending a letter code for each concerned. The authors I have selected are those who have in their writings drawn up concise classifications to which the reader can refer, thereby excluding such writers as Fr Gilbert Shaw and Dr Kurt Koch.

Among authorities who have made reasonably concise criteria for recognising demonic attack are the following:

Doctor Theodore Bovet (B), *That They may have Life*, p. 61.

Doctor Jean Lhermitte (L), 'Les possédés sont-ils des fous?', *Ecclesia*, No. 67, pp. 29–36.

Hal Lindsey (Ly), in his chapter, 'Diagnosing Demon Possession', pp. 150–66 in *Satan is alive and well on planet Earth*.

Professor T. K. Oesterreich (O), *Possession—Demoniacal and Other*, chapter 11, 'The external signs of possession,' pp. 17–25.

Doctor R. K. McAll (Mc), 'Demonosis or the Possession Syndrome', in *The International Journal of Social Psychiatry*, Vol. XVII, No. 2.

Rev. John Nevius, DD (N), in *Demon Possession* (originally *Demon Possession and Allied Themes*), and summarised by Prof. Merrill Unger in *Biblical Demonology*, p. 83.

The *Roman Ritual* (RR), in its rubrics on Exorcism, printed as an Appendix below.

Doctor P. M. Yap (Y), 'The Possession Syndrome', *The Journal of Mental Science*, Vol. 106, No. 442.

The picture which emerges from these writings is wholly consistent with the selection of present-day cases in the preceding chapter and shows that, as Oesterreich has written, the New Testament accounts 'even should they be recognised as of little or no historical value, bear in themselves the stamp of truth. They are pictures of typical states exactly reproduced.'

## Some Symptoms of Acute Demonic Attack

(A) *Change of personality* (O) (N) (Ly)
Resulting in change of intelligence (Ly), character (N), demeanour (Y) and appearance (O).

(B) *Physical Changes*
  (i) Preternatural strength (B), (L), (Ly), (O) and (RR).
  (ii) Epileptiform convulsions (Mc), (N), (O); foaming (N).
  (iii) Catatonic symptoms (Mc); falling (N).
  (iv) Clouding of consciousness (Mc), (Y); anaesthesia to pain (Y).
  (v) Changed voice (Mc), (O), (Y).

(C) *Mental changes*
  (i) Glossolalia (L), (RR), (B); understanding unknown languages (B), (L), (RR).
  (ii) Preternatural knowledge (B), (N), (R), (RR).
  (iii) Psychic and occult powers (Ly), (RR), e.g. clairvoyance (B), (RR); telepathy (L); and prediction (L).

(D) *Spiritual Changes*
  (i) Reaction to and fear of Christ (B), (Mc), (N); causing blasphemy, etc. (O), (Ly).
  (ii) Affected by prayer (B).

(E) *Deliverance Possible in the Name of Jesus.* As this is a diagnosis in retrospect it falls outside the range of pre-exorcism symptoms although Bovet, McAll and Nevius include it.

(Doctor W. Menzies Alexander's book *Demonic Possession in the New Testament—Its Relations Historical, Medical and Theological* in spite of its promising title has not been included in the above. He has two criteria for diagnosing possession cases. At the natural level, mental derangement, and at the supernatural level a confession of Jesus as Messiah. Because of the latter he is led to conclude that all genuine possession cases were restricted to the lifetime of Christ. Had he broadened the supernatural to a 'recognition of Jesus' he would have avoided his curious conclusion.)

The various 'possessed' states can also be summarised, although such an outline would be more of a hindrance than a help if it were presumed that each label indicated an exclusive state, and that the various states could not overlap or merge.

The division between 'true' and 'false' is based on the popular use of 'possession' as a term to denote *demonic* possession.

1 *False Possession* (but in no way implying 'unreal')

    (*a*) *Psychogenic* (i.e. originating in the mind).
        (i) By suggestion
        (ii) By autosuggestion
        (iii) By projection—whether self-induced or by another
        (iv) Delusion
        (v) 'Passivity phenomena' †
    (*b*) *Medical*—symptomatic epilepsy, etc.
    (*c*) *By living person(s)*.
        (i) Relations
        (ii) Occult manipulation
    (*d*) *By earth-bound spirits*.
        (i) By invitation
        (ii) By accident

2 *True (Demonic) Possession*

    (*a*) *Due to:*
        (i) Accident, e.g. Heredity, Place, Occult experience and healing, Occult transference and curses;
        (ii) Invitation knowingly, e.g. Devil subscription;
        (iii) Invitation unknowingly, e.g. mediums.
    (*b*) *By:*
        (i) demon;
        (ii) demons.

† The patient tells us that his thought, feelings, speech and actions are not his own,' Mayer-Gross, Slater & Roth, *Clinical Psychiatry*.

(c) *Degree*: ‡
    (i) Partial/'Lucid'/'external demonopathy';
    (ii) Complete/'Somnambulistic'/'internal demonopathy'.

Since, as I have frequently stressed, man is not a tripartite being but a whole person, it is most unlikely that the mind and body are ever unaffected by a troubled spirit. The possible computations of symptoms are therefore endless. One of the few pieces of diagnostic writing relating the demonic to bodily and mental ills is the essay by Dr Lechler in Part II of Kurt Koch's *Occult Bondage and Deliverance* (published by Evangelization Publishers, W. Germany).† Doctor Koch himself writes of Dr Lechler, 'The judgment of this Christian psychiatrist is weighty. For he is not only a specialist in this field, but he is also regarded in Christian circles as a counsellor with charismatic gifts.'[1] The following five quotations of Dr Lechler's will, I trust, encourage the reader to refer to their source and incidentally explain why I have been unable to summarise his findings.

1 '. . . a possessed person, though he may be restless and even driven into a rage at times, will nevertheless remain sane in his thoughts.'

2 'While the mental patient will speak in extravagant tones of the demons he alleges to be living inside himself, the possessed person avoids all mention of demons as long as no one approaches him on a spiritual level.'

3 'The voices which a patient says originate from strange people . . . are . . . usually . . . of a pathological nature . . . The satanic voices heard by a possessed person are of a completely different nature. . . . In general then, if the voices are demonic in origin they will attempt to lure the person away from God, whereas if they are the result of some mental abnormality they will speak of unnatural and nonsensical things.'

4 'Experience shows that in the case of schizophrenics, a person who continually talks about being possessed is in fact deluding himself. On the contrary a person who is

‡ For a selection of the numerous terms designating the degree of demonic influence, see the beginning of Chapter Five.
  † Available in USA from Kregel Publishing House, Grand Rapids, Michigan, and in England from Hughes & Coleman, Spar Rd, Norwich.
  [1] *Christian Counselling and Occultism.*

really possessed will never let the idea of possession enter his head, even if there is no other explanation for his condition.'

5 '. . . if blasphemous thoughts arise in a person's heart and are consciously expressed without the slightest remorse, they will in almost every case be promoted by the devil. On the other hand, if thoughts force themselves upon a person, and instead of being expressed are abhorred and genuinely repented of, they will most likely be of a pathological nature. A demonically affected person will care little about blasphemous thoughts, but the mental depressive will lament the fact that he thinks such things.'

## EXORCISM

There are, broadly speaking, only two sorts of exorcism; that which is undertaken in the name of Christ, and that which is not. I shall designate the one '*Christian exorcism*', and the other 'Non-Christian'. An example of the latter comes from the late Estelle Robert's autobiography *Fifty Years a Medium*, which I shall quote in full because it shows, among other things, that the 'demonic manifestations' which Christians describe are not due to inaccurate reporting swayed by loyalty to the New Testament accounts.

I was astounded by the transformation that confronted me. The pleasant-faced girl with whom I had spent the past four hours had in some Jekyll-and-Hyde metamorphosis changed into a coarse-featured foul-mouthed man. It is difficult to explain. The features were as before, yet different in some indefinable way . . . the voice, too, was completely different. It had dropped several tones, and the words it now uttered belonged to the gutter. With bold effrontery the creature sprawled into a chair and dared me to take a step forward. Offering dire threats of injury if I did not obey his commands, he boasted of his strength and his determination to manifest in the girl's body whenever he felt so disposed.

. . . With absolute certainty I knew that Red Cloud was with me . . .

. . . As I began to advance on the intruder I was met with a volley of oaths and obscenities. I told him that he must forsake the girl's body for all time. At this he screamed further threats of violence . . .

... under Red Cloud's guidance [I] placed my two hands on the creature's forehead. The cry this action produced can be described only as a scream of terror, followed by sobbing entreaties to leave him alone. Again I urged him to leave the girl's body. Again he refused ...

[After placing both her hands on the girl's head, there came] ... a cry of terror, followed by the frightened sobs. Then came silence, broken a few minutes later by the voice of Red Cloud breaking into my consciousness with the words: 'All is over. He will return no more.' With the entity's departure, the girl quickly returned to normal.

She recounts another exorcism in which Red Cloud had temporarily allowed the spirit to control her. From the account of the witnesses (for Mrs Roberts was in a trance state totally unaware of what was taking place), it was a raucous, rumbustious performance 'in which the threats and screaming blasphemies uttered through me eloquently betrayed the spirit to be of a very low order'.[1]

Other 'Non-Christian' exorcisms include not only mediumistic but ritualistic and magical approaches to the problem, examples of which abound in anthropological and sociological studies of primitive (and not so primitive) cultures. Doctor Yap's success with 'insulin or electroplexy' (i.e. ECT) suggests that the driving out of some malign intelligence can be accomplished by more physical means, and Wickland's mediumistic exorcisms with expulsion by static electricity applied to the patient, provide an interesting similarity.[2]

CHRISTIAN EXORCISM

For some this is a contradiction in terms, because they point out, rightly, that Christian expulsion of demons has nothing to do with entering into any relationship or pact with them, as the term suggests. The two New Testament references are instructive. (i) The High Priest says, '*I put you on oath* (*exorkizō*) by the living God to tell us if you are the Christ' (Matthew 26:63). (ii) It is only the poor unfortunate sons of Sceva who are

---

[1] Note that in the New Testament the word 'demon' (Gk. *daimōnion*, *diamōn*) is used *less* than 'spirit' (*pneuma*) in describing exorcism, as distinct from discussing it. Such spirits are often described as 'unclean' (Mark 3:11), or 'evil' (Luke 8:2).

[2] *Thirty Years Among the Dead.*

described (Acts 19:13) as *exorkistēs*. The avoidance of any sort of pact or agreement between minister and spirits is sound and essential; and practical rather than theological considerations are sufficient to make anyone wish to avoid emulating the Sceva family.

Some have sought to replace the term by 'dispossession', 'redemption' or 'liberation', and so on, but as language in general always tends to become less precise, and general usage is affected little by semantics or technical accuracy, it seems possible only to retain the word and to try to educate people about its two distinct uses. (Perhaps future editions of the Exeter Report, if the commission agrees, might be entitled *Christian Exorcism*?)

The casting out of demons is the work of God through his Church and a sign of the coming of his Kingdom, the doing of his will, and the deliverance from evil for which every member so faithfully prays; it is God's action, not ours, because the Kingdom, the Power and the Glory belong to him not to us.

It is not a fight-to-the-death between the natural and the spiritual, nor is it, as Canon Pearce-Higgins has maintained, 'the gift of some spiritually and psychically gifted clergy'. It is not a contest of psychic powers or wills described in Freudian terms of demonic archetype, nor is it, in Christian terms, an externalised battle between the new nature and the Old Adam. Christian exorcism is not the externalisation of basic drives and impulses in order that they may be recognised and renounced, however much Christ would bless such a process, nor is it an accommodation to the delusions of the mentally ill by supplying them with a therapeutic ritual. It is not the action of a diminishing Church to publicise the reality of a diminishing God—a God-of-the-Gaps in medicine and psychology. Christian exorcism is not a deliberate return to earlier Christian practices on the naïve assumption that the Church should, or can, return to the Apostolic era, or a retreat from the challenge of evolving a Space Age spirituality. Nor is it, as some have maintained,[1] '*part* . . . of a revival of a magical world-view'. It is not a defence against spiritual armies which are about to overrun us.

It is instead a demonstration in power and love of the Lordship of Christ over his world; the 'manifestations' outlined in the

[1] F. B. Welbourne, *Theology*, Vol. LXXV, No. 629. November 1972.

last chapter are demonstrations *against* power, not demonstrations of it. The demons, as I vividly recall Dr Frank Lake saying in a lecture,

> * . . . do not have that kind of reality which requires them to be destroyed, but they 'go to their place' *until* they take their place in the triumphant train of Jesus Christ. (See Colossians 2:15)

St John's silence about exorcism[1] should not be taken to undermine the authenticity of possession, but rather to supply the framework in which it can be understood: 'Now [i.e. in the Cross of Christ] is sentence being passed on this world, now the prince of this world is to be overthrown' (John 12:31).[2]

In Christ were created

> . . . all things in heaven and earth: everything visible and everything invisible, Thrones, Dominations, Sovereignties, Powers—all things were created through him and for him. (Colossians 1:16–17)

Hence James writes, 'the demons have the same belief [in God], and they tremble in fear' (James 2:19). In practical terms, as one minister put it to me, 'the demons are much more afraid of us than we are of them!' The Bible is more concerned to proclaim the *defeat* of such powers, than to describe their ancestry. Whatever that may be—and there are a number of authors who have given the matter their attention[3]—it has not taken place beyond the bounds of Christ's rule. Christ is their Lord as well as ours, and they have to obey him for no other reason than for what he is. Those who are 'in Christ' share the authority which is Christ's by right and theirs by adoption and commission.

> 'Here is a teaching that is new,' they said, 'and with authority behind it: he gives orders even to unclean spirits and they obey him.' (Mark 1:27)

---

[1] But note the similar way of describing Judas in Luke 22:3, and John 13:2.

[2] See especially H. Schlier's *Principalities and Powers in the New Testament* (Burns and Oates). 'Overthrown' is the same Greek verb as the one which I described as 'chucking out', and is translated 'cast out' in the AV, and 'thrown out' in Beck's *The New Testament in the Language of Today*.

[3] e.g. Unger's *Biblical Demonology*; Langton's *Satan—a Portrait*; Chafer's *Satan—His Motive and Methods*.

Part of the people's astonishment was due to the astonishing difference between exorcism and Christ(ian) exorcism; it is the authority of Christ and in Christ that makes the latter so distinctive. When sending the Twelve on their mission we read:

[He] . . . began to send them out in pairs, giving them authority over the unclean spirits.

The distinction between the healing of sickness and the casting out of demons is explicit in the synoptic Gospels (e.g. Mark 1:32; Matthew 8:16; Luke 6:17) and Paul Tournier expresses a view contrary to most commentators when he sees the terms 'healing the sick' and 'casting out demons' as synonymous.[1]

There are indications in the Gospels that some cases were acute and others not so. In Christ's healing of the Gerasene demoniac there is an indication (Mark 5:8) that Jesus' commands to the spirits had been going on for some time, as the Greek imperfect tense is used. On another occasion reported in the synoptics, Luke says that he 'rebuked' a high fever (Luke 4:39). Since this follows the crowds' astonishment at his authority over unclean spirits, it is probably more than a literary device of 'personifying the fever' (Creed)—an implication that there was something behind or within the illness best approached by an authoritative 'rebuking' as, according to the same author, Jesus rebuked the spirit in the epileptic demoniac (Luke 9:42). The story of the healing of the Syro-Phoenician/Canaanite woman's daughter suggests an exorcistic healing at a distance (Mark 7:25–30, Matthew 15:21–8), and perhaps also Jesus' reservations about such a ministry.[2]

Christian exorcism may be either a *petition* to God, as in the Lord's Prayer and the tradition of the Eastern Churches, or a *command* addressed *not* to the demoniac but to the demon(s):

Paul lost his temper one day and turned round and said to the spirit, 'I order you in the name of Jesus Christ to leave that woman.' The spirit went out there and then. (Acts 16:17–18)

---

[1] *A Doctor's Case-Book in the Light of the Bible.*
[2] cf. Acts 19:12. For the New Testament miracles including healing at a distance see Loos, *The Miracles of Jesus* (Brill). To suggest that it was not a miracle at a distance (Taylor, *The Life and Ministry of Jesus*) but that Jesus' statement of the demonic departure was due to 'a confident assurance based on supernatural knowledge' is to explain one difficulty by another difficulty.

The distinctions between the acute and more mild states suggested by the New Testament are as valid today, and are important. For clarity's sake I used examples from the acute cases in the last chapter—or at least of acute manifestations. The contemporary Roman Catholic distinction is between 'major' and 'minor' exorcisms relating to the acute or mild degree of 'obsession' or 'possession'. On the authority of D. M. Prummer's *Manuale Theologiae Moralis*, Fr Tugwell O.P. writes:

> Even short of fully-fledged public exorcism ['major'], which the Church prudently reserves to the discretion of the Bishops, there is often need and opportunity for all the faithful to give battle in the Spirit. Private and unofficial exorcism in the name of Christ is within the competence of any Christian, lay or clerical.[1]

Exorcism at a distance is only rarely undertaken. Prebendary Henry Cooper in an interview with Richard Baker on BBC 4 said that he had, on one occasion, said a prayer of exorcism over the phone, and Fr Neil-Smith recalls:

> I was awakened about three in the morning by the telephone. At the other end of the line was one of our African members [i.e. of his church] who said he was being set upon by demonic forces. He sounded desperate, and as he lived some distance away, I performed a short exorcism over the telephone which seemed to quiet him a little.

But, continues Fr Neil-Smith's account, 'I asked him to come and see me the following morning.'[2] Father Neil-Smith both knew the person and, as the full account makes clear, embarked on a prompt follow-up, and even traced the real cause to another person's amateur magic. Although the actual healing is hardly different from that which every congregation presupposes when it embarks on prayers for the sick, exorcism at a distance could, by less careful clergy, divorce the action from the Christian community and the patient from adequate after-care.

A policeman who comes across a would-be intruder does not first retreat to his office and look up in his handbook what phrases to use authoritatively to drive him out. His authority lies not in a formula but because he can speak in the name of the

---

[1] *Did you receive the Spirit?* (Darton, Longman & Todd).
[2] 'The Flesh and the Devil', *Frontier of Belief*, No. 88, *Man, Myth and Magic*.

law. Whatever words he might use, they will convey the same message—*get out, and don't come back*. According to his assessment of the intruder and the temporary nuisance he might be, the policeman might forbid him to be violent or repeat his order to get out.

Such an analogy answers most queries there might be about the Christian use of a formula. It is probably a matter of training or temperament whether the law expresses itself formally, 'Halt, who goes there?' or informally, 'Oi! 'oo d'you think you are?'

The range from formality to informality is just as marked in those wielding the authority of Christ, from Rev. Donald Omand's translation of the Latin:

> Go forth thou deceiver, full of all evil and falsehood, the persecutor of the innocent. Give place thou wicked one; give place thou evil one; give place to Christ.[1]

to Pastor Richard Bolt's

> *. . . after three, you're going. One—two—three . . .!

The Apostolic Church healed in the Name of Jesus, not because they regarded it as magically significant, but as signifying that it was not they who were healing, a fact that Peter makes very clear in Acts 3. It is well known that the Name in Babylonian and Assyrian demonology was of foremost importance in using 'words of power'. The fact that Jesus' name could be used in this way successfully (Mark 9:38) does not indicate that this was the Church's use of it. The fate of Sceva's sons has already been referred to and illustrates the dangers of confusion about this.[2] Those who feel that a formula is necessary will find them printed in the Appendix to Michael Harper's *Spiritual Warfare*, and, of course, the *Exorcism* Report gives a great deal of useful advice and needs to be read in conjunction with this study.

The form of words will, for quite obvious reasons, usually include three items, a command to the demon(s) to:

> (i) harm no one;
> (ii) to come out;
> (iii) to go somewhere else.

---

[1] *Experiences of a Present Day Exorcist.*
[2] For a general discussion see Langton's works, *Essentials of Demonology, Good and Evil Spirits*, etc.

(i) *To harm no one*. The padre in Example 1 of the last chapter might possibly have fared better had he been taught this. Be that as it may, I know one well-known person within the deliverance ministry who only learnt this the hard way, and now has an injured back. Some might feel that it would not be time wasted to add to this a prohibition to enter anybody else.

(ii) *To come out*. Since spatial terms are the most obvious to use, this should never be said without a clear idea of what will be *going in*, since a vacuum is abhorred here as elsewhere. A 'blessing' and infilling of the Spirit of Jesus begun and maintained is the other side of the coin. It has become clear to me that in a number of cases the spiritual clearing-out and renewal process can be described (somewhat negatively) as exorcism, and positively as a blessing. There are recorded examples of instantaneous release from drug dependence as a result of either exorcism or the Baptism in the Holy Spirit. This is important, for it probably indicates complimentary truths about the spiritual reality of exorcism and the spiritual reality of such 'Baptism'. Namely that, in spite of the term, much of the reality of exorcism is a putting in; and in spite of the 'Baptism' term, a great deal of that reality may be a driving out. If the occupants of a large house are suddenly replaced by others, it could either be viewed as a rush out of the back door, or a rush in through the front. I hope that the 'front door' view-point will be maintained in spite of so much back-door terminology with which this study has had to be concerned: '. . . it is through the Spirit of God that I cast devils out . . .' (Matthew 12:28). The Gerasene demoniac is told, 'Go home to your people and tell them all that the Lord in his mercy has done *for you* [italics mine]—not, notice, all that the Lord had done *to them*, i.e. the spirits.

(iii) *To go somewhere else*. The Examples of the last chapter will made it clear that any normal person would instinctively wish for not only simply a coming out of himself, but also rather a total driving away from him, the situation, and the place. In his exorcism of the epileptic demoniac, Jesus commands the spirit, 'come out of him and never enter him again' (Mark 9:25). As Michael Harper says, 'We only have a mandate to cast the spirits out, not to tell them where to go. None of the ancient rites of exorcism tell the evil spirit where to

go. There are some people who tell the evil spirits to go to the
lake of fire or hell . . . the only thing we can do is to hand them
over to the sovereign power and authority of the Lord Himself.'
(*Spiritual Warfare*)

To send them to the Pit or the Abyss (Revelation 20:1–3) is
not only a little presumptuous, but implies that the 'minister'
knows the exact nature of the evil with which he or she is confronted as well as God's immediate purpose for it prior to join-
ing in the Triumphal Procession of Christ. A form of words
suggested by the *Exorcism* Report (p. 37) concludes:

> . . . that harming no one you depart from this creature of God,
> N., and return to the place appointed you, there to remain
> forever.

By 'place' here is meant a 'state', as Dom Robert pointed out
once in a television interview.

To include the three items of harming no one, coming out,
and going to where God wants them to be is not to resort to a
magical use of formula. I cannot resist pointing out that Dr
Christopher Woodard's account of a suggested exorcism prayer
not only omits both the command to harm no one and to go to
its place, but is printed only two pages away from the account
of the army padre who died and who *also* imposed no such
restrictions on the demons.[1] The demons will do what is said in
the name of their Lord, but they are malign not benevolent
intelligences, and an unquestioning response to suggestions and
gentlemanly hints are not of much avail. If the cases show
resistant and reluctant obedience to authority, it is not to be
supposed that in those that come our way, they will necessarily
be mild and submissive, and not take advantage of us at every
turn. There is a well-known story of the exorcist in the Middle
Ages who learnt a 'lesson he would never forget', after mock-
ingly banishing a demon to one of the smaller rooms of his own
house!

The question about enquiring the name of the demon remains
something of a puzzle, but it makes most sense if seen in the
context of authority and the practical necessity of bringing
some precision to the command. I do not believe that Christ
has more or less power over a demon because the exorcist
happens to have enquired about its name. What it is possible to

---

[1] *A Doctor's Faith Holds Fast.*

believe is that, as any Sergeant Major demonstrates, the effectiveness of authority is very much dependent on commands
being unequivocal. Whether a name is ascertained or not, it has
in any case to be made clear both to the patient and to any
occupying intelligence, who is being addressed. To find out
the name of the demon (the name given might be Lust, or
Hatred, or Anger, Witchcraft, etc.) enables the Church to see
that such things are replaced by their opposites in the after-
care of the person, particularly where the names given are
immoral. The Roman Ritual regards the enquiring of the
demons' names and number as a necessary action, while Pentecostalist tradition is just as strong. It is not a point which we
should get either hysterical or phobic about. It is a valid terminology, and a reminder that it is with intelligences that we
are dealing. To give them a name-label is not so very strange
once it is accepted that they should be addressed in speech in
the first place.[1]

Derek Prince tells of a young person who wanted to strangle
his girl friend. He said, 'I'm not necessarily quarrelling with
the psychiatrist's diagnosis. I'll use different language and suggest a different remedy . . . That's what the psychiatrist calls
a fixation, but I will call it demons of hate and resentment. If
you accept my diagnosis I'm prepared to apply my treatment.
He said, "I will". I said, "You can be delivered". I instructed
him and emphasised that he could not be delivered until he had
forgiven his father.'

Whether the reality is described as 'demons of hate and
resentment' or a 'fixation' is unimportant, *providing the person
receives appropriate treatment and is healed*. If it is purely mental
illness, the psychiatrist will rid him of such 'demons'; if it is a
genuine demonic affliction the Christian minister will rid the
person of his fixation—either way, those concerned will be co-
operating with Christ's promise of life more abundantly.
Christ's healing work will not, however, be forwarded by our
'hang-ups' on terminology.

Jesus' injunction that the demons should not speak (Mark
1:34) seems in its context to be conditioned by the time and
place of his ministry, and is generally taken to be part of what

[1] For some interesting sidelights on this see Dr Rollo May's sections on
'Naming the Daimonic' and 'Naming the Daimonic in Therapy' in his
*Love and Will* (Souvenir Press).

the commentators call the 'Messianic Secret', rather than an authoritative precedent against allowing conversation with them. For in the same Gospel there is the detailed case of the Gerasene demoniac (which took place in Gentile country) and which not only included talking with the demons, but encouraging the man to broadcast his cure.

Jesus taught that the strong man of the house has first to be *bound* ('tied up' in modern translations) before what belongs to him is removed (Mark 3:27, Matthew 12:29 and Luke 11:22–3). The context in each gospel shows clearly that the strong man is Satan. His 'goods' are his human victims, 'his "whole armour" represents the host of demons. The stranger who comes upon him and defeats him is Jesus himself, as God's representative, armed with divine power' (Manson, *The Sayings of Jesus*). 'Binding' according to this is primarily of Satan, and incidentally of the demons. 'Binding' based on these passages (and by some in Matthew 16:19), has come into deliverance terminology to describe the restraining by Christ of the activities of the demons. Perhaps it is better described as a counter-binding, for as Luke records, it is Satan who binds. 'This woman . . . whom Satan has held bound these eighteen years—was it not right to untie her bonds on the sabbath day?' (Luke 13:16).

Such restraining has already been apparent in the commands to harm no one, to depart never to return, etc.

The practical use of binding is well illustrated in this passage from Daphne Buckley's *The Ministry of Exorcism*, and should be borne in mind when considering the right action in what would appear to be an emergency situation.

> Violence caused by demons should be bound by a command in Jesus' Name. This is easier than physically holding a person, and also kinder to the human body, for they can be hurt with a tight grip on their arms and body. Also demonic strength is multiplied beyond normal human strength and seems to increase if they are held, whereas a stern command to stop the violence in Jesus' Name *has* to be obeyed.[1]

I remember staying for a short while in a home of healing where the deliverance ministry was regularly undertaken. One

---

[1] Available from Full Gospel Deliverance Crusade, 9 Corbett Rd., London.

boy there was a very acute case of possession—in fact one of the severest cases they had come across. During my second evening there I was amazed to see the person concerned quietly sitting in a corner while everybody else sang heartily about there being Power in the Blood of the Lamb. Vainly imagining that I knew some of the elementary things about exorcism, I nervously asked about our safety—only to be met with the matter-of-fact reply that at the end of a period of ministry that day, the demons had been *bound* until he was due for another session. In fact, I later learnt that in such a community where a number of people had trouble of this nature, the Community simply could not function if emergency prayer-sessions were happening all the time. There was a time set each day for 'ministry' as they termed it, and anyone causing any disturbance was 'bound' until an appropriate time.

(In suggesting that *they* were bound is to use the same short-hand by which we talk of people being exorcised. In both cases it is of course *the demons*.)

The difference between exorcism and binding, is between 'chucking out' and (if you'll forgive another slangy expression) 'shutting up'.

I was visited once by a Pentecostalist minister who had stumbled on a *very* acute case involving three or four adults and their home. He had apparently cleared the situation only to find that some time later all the phenomena resumed. What in fact had happened was that having no experience of exorcism and never having previously given it any thought, he had most effectively *bound* all powers that were causing chaos, but had not banished them.

Jesus, while happily touching lepers, appears not to have ministered to demoniacs by touching them in any way.[1] I do not think the reason is very mysterious. The action of touching someone is prompted by feelings of sympathy, compassion, tenderness and so on. If you recall the demoniacal behaviour of the Examples in the last chapter, it is normal not for one's compassion to be less, but when the demonic is trying to avoid its imminent defeat, to have feelings of tenderness for the *person* eclipsed by righteous anger at the cruelty and suffering

[1] The account in Luke 13:10–13 of the woman with the 'spirit of infirmity' is usually regarded as the exception, unless J. B. Phillip's 'ill from some psychological cause' is accepted, which resolves the problem nicely.

caused by the *demonic*. Some appear to have tried to make the laying-on of hands a theological debating point; a more obvious approach might be to suggest that just at that time it is not very natural and not very appropriate. The anger of Paul to the demoniac fortune-teller may have been more than impatience.

Laying-on of hands will almost certainly be used for the subsequent blessing of the person. There may be a danger of some temporary evil transference taking place if they are used for the actual exorcism. The *Exorcism* Report says that the exorcist 'may . . . sprinkle the person with holy water'. In the next chapter I have something to say about holy water; suffice it here to point out that it is an expression of the prayers of the Church in a way that is impersonal rather than involving the personalities concerned. If in an ordinary laying-on-of-hands service a person reacts in a strange way, there is some expelling to be done before further healing. In *Spiritual Warfare*, Michael Harper tells how on an occasion when Dennis Bennett was giving the laying on of hands to a row of people kneeling quietly awaiting God's blessing he

> moved on to a minister and laid his hands on his head . . . He [the kneeling minister] began to growl like a dog and to flail his arms in all directions. He slipped from his chair and went into a coma . . . One realised that one was face to face with another power that had been exposed by the Holy Spirit and made to demonstrate its presence. Later . . . the minister agreed that it was necessary to expel these evil powers. But the moment the name of Jesus was mentioned, he went into another coma, his legs shot from under him, and he lay spreadeagled and inert on the floor. Bending over him and binding the enemy power, the spirits were commanded to leave in the name of Jesus. He opened his eyes, blinked, got to his feet, brushed himself down and smiled blandly. He had been delivered.

The items in this succinct account of ministry are by now familiar to the reader. Firstly, the exposing of the demons by the Spirit of Jesus; secondly, their panic-stricken reaction causing physical manifestations and temporary unconsciousness; thirdly, reaction to the Name of Jesus; and finally, deliverance in the Name of Jesus by the binding and driving out of the demons.

Michael Harper forestalls his readers' queries that a Christian minister could be in such a state, by reminding them of the fact that Jesus' first exorcism was of a man in the synagogue (Mark 1:23 ff.).

Derek Prince, an authority on the subject, and author of the booklet *Expelling Demons*, in conversation with Don Basham said:

> . . . Let me tell you about my own deliverance . . . People look surprised when I admit to having harbored a demon—as though it made me a kind of second-class Christian . . .[1]

Derek Prince was formerly a Professor of Logic and Philosophy at Cambridge, and considers that '*having* a demon' in the New Testament sense is no more impossible for the Christian than being ill, and points out that when a 'flu bug enters us we do not regard ourselves thereby as less Christian. He later prayed, after confessing his anger as sin, for the Lord to remove anything in him which did not acknowledge Christ's kingship. He was delivered, alone—for it is by the Spirit of God that demons are expelled. My acquaintance with Christians now engaged in this work indicates that such ministry has not infrequently followed their *own* deliverance, thus underlining what I tried to indicate above that 'exorcism' properly understood can be viewed as an infilling.

It ought not to be surprising that those who are engaged in the Lord's work are targets of attack. A Christian psychiatrist I know well once invited me to see, with him, another minister whom he thought might have had some spiritual problem of this nature. The three of us chatted happily together, and when 'Jesus' was introduced into the conversation, the minister showed no sign whatever of being in any way disturbed. He periodically had attacks in which he went semi-conscious and virtually unable to speak, and it was these 'attacks' which were troubling him. We noted that they were sometimes when he tried to preach. I asked him when he experienced his first attack. He immediately recalled the occasion—a Sunday morning in church. He had gone up in the pulpit and had 'come over all queer', and the people could not hear him, and he just had to stop preaching.

[1] Related by Don Basham in *Deliver Us From Evil*.

'What were you preaching about?' I asked.

'*Jesus*', he said.

'I'm glad to hear it!' I smiled. 'Did you often preach specifically about Jesus?'

'Now you come to mention it, no,' he replied. 'I had preached other things for many years but the week before this, I realised that I was not being true to my calling to 'preach the Gospel', and I decided that the following Sunday I would give them the Christ-centred message that they had lacked for so long . . .'

This minister did not growl like a dog or fall spreadeagled on the floor, nor were there any manifestations even during prayer. One might deduce from this that there was nothing demonic then present, and that no exorcism would have been of any avail because there was nothing there to cast out. Instead spiritual direction in the Christian life and guidance in disciplined Christian living, and some teaching about how to *put on* the armour which God supplies (Romans 13:12, Ephesians 6:11) rather than just believing it exists would be what was needed. Together with this some closer integration with the Body of Christ (and employment by it is no guarantee of 'integration') so that he not only knew but felt that it was not an individual battle but an attack on the Church, against which the Gates of Hell itself will not prevail (Matthew, 16:18).

In order to convey something of the reality of demonic possession I have quoted a number of cases illustrating the manifestations of the demonic. Just as the departure of the demons is certain under the authority of Jesus, so their manifestations against God's power are similarly under the authority of our Lord. A number of ministers (using the term for the one who 'ministers' the exorcism, rather than implying only ordained persons) when confronted by such cases (i) find that the demonic manifests itself without warning, or (ii) in order to 'know the enemy' (cf. 1 Corinthians 9:26b) they command it to expose itself. Others (iii) forbid any manifestation whatever in the Name of Christ, in which case the deliverance is accomplished with no external indications of its having taken place. The latter requires great faith on the minister's part, but no less than the detachment required of ministers in the other situations. As my 'chucking-out' terminology was used to emphasise, the demonic is not a thing to be involved with, but to fight against. It seems all too easy to confuse the two, and the detailed cases of Roman Catholic exorcisms in *Satan in the Modern World* seem to my mind to err in this direction.

Frequently demoniacs require more than one session of exorcism, but in less severe cases when a person seems completely delivered is it a sign of failure to need another exorcism at a later date?

A possible analogy might be made between the quick daily dust, the weekly more thorough efforts in a room, and the annual spring-clean. A spring-clean ought not to be necessary, and indeed would not be so if the daily dust were more thorough. The spiritual life is not unlike this. Our spiritual cleanness (whether of our home or ourselves) depends on the daily discipline, the weekly effort, and such spiritual spring cleaning as houseparties, retreats or Confession. Should a spiritual spring-clean involve the casting out of unwanted influences, I should want to cry not 'failure' but 'success'!

Because of our Lord's respect for human choice, there are times when the patient is either unwilling or not yet ready for such ministry, and where Christ is prevented from bringing wholeness and renewal.

Most frequently the sufferer is ashamed but not repentant. Maxwell Whyte has some wise words about this:

> It must be emphasised that no person can be delivered if they are not willing to confess their need and their great desire to be delivered. We will save ourselves a lot of time and energy and trouble if we make quite sure that the person does really want to be free. Strange as it may seem, some people will come for deliverance, but deep down in their hearts there is still some love left for their sin. (*Dominion over Demons*)

Rubric 12 of the Roman Ritual says, 'The subject if in good mental and physical health should be exhorted to implore God's help, to fast, and to fortify himself by frequent reception of penance . . .' Derek Prince says that 'Resentment and an unforgiving spirit are two of the commonest hindrances to deliverance,' and advises a ministry which expects of the the patient humility, honesty, confession, renunciation and restitution.

The deliverance programme will be much wider in scope.

This subject was considered by a working party on Spiritualism and the Occult at the 1971 Evangelism Congress in Amsterdam, and their seven guidelines were drawn up by Mr R. Kriese of Germany.

> . . . some of the important points to be settled when counselling persons in touch with occultism:
>
> (a) A full conviction and confidence that only Jesus Christ can deliver.
> (b) Anything that has to do with occultism: books, objects, etc., should be destroyed.
> (c) The person should stop any contact with occultists and spiritists.
> (d) Confession should be made by the person during conversation of things in which he has been involved.
> (e) The person should say a prayer† with the counsellor to indicate that he wants to stop all such things.
> (f) The counsellor should give the assurance of forgiveness of all sins . . . and claim in the name of Jesus Christ, deliverance of the person.
> (g) The counsellor should direct his contact to a prayer group which would be able to pray with him and look after him, because deliverance must be followed by consolidation in the faith and linking with a local body of believers.[1]

In a paper given to the William Temple Society at Bournemouth, the Rev. Alan Harrison gave the following as a deliverance programme:

> (a) Recognition that the person can only be delivered through Jesus Christ.
> (b) Every object of sorcery to be absolutely destroyed.
> (c) All contacts with mediums, etc., broken.
> (d) Confession and renunciation, with absolution and freeing in the Name of Jesus.
> (e) The support of the prayer group.
> (f) Building up into the Body of Christ and 'the means of grace'.
> (g) Complete surrender.[2]

---

† This probably means (unless the person is familiar and at ease with prayer/praying aloud) that the counsellor first explains an outline of a prayer to the person, and if he assents to it, he says it phrase by phrase after the counsellor.

[1] *Official Reference Volume of European Congress of Evangelism—Evangelism Alert* (ed. Kirby).

[2] 'Techniques of combating the Devil' (private tape).

After careful checking, I can state that the two lists were drawn up *quite independently*. Some things are learnt only by experience, and true experience in these matters is the same the world over.

Michael Harper, in his concluding chapter of *Spiritual Warfare* makes many of the same points, his headings are:

   (i) Repentance
  (ii) Deliverance:
     (a) Resisting
     (b) Binding and loosing
     (c) Casting out
 (iii) After care:
     (a) Filling
     (b) Healing
     (c) Self Discipline
     (d) Faith
     (e) Praise

Having already commended the book, I will presume that many readers will want to refer to it in this connection and note for themselves the similarity of content to the sources I have quoted more fully, as well as drawing on the conclusions of a balanced approach, not always apparent in authors on the subject.

Failures, then, can be due to the patient, but this is in fact as much the failure of the counsellor, for embarking on a deliverance ministry when the person is not yet ready or prepared for it. The main cause of failure would seem to be that the exorcism has been taken out of the context of deliverance and salvation, or separated from the Healing Community of God's Church. A diagnosis of the demonic when it is not present will be a waste of time all round—and will certainly not improve the patient if mentally ill—although I think the dangers of this are much exaggerated by general ignorance and mistrust of what Christian exorcism involves.

Some failure is due to the 'minister's' lack of authority and suitable intention. There is a well documented case, with a number of witnesses, of a Roman Catholic exorcism:

> An interesting point about the third session was the admission by the devil [i.e. demon] that he had been greatly helped in the first period of possession by the incredulity of the priest who would not believe in the presence of a devil in the possessed woman, and therefore was opposed to exorcism.[1]

[1] *Satan in the Modern World.*

Such authority is not guaranteed by a fervent working-up of religious intensity on the part of those involved, indeed, the need to do this might indicate that deliverance was being undertaken by the mustering of religious power rather than an emptying of self to be the channel of God's grace. The main reason why the demonically afflicted are not healed is that the demons are not driven out or away by someone speaking in the authority of Christ. I wonder how many demons have chuckled when a priest's ministry to the trouble they are causing has consisted solely of 'Yes, aren't the flowers lovely, God bless you, and I'll pop in next week.' That quotation is not gleaned from a written source, but from my own words in sick-visiting, when British mistrust of fanaticism coupled with a basic shyness, together with a lack of spiritual discipline and the discernment which comes with it, have combined to make me take the line of least resistance, when a line *of resistance* in the Name of Christ might have brought healing. I wonder whether Screwtape ridicules those we term 'fanatics', or whether he is afraid?

Father Gilbert Shaw has written:

> The essential condition for exorcism is the cognition of that which is to be cast out. A vague good will and intention to benefit sufferers is not likely to be effectual.[1]

## THE EXORCIST

It might appear logical to have considered the Exorcist somewhat earlier, but in practical terms a discussion about those involved in deliverance can only follow when the reality of demonic encounter and Christ's victory has first been established, and some of the many misconceptions about exorcism cleared away. The reader who is firmly convinced that such a ministry is 'not for me', has, by elimination, at least narrowed the field of possibilities to 'someone else'!

Tertullian's statement that any Christian who cannot exorcise should be put to death, is a penalty not now in force—although the truth which he was trying to emphasise is. It is the work of the Holy Spirit in and through the Christian which makes real the victory of Christ; it is not primarily a gift or a specialist

[1] 'Exorcism in Theory and Practice', Part 1, *St Raphael Quarterly*, Vol. 4, No. 6, May 1961.

vocation, but is part of the extension of Christ's kingdom which is both the prayer and the calling of all those who acknowledge him as king.

My introduction to this ministry came via an elderly welfare worker who one day paid a private visit to a troubled family, and was faced by a situation in which he knew as a Christian that there was only one thing to do—to pray to Jesus to drive out the trouble; which he did. Many people, unordained men and women, have found themselves *in* the ministry by an emergency situation in which they simply had to act on the prompting of the Holy Spirit. In a Jean Darnall newsletter was once printed the story of a young woman called Nancy. Her grandmother was a white witch, and gradually Nancy found that she had no choice but to obey her. When she was staying at Sir Thomas and Lady Faith Lees' home, the doctor described her as:

> . . . the worst case of self-inflicted injury I know. If she went to a psychiatrist every day for the rest of her life I don't believe she would be healed . . .
>
> . . . Tom and Faith had just been filled with the Holy Spirit and Nancy was the first person they had prayed for for any kind of healing . . . one day Tom almost in exasperation shouted, 'In the Name of Jesus Christ get out'.† Not knowing wholly what he was doing he had cast out the demons that had been vexing Nancy's life. Immediately she quietened down and then slept.[1]

I interviewed two very well known Anglican priests and asked each of them the same question. 'What is the ratio, in your experience, between the number of cases of demonic infestation of *people* and of *places*?' One confidently replied, 'About one person for every hundred places.' The reply of the second was, 'About one place for every hundred people'! They were *both* right, for the simple but vitally important reason that God's plan for his Church is that one of them should deal primarily with places and the other with people, and he has equipped them accordingly. It is the ministry of the Spirit through God's Church, and while it is possible to make generalities about the Spirit's working, his actions are not

---

† Compare the example of earliest Christian exorcism on record (quoted in the *Exorcism* Report), of a nun, the one word '*Exi!*' (*Get out!*).

[1] Published at Post Green, Lytchett Minster, Dorset.

always predictable (John 3:8). This may mean *more* order, not less, for as I recall Fr Neil-Smith pointing out, the Holy Spirit will *restrain* as well as prompt.

The Roman Catholic distinction between 'major' and 'minor' exorcisms which I mentioned above and their allowance of 'private and unofficial exorcism in the Name of Christ . . . by any Christian, lay or clerical' reaffirms the corporate nature of the deliverance ministry, however much it might be advisable to draw on those with more experience. Prebendary Henry Cooper has always maintained that such ministry should not be regarded as the work of 'specialists', but should, with appropriate training and instruction, form part of the ministry of the local parish priest. 'If', he writes, 'a priest of ordinary capacities can serve as a pastor in a parish and provide his people with spiritual needs why cannot he equally be used to declare the over-mastering love and power of God in all circumstances, including possession and infestation by evil? . . . I do not think that either the healing ministry nor the ministry which ejects evil should depend upon special gifts for that would mean deprivation to most parishes . . . I should . . . like to challenge the episcopal assumption that the ministry of exorcism is a matter for specialists, for that presupposes that it requires a *gnosis*, a knowledge of a human kind.' (*Deliverance and Healing*)

The Anglican policy by way of safeguard in the matter is that 'No exorcism of a person may take place, therefore, without the explicit permission of the diocesan bishop of the place where the exorcism occurs, given for every individual case concerned. This is clear from Canon LXXII of 1604. . . .' I understand however that obedience to Canons applies only to those now in force, and the Church of England has in its Revision of its Canons chosen, for some reason or other, neither to include it *nor* revise it, hence Prebendary Cooper's plea for some episcopal guidance on the matter (*Church Times*, May 8th, 1970). Until there is some such guidance, the situation will continue in which priests use their discretion according to the nature of the case drawing on the experience of the 'Diocesan exorcists' if they feel the need to do so. The Report's plea for duly appointed exorcists in each diocese, who would act without (one imagines) explicit permission given *for every individual case concerned*, makes the theory a little more practical, and needs to be taken in conjunction with it. Official recognition of the policy quoted in Prummer's *Manuale Theologiae Moralis* above, page 164, would seem realistic now that exorcism has come to be regarded as the ministry of the Church and not a priestly ritual. Doubtless a very small minority may misuse such a policy; this may be better than the majority having, as at present, to ignore it. It does not take much reading between the lines of many cases quoted to see that obtaining episcopal permission was either impractical or unnecessary.

Those familiar with the books of Daphne Buckley, Elsie Salmon, Katherine Kuhlmann, Agnes Sanford and Anne White[1] or who know of the ministry of Jean Darnall or Jean Orr, will know that neither the understanding nor the practice of deliverance is the prerogative of the clergy. Agnes Sanford's 'usual pattern' of ministry, for instance, is as follows:

> First of all I pray, usually in silence, for myself and for this person to be surrounded with protection.
> Secondly, with or without the laying-on of hands, I command the invading spirit in the name of Jesus Christ to leave the person . . . using . . . any words which come to mind . . .
> Thirdly, I give thanks that the evil has departed. Often I sense this very definitely, but even if I feel nothing I give thanks anyway as an act of faith. And I direct this departed thing into the hands of Christ who will know how to deal with it. I do not condemn it or hate it, for there may be something in it which can be saved. I only place it under the control of Christ, and forbid that it shall ever come back to this person or to anyone else . . .
> Fourthly, I pray that the love of Christ will come in quickly and fill up the empty places where this used to be.
> And finally, I pray that the person may be surrounded from this time forth by heavenly protection so that nothing can come near him to trouble him.

She adds that, 'A minister, if only he believes the truth of it, can always do this work, for the authority is passed down to him in his ordination and the devil knows it.' But, one might ask—do all the clergy?

---

[1] e.g. *The Ministry of Exorcism, He Heals Today, I Believe in Miracles, The Healing Gifts of the Spirit*, and *Healing Adventure*, respectively.

Towards the end of her chapter on the 'Deliverance Ministry', Anne White wrote this constructive criticism:

> The claim that Apostolic healings were only for that particular age is now being disproved where the Church is trying to minister on a higher plane than Jumble Sales, bazaars and art clubs. Although some people are drawn to the Church by such measures, spiritual revival has not been conspicuously present through these media. On the other hand, evangelism leading to conversion is one of the accompaniments of the healing ministry.

Those who are concerned about 'evangelism' and 'conversion', or 'outreach' and 'mission' as they tend to be called nowadays, might reflect that there is a common link in that evangelism, conversion and deliverance are *all* accomplished by God's Spirit. It follows that each of these facets of the Gospel occurs where the Church is open to the moving of his Spirit, and it may be deduced that it is the ministry of individuals who are similarly open to the Spirit's working through them. Perhaps this is the only real classification that can be made. This does not mean that everyone with an experience of the Holy Spirit in some way is called to exorcise, but it does mean that it will be from people in whom the Spirit dwells that God will call out his ministers. Clergy who might feel that this is equating such ministry with the 'charismatic movement' need only re-read their ordination service to correct that impression, for it would be hard to find any formal expression of Christian hope more concerned with the infilling of the Holy Spirit.

There are dangers in undertaking this ministry. The least important is the physical danger—it is the spiritual dangers that need be faced. The greatest of these is clear from Jesus' warning in Luke 10:17—the only occasion when rejoicing is discouraged in the New Testament.

> The seventy-two came back rejoicing. 'Lord,' they said 'even the devils submit to us when we use your name.' He said to them, 'I watched Satan fall like lightning from heaven. Yes, I have given you power to tread underfoot serpents and scorpions and the whole strength of the enemy; nothing shall ever hurt you.'

Jesus adds:

> *Yet do not rejoice that the spirits submit to you . . .*

Pride in success—even as successful soldiers of Christ—sows the seed of a belief that it is us, not the Spirit of God by whom demons are cast out. This is magic, even if couched in Christian terms, and constitutes a far greater danger than any of the physical manifestations that have been related. Once magic is embarked on the only way to ensure comparative success is by acquiring power and more power. The scribes thought that Jesus was operating in this way when they accused him of black magic—'Beelzebub is in him' and 'It is through the prince of devils that he casts devils out' (Mark 3:22). Matthew and Luke make clear Jesus' contrary claim that it is by the Spirit or finger of God and not by superior demonic power that these things are accomplished. Mark omits this actual reply, but makes it very clear that their allegation of the power of *evil* spirits was a blasphemy against the real source of his power—the Holy Spirit (Matthew 12:24, Luke 11:15 and Mark 3:29–30).

> Lord Jesus, please cleanse my heart and fill it with your Holy Spirit for the rest of my life.

This prayer was made by a Chinese woman at the prompting of her woman doctor who regarded her as demon-possessed. In recording the case Leslie Weatherhead states that her doctor said, 'From that moment she was well.'[1] More frequently the Holy Spirit heals through a 'minister', though whether he should hold a Dip. Ban. as the following poem suggests is doubtful:

> Whoever you are, you'd better start vanishing—
> You don't stand a ghost of a chance against me;
> I've taken the Church's Diploma in Banishing,
> And I exorcise often and regularly.
> I'm honoured to be on the Archbishop's list
> As a fully qualified exorcist.
>
> You've lost your respect for the curate and vicar,
> And even the Bishop has left you unmoved;
> You'd better go now—or if possible quicker—
> To ensure my professional prowess is proved.
> For no decent demon can ever resist
> The power of a qualified exorcist.

[1] *Wounded Spirits.*

Of devils and poltergeists, spirits and spectres,
I've studied the habits and customs and vices;
I'm fully equipped with demonic detectors
And all the most modern techniques and devices.
No goblin or ghost should agree to be laid
By a layman untrained in the tricks of the trade—
If you've got any spirit you'll surely insist
On a properly qualified exorcist.[1]

Parodies should always prompt us to re-examine the original, and the *Exorcism* Report (SPCK), with which the poet was so obviously familiar, gives detailed suggestions for the Christian ministry to both people and places, suggested forms of prayers to use, and advice on purely practical matters: the recommendation, for instance, that the suffering person be sat in a deep armchair since, if there is the slightest possibility of falling unconscious, marble chancel steps are among the worst places to do it. To outline such details would involve reproducing most of that publication. I will presume, therefore, that it will be read in conjunction with this study by those who want practical guidance on the deliverance ministry. As I mentioned in an earlier chapter, the actual Report (excluding the Appendices) was written before the interdenominational, charismatic and lay factors had really emerged, but in spite of this it will remain relevant and authoritative on these matters until such time as it may be superseded by the 'episcopal guidance' that many clergy are looking for.

The 'property qualified exorcist'—with or without his Diploma in Banishing—will probably always be necessary, however well-instructed local clergy become on these matters, to act in an advisory capacity, perhaps to share ministry together,† and to bring his experience to difficult and very acute cases. The role of the local minister remains of the utmost importance even when a specialist of some sort is brought in. The *Exorcism* Report fully acknowledges this:

> . . . in every case where exorcism is decided upon, the utmost effort must be made to train the patient in the practice of the Christian Life. This is, of course, the main responsibilty of the parish priest . . .

[1] John Irwin, *Cambridge Evening News*, April 25th, 1972.

† The disciples were sent out 'in *pairs*, [with] . . . authority over unclean spirits' (Mark 6:7).

. . . the after-care of the patient will also devolve upon the parish priest . . . and the importance of the work cannot be over-stated.

The 'qualified exorcist' does not exist to absolve other ministers from the obligation to take seriously and interpret evil manifestations, nor to draw on the resources of Christ to deal with them.

The actual exorcist, whoever that may be, acts only out of *compassion* for the sufferer, for even the disturbance of places is basically a ministry for the people involved. The ministry must not be approached in an experimental way, or out of curiosity; people are not guinea-pigs for spiritual or psychical speculation. I have grave doubts about some Pentecostalists and some parapsychologists who approach these situations armed with taperecorders, although the latter have more reason to do so.

Although the minister is prompted by his compassion, this must not lead to emotional involvement. William Sargant in his *Battle For The Mind* warns that possession, conversion and all similar conditions can be avoided by emotional detachment. Father Gilbert Shaw, writing from a very different view-point, taught that:

. . . thoughts of doubt, anger, disgust, or impatience as expressions of selfhood, may provide contact for the demonic spirit to act upon the exorcist, to weaken his prayer and even nullify his action . . . if there is to be feeling it should be of grief for sin, and of Divine compassion for it.[1]

The *authority* of the minister is something which is *given*; so we read that Jesus '*gave* them power and authority over all devils and to cure diseases, and sent them out to proclaim the Kingdom of God and to heal' (Luke 9:1–2). A few years later, the same author records that 'Satan entered into one of them' (Luke 22:3). Judas Iscariot had been given authority, an 'extrinsic' authority which was his by virtue of his position, yet this was not sufficient for him to recognise and claim authority in his own life. An 'intrinsic' authority † on the other hand is an authority which belongs to the *person* as such and not his position. Most writers on the subject presume the former and

[1] 'Exorcism: Its Application', *The St Raphael Quarterly*, Vol. 4, No. 7, August 1961.

† I owe this distinction to the Bishop of Durham, see J. Habgood's article in *Regina*, 1972, Queen's College, Birmingham, on 'Authority'.

insist on the latter. The former authority—by virtue of the position held—belongs to priests and ministers, but in this connection I wonder whether authority has not only to be *given*, but *received and used* before it becomes real? One knows of certain ministers who, like sleeping policemen, have authority but do not exercise it. Experience would suggest that any person *in Christ* inherits *an* authority as his soldier and servant. Since those 'in Christ' become 'new Creatures' and have a 'new mind' (Romans 12:2) the intrinsic authority increases with the sanctification of each individual.

The authority of the exorcist is an authority given by Christ who is reported in Matthew 28:18 as saying, 'All authority in heaven and earth has been given to me. Go, therefore . . .' It is on such authority that our going depends. It is the *Church* against which the gates of hell will not prevail (Matthew 16:18), it is the Church that has been given authority, which becomes real in those of the Church who take it and wield it.

I once said during a talk on the subject of Deliverance, that there were three essentials: A life of prayer; the work of Christ; a sense of humour. Only afterwards, in preparing this manuscript, did I see its possible Trinitarian source, which gave me the courage to reproduce it here in the hope that what was a fairly flippant comment might indicate something quite important. Be that as it may, the Life of Prayer is the first essential. In the fifteen rubrics I contributed to the *Exorcism* Report in Appendix III (The Exorcism and Blessing of a Person) I suggested that, 'The priest should prepare himself, and those whom he selects to be present, by confession, prayer and fasting, and, if possible, communion together.' Some of those deeply involved in the ministry (as distinct from writing about it) kindly wrote that although they agreed with the suggestions, it did give the impression that the minister concerned could spend half a day in spiritual preparation! Prebendary Henry Cooper in a letter to me pointed out that they were 'somewhat perfectionist', and made the very important point that 'Working priests ought always to be in a state of grace and to have fulfilled the conditions you mention. One never knows what is around the corner . . .' Two of these conditions were that the priest should undertake the exorcism only 'in a state of recollection and confident of our Lord's victory over evil in general and in the situation confronting him.'

The minister makes real the victory of Christ by himself being *in* the victory. Schlier points out in *Principalities and Powers in the New Testament* that the '. . . struggle against the principalities fundamentally begins in and with myself'. Enemy-infiltrated territory is open to occupation, hence the New Testament's warning about unrelenting anger which '. . . will give the devil a foothold'. This is true of every Christian, but especially true for those involved in the ministry of deliverance, for the struggle of good overcoming evil can take place 'within the exorcist' (*Exorcism* Report). Sometimes this invisible battle and defeat can be 'seen' by its effect on the afflicted person or on the minister. This explains the apparent 'pushing' which so many have seen on the film clips which have repeatedly been shown on television in recent years. As a correspondent wisely wrote about them, 'They do not make much sense to look at, because we cannot see the invisible.' The minister concerned has said, 'The vibration is caused by the evil force within the person and the power of God.' Elsewhere he has been reported as saying, 'It appears that one is having a struggle with the person, but it is not that at all. It is the evil force of the person having received the impact of the power of God through my hands.'[1]

If such ministry can involve a confrontation in this way with the forces of evil†, the importance of the minister's spiritual invulnerability becomes acute. Hence the stress to be living 'in a state of grace' or, to use different terminology, 'close to the Lord', and to draw on all the spiritual resources available within (and even outside) one's Christian tradition: prayer; confession; Holy Communion; fasting, etc. The tendency for some New Testament manuscripts to add 'fasting' to prayer (e.g. Mark 9:28, Acts 10:30 and 1 Corinthians 7:5) suggests that early Christians in practice linked the two. Blumhardt, Wesley and Pastor Hsi linked it not only with prayer but with deliverance. Pastor Peter Scothern—I noted above (Chapter Five) in the epileptic case quoted—wrote, 'I recognised my weakness and lack of power, so I spent two days in prayer and fasting.'

[1] *Yorkshire Post*, November 16th, 1970, and Russell Miller 'The Ghost Hunters', *Mirror Magazine*, January 1970.

† A factor which many feel adds weight to the New Testament witness against laying-on of hands.

Pastor Hsi, known as 'the Conqueror of Demons', was severely tested by the affliction of his wife: 'suddenly her nature seemed changed . . . rapidly fell a prey to deep depression . . . against her will, she was tormented by constant suggestions of evil, while a horror . . . seemed to possess her. She was not ill in body and certainly not deranged in mind. But try as she might . . . she seemed under the sway of evil powers against which resistance was no avail. Especially when time came for daily worship, she was thrown into paroxysms of ungovernable rage . . . in the seizures which became frequent she would use language more terrible than anything she could ever have heard in her life. Sometimes she would rush into the room, look like one insane, and violently break up the proceedings, or would fall insensible on the floor, writhing in convulsions that resembled epilepsy . . . local doctors were powerless and all the treatment he could think of unavailing.'

Not surprisingly, the 'Conqueror of Demons' came to the diagnosis with which my reader is now familiar. But, interestingly, 'pray as he might the poor sufferer only grew worse'. Knowing the power of prayer coupled with fasting he:

> . . . called for a fast of three days and nights in his household, and gave himself to prayer . . . Then without hesitation he went to his distressed wife, and laying his hands upon her, in the name of Jesus, commanded the evil spirits to depart and torment her no more. There and then the change was wrought. To the astonishment of all except her husband, Mrs Hsi was immediately delivered . . .
> . . . For the completeness of the cure was proved by after events. Mrs Hsi never again suffered in this way. And so profoundly was she impressed, that she forthwith declared herself a Christian and one with her husband in his lifework.[1]

Arthur Wallace mentions Pastor Hsi in a chapter entitled 'They Fasted to Deliver' in *God's Chosen Fast* (Victory Press). This is nothing new to the Roman Church as it makes clear in rubric 10 about exorcism:

> Wherefore he will be mindful of the words of our Lord (Matthew 17:12), to the effect that there is a certain type of evil spirit who cannot be driven out except by prayer and fast-

[1] From *Pastor Hsi—Confucian Scholar and Christian,* Mrs Howard Taylor (Overseas Missionary Fellowship).

ing. Therefore let him avail himself of these two means *above all* [italics mine] for the imploring of the divine assistance in expelling demons, after the example of the holy fathers; and not only himself, but let him induce others, so far as possible to do the same.

There is naturally emphasis given to prayerfully putting on the armour which God provides, and there are a number of Christians who mentally put it on piece by piece (Ephesians 6:16 ff.). Without in any way wishing to detract from the analogy of armour, it is not, I think, the whole truth to regard our position as of a defenceless child unprotected by its Father. Indeed, as has often been noted, there is no armour for the back—so even this analogy is not meant to indicate anything but attack. The armour is an additional protection rather than our only protection. Providing we are looking 'for the things that are in heaven . . . not on things on the earth', and provided we die daily, the life we have is 'hidden with Christ in God' (Colossians 3:1-3). Protection is more dependent on where we are than what we wear. An armour-formula could become (like any other Christian action or affirmation) magical—at every level this must constantly be guarded against, as the late Edgar Trout used to teach about the phrase 'The Blood of Christ'. The Blood of Christ is so meaningful in this connection because, as Calvin so finely put it when commenting on Colossians 2:15:

There is no tribunal so magnificent, no throne so stately, no show of triumph so distinguished, no chariot so elevated, as is the gibbet on which Christ has subdued death and the devil, and trodden them under his feet.[1]

According to Revelation 13:11, the angels' victory over Satan in the heavenly war is 'by the blood of the Lamb', and the meaning is clear if the context is noted. The voice shouts:

Victory and power and empire for ever have been won by our God, and all authority for his Christ, now that the persecutor . . . has been brought down. They have triumphed over him by the blood of the Lamb . . .

Christians have different ways of affirming and declaring the victory of Christ. The phrase 'the Blood of Christ' declares it

[1] Quoted in James Stewart's 'On a Neglected Emphasis in New Testament Theology', *Scottish Journal of Theology*, Vol. IV, September 1951.

audibly, the making of the Sign of the Cross declares it visibly. Since they are shorthand expressions for the total work of Christ they reaffirm his position, the position of those 'in him', and, negatively, the defeat of the rebellious powers. They are, somewhat incidentally, therefore, declarations of protection. This accounts for the expression used by some Pentecostalists that 'No demon can pass the Blood line', and for the protection of the Sign of the Cross that so many Christians have found in situations where they did not know what to do. A parishioner described to me what happened in a wood one day. Walking up behind her came a man in a long flowing cloak with what she described as 'an *evil* face'. She said, 'As I was a bit anxious I made a short prayer to God, and as I often do, the Sign of the Cross. Do you know what happened next?—it was most extraordinary—I looked around, and there he was running as *fast* as he could . . .' The exact nature of this pantomime occurrence may never be known, but whether really in the wood, or in a dream, it is an authentic story of Christ's action.

St Patrick's Breastplate, as it has come to be called, was written as a divine protection against idolatry and witchcraft, and the woman's action could equally well be described as 'putting up the breastplate'—a good spiritual exercise for *all* Christians who wish to live as soldiers of Christ (2 Timothy 2:3), as well as of particular importance to any who are wanting protection. The central part of the hymn reaffirms the Presence of Christ:

> Christ be with me, Christ within me, Christ behind me, Christ before me, . . . Christ below me, Christ above me . . .

and could be termed a *Prayer of Affirmation*. This is the title of a book (by the Rev. W. Mauleverer, published by A. James) that many have found helpful. Such prayers are particularly appropriate in any 'evil' situation because instead of affirming our own inadequacies, they affirm the adequacy of God, and turn the person away from the supposed source of fear to the real source of faith. It is very easy in prayer to put oneself before God, whereas its essence is to put God before self. One simple expression of this is affirming Christ's position and one's love of him by the one word JESUS . . . 'which is above all other names, so that all beings in the heavens, on earth and in the under world should bend the knee at the name of Jesus and that every tongue should acclaim Jesus Christ as Lord . . .' (Philippians 2:9–11).

## AFTER-CARE

In the following chapter I shall discuss apparent evil infestation of places. Although these few comments on after-care precede it, this does not imply that after-care is limited to the exorcism of people. Places and people are inextricably bound together. An infested place is not even recognised as a disturbance until its influences impinge on people. The ministry involving places is usually a ministry to distressed people and the causes of their distress.

After-care, whether of someone wanting to come out of witchcraft, of someone who has suffered demonic attacks by accidental involvement in dangerous things, or of a family who seem to be the centre of psychic disturbances—in every case after-care is simply the building-up in the Christian life, and the necessary renouncing of and breaking away from all contacts with a previous way of life which was either contrary to this commitment, or which make the person spiritually vulnerable. The *Exorcism* Report states:

> . . . Our Lord tells us that when the evil spirit is gone out of a man the house, if left empty, will be reoccupied by evil and the last state worse than the first. Those who have been exorcised must be warned about this, and encouraged *by all means possible* [italics mine] to lead a prayerful life in union with the Church, to study Holy Scriptures, and to receive the sacraments regularly.

Jesus said to a sick man whom he had healed, 'Now you are well again, be sure not to sin any more, or something worse may happen to you' (John 5:14). Our Lord had previously asked him whether he wanted to be well (verse 6), and the implication may be that having been ill for nearly forty years he would find it hard to carry the responsibilities of health, and may have preferred the attention of others which his sickness attracted. There is no record given of any previous sin to cause his illness, perhaps it was simply his desire to hold on to it that constituted the sin which he had to discontinue. There are some people who need sickness as much as others need health, as any doctor, psychiatrist, welfare worker or priest will know from hours spent with them. The effectiveness of after-care will depend very much on how it was previously established that the sufferer wanted more than a relief of symptoms. The cancer patient who will not cut down smoking, or the overweight person who will not cut down eating have their spiritual counterparts, human nature being what it is. That is why incorporation into the 'divine nature' (Philippians 2:6, NEB) of Christ is not denominational blackmail, but spiritual necessity.

The subsequent blessing and healing, and incorporation into the Body of Christ and strengthening will draw on all available resources of the Church. After-care cannot exist unless it is corporate in this sense. While it may, and perhaps should, involve such sacramental means of grace as Confession and Absolution, Laying-on of hands, Holy Communion and even Unction, these cannot rightly be undertaken if theologically or practically divorced from the local 'Church'. It alone can offer the acceptance, fellowship, teaching and encouragement that spiritual convalescence requires. In an age when many expect nothing from the Church, praise God that there are some who must look for *everything* in the Church. Will they find it? James Davidson Ross in *The Heart Machine* writes:

It is a damned silly Church, and it is wasting a lot of its time and most of its opportunities, but it is still the Church of God. And those people who would like to get rid of it all . . . are wrong. Because underneath all the clutter it is still the Church of Christ, and it works.

# CHAPTER EIGHT

# PLACES

From ghoulies and ghosties
and long leggety beasties
and things that go bump in the night,
Good Lord, *deliver* us.

ALTHOUGH PSYCHIC RESEARCH and psychology might be able adequately to classify such phenomena, it is still for *deliverance* from such things (whether objective or subjective) that people go to the police, the psychiatrist or the priest.

Surveys show that five million people in Britain claim to have experienced visual or audible proof of the 'supernatural' by hearing, seeing or being touched by an allegedly 'supernatural being'. Such meetings are not always unsought. Pan-American Airlines offer 'Psychic Tours of Britain' (complete with séance) to our American friends, while ghost-hunting is an increasing activity of the British. John Harries' *The Ghost Hunter's Road Book* and Peter Underwood's *A Gazetteer of British Ghosts* furnish the would-be ghost-hunter not only with the authentic stories, but the best 'viewing' times and the recommended hotels nearby.

There is, however, a world of difference between fear experienced by choice from fiction, film or fun-fair, and being—as we put it—'haunted' by fears, whether from within or without, over which one has little or no control.

Some will be inclined to dismiss the whole subject of ghosts and poltergeists and, if they are not pastors—in the widest sense of that word—they are entitled to do so. The pastor cannot dismiss anything which is real to the people who turn to him for comfort and guidance. This is not to say that he has to accept without question the objective reality of every hallucination and fantasy which is described, but that he must at least start from a position which acknowledges that things may have a genuine reality for others irrespective of his own perceptions and beliefs.

The vicar who allows himself to be cheered by the fact that one parishioner told him of feeling 'a great peace' at his service, must also allow himself to be disturbed when another parishioner telephones at two o'clock in the morning to complain of an 'uncanny atmosphere' at home. Both experiences are likely to be real to the people themselves otherwise they would not have mentioned it; probably neither experience could be proved or disproved. It would be very arbitrary of him to describe the former as genuine and the latter as 'imagining things' on account of having read more theology than psychic research. There are, unfortunately, enough stories going about of clergy (and even of a Bishop) rushing into unfamiliar situations, not to listen and understand, but to pontificate on what cannot happen and immediately to imply that the people concerned are deluded. It is not the ministry of the Church to make even more acute the anxiety of domestic situations which she has been invited to *heal*.

Because ghosts are mental 'projections', Dr William Sargant said, on television, that 'ghosts *do not exist*'. It is not the place here to discuss at any length the nature of existence and reality, but simply to draw an obvious analogy from the term 'projection'.

What *exists* on a cinema screen is no more than a succession of varying patches of light. Those who wished to be 'materialistic' about it (though I cannot imagine anyone being so foolish) would find the amusement or fear experienced by the audience quite inexplicable, because the causes for such emotions—cowboys, Indians or monsters—never existed. Such reality and existence as they had was sufficient to touch people deeply, to rouse their emotions of love or hate or fear. If a vast industry can build itself on an illusion, there must be some 'reality' about it!

Similarly it seems pedantic to say that ghosts 'do not exist'. Such things are all too real to a great number of people to be dismissed so easily, although the *nature* of their existence invites a wide spectrum of theories and opinions.

One has only to ask which way the Matterhorn leans, or whether turquoise is a bluish-green or greenish-blue, to be reminded that perception and interpretation vary from viewpoint to view-point and from individual to individual.

Nowadays most educated people know that bats squeak, so

it is no longer said (as I imagine it once was) 'I can't hear them; therefore you must be imagining things; therefore they can't be squeaking.' Such a statement appears amusing, although in other spheres of learning today, much the same is said.

In the purely hypothetical case of a sick patient describing his late Uncle Ebenezer standing at the end of the bed, his perception would be described as abnormal by a group of doctors, yet with equal unanimity, a group of mediums or 'sensitives' might state that the patient was not suffering from hallucinations because his perception was no different from their own.

I believe the time is coming when it will be seen not as intellectual superiority but intellectual dishonesty to dismiss automatically or ignore the testimony of those whose experience does not easily fit in with one's preconceived ideas.

Aldous Huxley when considering the theory of demonic possession wrote:

> There is nothing, so far as I can see, self-contradictory in the idea of possession. The notion is not one to be ruled out *a priori* on the grounds that it is 'a relic of ancient superstition'. It should be treated rather as a working hypothesis, which may be cautiously entertained in any case where other forms of explanation are found to be inadequate to the facts.[1]

It is as a 'working hypothesis, which may be cautiously entertained' that the following remarks about disturbed places are made.

The evil infestation of places figures prominently in 'horror' fiction, and 'ghosts' continue to be the subject of scientific, journalistic or simply hysterical writing. The pastoral situation created by such occurrences (whether genuine or imagined) and the appropriate action of the caring Church occurs rarely in print.

The Rev. Donald Omand spends a chapter of his book *The Experiences of a Present Day Exorcist* (Kimber) in describing the action he took at the 'House by the Polluted Well'; Michael Harper in *Spiritual Warfare* tells of the time when he experienced at night uncharacteristic feelings of 'gloom and fear, particularly of death'. He relates how his home was exorcised by

---

[1] Quoted in *Towards the Death of Satan*, by H. A. Kelly, from Huxley's *Devils*.

Dom Robert Petitpierre, who, he writes, 'has wide experience in such matters', and he concludes that the Church needs to 'claim buildings as well as people for the Lordship of Christ'.

The report of the Bishop of Exeter's Commission, which included two Roman Catholic priests among its members, took the infestation of places as a serious possibility:

> Places—churches, houses, towns, countryside—may be strained and influenced by a variety of causes, and frequently more than one of them at a time.

The *Exorcism* Report continues by listing six causes: souls of the departed; activity of magicians; human sin; place memories; poltergeist; and demonic interference. Although only the latter can or need be 'exorcised' in the literal sense, a brief comment on the non-demonic causes of disturbance is necessary.

The order chosen by the Exeter Commission of the causes was made to group together the purely human at the beginning of the list—the first three items in fact. I shall depart from their order, however, and deal firstly with the two types of ghost.

## 'Ghosts'

In ordinary speech almost any phantom 'appearance' is described as a 'ghost', whether it is of a person, a stage-coach or a battle. The use of the term 'poltergeist', meaning literally *noise-ghost*, does nothing to lessen the confusion.

The majority, some would put it as high as ninety per cent, of 'ghosts' are neither personal nor demonic. True, they may appear to be a person, but are no more personal than a series of photographs flicked with the thumb to cause movement. As such they are neither a soul seeking forgiveness nor an evil intelligence needing to be banished.

They have been described as 'impersonal traces of earlier personal action, and seem to be caused either by habitual actions or by actions accompanied by violent emotion'. Canon Stafford Wright uses the word 'imprint', and one theory commonly put forward to explain it uses the analogy of the film. In Rodney Legg's *Guide to Dorset Ghosts*, we read:

> These imprint shadows called ghosts are often left by people who perform the same action continuously throughout their lives with great devotion. There are simple ghost stories con-

cerning the shoemaker who was heard banging every night,
the priest at Silton Church who glides silently towards the altar
then slips into the vestry . . . There are a number of stories
that suggest the ghost has appeared not through violent emotion
but through repetition. . . .

If a ghost is a shadow, a kink in the ether, there is no reason
why it should not be like a length of cine-film, useless and
unseen without a projector. Then we [i.e. certain psychically
sensitive people] come along and our brains act on the film to
make it run, we see it and think it is something external to
ourselves, which, to some extent it is for other people can see
it . . . it only requires one person with the right type of brain
to unconsciously produce the local ghost for a whole multitude
to see.

This it seems is a 'workable hypothesis' and can account for the
more obviously non-personal apparitions as well as many which
appear in human form.

John Harries' *The Ghost Hunter's Road Book* is a mine of
information not of real 'ghosts', but of these 'imprints' or
'place-memories' to use the Exeter Commission's phrase. Here
is an obviously 'impersonal' phenomenon:

North from Melrose the A7 becomes a very busy road . . . After
Stow as far as the junction for Heriot . . . the vehicles may be
augmented by a spectral lorry, sometimes on the road itself
and at others on adjacent tracks and running across streams
unsuitable for anything but a tank. Pedestrians and cyclists
have been sufficiently alarmed to dive for safety, and if local
press stories are to be believed the lorry has been the cause of
many accidents when motorists have swerved out of its way or
blithely followed it off the road.

The B2167 near Lamberhurst in Kent, and the Coventry–
Rugby road also have such phantom vehicles; the frightening
thing about the latter is that the lorry 'fails to pull to the left
as the oncoming driver naturally expects it to do. Because of
its speed it is on top of the approaching vehicle before the driver
can brake or take evasive action. There is no impact and the
lorry gives the impression of enveloping the other vehicle, fading
as it does so.'

Elsewhere the story is told of a monk which motorists from
time to time saw crossing the road. When the road was lowered
by putting it through a cutting, reports came in of motorists

seeing a monk 'floating' across the top of their vehicles. This amusing change indicates that the monk was nothing more than an 'imprint' of that particular place.

Such apparitions account for most 'ghosts', and if it is understood that they can exert no influence, can cause no direct damage, that they are simply bits of atmospheric 'film', that they are quite impersonal, then they are best ignored. Their disappearance in any particular situation, or rather 'non-appearance' can only be accomplished by the removal of the person who is unconsciously acting as a 'projector', most often a teenage girl. Such a step would be as inappropriate as exiling grandad because to some people the house smelt of his tobacco!

I remember after reading a paper at a healing conference, that the host began the question-time by relating how only the week previously his communion rail according to some, had an unfilled place, while according to others the row had been full. The extra 'person' was someone who had recently died, and who had regularly received communion not only at that church, but always at *that same place* at the communion rail. Was it her ghost? Had she 'returned'?

I thought not. The restless soul who occasionally lingers on after death is almost invariably too attached to things of the earth, or bound by habits and sins. They most frequently need forgiveness and reconciliation—things which the woman at the altar-rail had received and renewed weekly for as long as others could remember. She, or more correctly it, was just a place-memory, imprinted there (in the words of Rodney Legg's book already quoted) by a person who performed 'the same action . . . throughout their lives with great devotion'.

Had she been one of the souls of the departed, she would have earned the Exeter Commission's epithet as one of the 'ghosts *proper*' and it is to those that I must now turn.

St Augustine's observation that 'our heart knows no rest, until it may repose in thee' describes very well the spiritual state of real departed souls who from time to time make their presence known in a plea for help. A Sunday paper recently gave an account of a ghost which I would quote even if it were entirely fictional, as it is virtually a blueprint of such cases.

A family in the Midlands living in a council house with their two children are troubled by a 'ghost'. The frightened children move into their parents' bedroom, while the ghost is heard to

stamp around the house as if in hobnailed boots and wheeze
his way up and down stairs. All the family hear him. The wife
sees him as a dark shape, the eight-year-old daughter draws
him and describes him as a 'little fat man with a red face. He's
old and has a walking stick.' The daughter of this 'Albert' was
called in and said the description fitted her father perfectly.
He had died fifteen years previously, shortly after falling down-
stairs there, having first sworn that if anything happened to him
he would return to haunt the house. It appears that he was a
money-lender and was always hiding money about the home.
The Suffragan Bishop of the Diocese, according to the newspaper, conducted an 'exorcism service' which 'was not a success'
with the result that the family are now urging the city council
to give them another home. I have rewritten the story rather
than quoted it because the Bishop's work is difficult enough
without broadcasting what may have been an error of diagnosis.

The story might be taken as a 'classic' of its type. 'Albert'
meets with a tragic death, having laid up for himself treasure
upon earth; and where his treasure is, there remains his love
(Matthew 12:19–21). He is heard and seen by more than one
person, and most clearly seen by a child. If the newspaper is
right and a real service of *exorcism* was conducted then it is
little wonder that the situation was not improved.

In *The Times* of the April 26th, 1972, Dom Robert Petitpierre
was interviewed, and in the course of it said:

> Real ghosts . . . are most often the souls of the recently
> deceased, the souls of people who have been so attached to their
> houses or gardens or material goods, that they find it hard to
> leave them without some help. In this kind of case no exorcism
> is necessary, in fact it could make things much worse because
> you cannot exorcise a human spirit, only *from* a human spirit;
> Prayer is a much more effective solution.

Occult thinking is parallel in its assessment of such ghosts,
although it resorts to mediumistic answers to the problem. Nat
Freedland in *The Occult Explosion* writes:

> Surprisingly, classic occult theory has never attached much
> significance to ghosts. They are supposed to be merely low-level
> spirits who have probably died by violence and are too trau-
> matised to realise that they can now ascend to higher dimen-
> sions. A true occultist believes ghosts are to be pitied and

helped instead of feared. Usually a séance with a sympathetic medium is sufficient to make the ghost aware it is now time to leave the earthly plane. Exorcism rituals of banishment are only necessary for mean, stubborn ghosts who cling to their haunts in a misguided lust for vengeance.

From time to time, there appears a case of an apparent return of the departed for the benefit of those remaining. J. B. Phillip's description of two 'visits' by the late C. S. Lewis probably fall into this category,[1] and I share Canon Stafford Wright's opinion that the Chaffin Will case is another exception to prove the rule.

James Chaffin died in 1921 leaving four sons.[2] His only known will was written sixteen years previously and in it his property was left to his third son who died shortly after inheriting it. The second son had several visions of his father who said on one occasion, 'You will find my will in my overcoat pocket.' In the pocket was a paper saying, 'Read the 27th chapter of Genesis in my daddie's old Bible.' It was at that place in the Bible that the later will was found, by which the father had divided his property equally between the four sons. No medium was involved.

Such exceptions are rare. Most 'ghosts proper' are in need, and any actions which occur come usually either as means of identification or to make their needs known. If things are moved it is not the random chaos of poltergeist activity, but items which are associated with the dead person and their former habits. It is not so much that they have 'returned', but rather that they have never *left*. They long to leave and find their rest in Him. Their need is for the Gospel which may be 'proclaimed' by the Eucharist (1 Corinthians 11:27) and by the life of the family concerned. One Christian family successfully ministered to such a soul by giving him a nickname, and inviting him to meals and family prayers. He was soon at peace. Another departed soul used regularly to arrive in Church alone with the parson to hear the daily Morning and Evening Prayer and the Scriptures read aloud. He too met God and is at rest. Not infrequently the saying of confession on behalf of those bound by sin is appropriate.

[1] *Ring of Truth* (Hodder & Stoughton).
[2] *Christianity and the Occult* (Scripture Union); fully investigated in *Proceedings of the Society for Psychical Research*, Vol. XXXVI.

It is a pity that the whole subject of praying for the dead †
is abhorrent to some Christians. I suspect that their abhorrence
is a reaction against the dangers of *contacting* the dead—which
has nothing whatever to do with praying for them. The
Corinthians were baptised on behalf of the dead (1 Corinthians 15:29) and some meaning must be placed on the difficult
passage in 1 Peter 3 in which Christ 'went to preach to the
spirits in prison'. C. E. B. Cranfield's comments on this second
passage are relevant to the whole question of the departed.

> This verse indicates that that interval [between death and
> resurrection] is not without significance, and that in it, as at
> other times, Jesus Christ was active as the Saviour of the world,
> and that the scope of His saving activity is such that we dare set
> no limits to it.[1]

## POLTERGEIST ACTIVITY

I have chosen to head this 'Poltergeist Activity' and not
'Poltergeists', because the latter suggests that the trouble would
cease by the removal of a 'noisy spirit', whereas in both theory
and practice a 'spirit' is not usually responsible.

As far as poltergeist activities are understood at all—and that
is not very much—the consensus of opinion seems to be that the
energy emanates from the uncontrolled psychic side of a person.
A. R. G. Owen, a Cambridge don, after sifting the evidence of
two hundred cases found the one of Virginia Campbell most
convincing.

> A clergyman saw a pillow rotate under the girl's head, and a
> large linen chest lift itself up, travel 18 ins. along the floor,
> then back. A doctor heard weird knockings, a sawing noise
> inside a linen basket and saw inexplicable ripples passing over
> Virginia's pillow. A teacher at Virginia's school saw a heavy
> desk rise slowly off the ground, hover like a helicopter and land
> in a spin. After a careful investigation Dr Owen's verdict was:
> 'The happenings seem to be more consistent with a force
> originating in Virginia's body, rather than an entity outside
> her.'

Doctor Hans Bender, a psychologist at Freiburg University, has
made a videotape of poltergeist activity, and a surprising

---

† I refer the reader to *Prayer and the Departed* (Report) SPCK.
[1] *The First Epistle of Peter* (SCM).

number of parish clergy will, in company where they will not be ridiculed, admit to being called in to households which are troubled in this way. The Rev. Jack Roundhill's experience and reactions are fairly typical, and are taken from his account in the *Church Times*, August 29th, 1969:

> As a priest I have only twice been asked to exorcise houses and rid them of noisy, mysterious, invisible visitants. On the first occasion I went round to the house and found a lady of no particular Church belief, but who was troubled by knockings and bangings in the night. She had been told by a neighbour that vicars were able to 'do something about such things' and would I please oblige? Well, I was doubtful then, as I am now. I hummed and hawed a bit, but I agreed to say some informal prayers and ask God's blessing on the house and household. I felt that God at any rate would know what to do . . . I kept in touch afterwards, and as far as I know, the knockings and banging ceased from that moment, and there was no more mysterious and uncanny trouble in the household.

Strictly speaking Mr Roundhill's experience might not belong under the heading of poltergeist activity, but it is a fine reminder that we are dealing with situations about which more is unknown than known, and that the Church's ministry is neither solely nor primarily an analytical one, but one which exposes the situation—whether understood or not—to the wholeness which is the perfect will of our all-knowing all-loving Father. An open acknowledgment of one's own ignorance on the one hand, but of the power of God on the other is better 'equipment' to deal with the situation than any amount of mere knowledge. Christ's Lordship extends not only over the known, but the unknown—and there is a good deal more of the latter.

If, as seems likely, family tensions contribute to poltergeist activity, then the 'peace of God which passeth all understanding' is particularly appropriate. The cure of such things may be reached more satisfactorily by addressing oneself to the family situation than to a 'spirit'—noisy or otherwise.

The main difference between disturbances created by true 'earth-bound' or departed spirits and poltergeist activity, is that the departed are confined to a sort of charade to make themselves and their needs known, whereas the poltergeist activity is random, chaotic and mischievous although rarely is a person injured by it.

Of the vast range of reported phenomena, which the reader may find in any of the standard works on the subject,[1] one that particularly sticks in my mind as illustrative of poltergeist activity is the occasion when a housewife found the Sunday joint taken from the oven and placed on top of the pelmet! Sheer mischief—with nothing of the charade of the departed, nor of the attraction or malevolence of the demonic.

The *Epworth Poltergeist* in the home of the young John Wesley has become a well-known example of these things, and few authors on the subject can resist relating the story, which here I need only outline.[2]

According to John Wesley the occurrences began on December 2nd, 1716, when their servant heard a knock and a groan at the door at ten o'clock at night. He opened it and found no one there, and on his way to bed he saw a handmill turning by itself, and the noise, among others, of someone stumbling over shoes. The next day their maid dropped a trayful of butter when suddenly confronted with inexplicable knockings.

One day when Molly Wesley was sitting in the dining room, the door opened and the rustling of silk seemed to indicate that someone walked around her and then left by the door. She explained later that she had left quietly and slowly as she thought it useless to run since whatever it was could probably run faster than she. Christina Hole in *Haunted England* says that the 'almost lighthearted way in which the Wesleys treated their *poltergeist* is very astonishing', although she herself relates that Samuel Wesley refused to be advised to leave the place, saying that he would not fly from the Devil—little wonder they were not afraid.

Not surprisingly the children were less composed, but it is interesting to note that they were, according to their father, '. . . frightened in their sleep and trembled very much till it waked them'. Hetty trembled in her sleep prior to being woken by it and often the disturbances centred around her. This,

---

[1] *Can We Explain The Poltergeist?*, A. R. G. Owen (Garrett, New York, 1964). *Ghosts and Poltergeists*, Herbert Thurston, S.J. (Burns Oates, 1953). *The Story of the Poltergeist down the Centuries*, H. Carrington and N. Fodor (Rider, 1953).

[2] For a compilation of relevant passages from the family's correspondence see the entry 'Epworth Poltergeist' in *The Encyclopedia of Witchcraft and Demonology*, Robbins (Spring Books). Also *Ghosts*, Eric Russell (Batsford), *Ghosts and Hauntings*, D. Bardens (Collins).

wrote her mother, 'she took notice of and was much frightened, because she thought it had a particular spite at her'.

Samuel Wesley challenged what he called the 'dumb and deaf devil' and, according to his own words 'asked it what it was and why it disturbed innocent children and did not come to me in my study'. It did. The invitation was accepted but not graciously, and the Rector found himself pushed around there.

The knockings and bangs, once described 'as if all the bottles under the stairs had been dashed to a thousand pieces' used to come during the family's prayers, and Samuel Wesley wrote of the 'usual knocks at the prayer for the King'. This is generally taken as a sign of Jacobite sympathies, though if the communication was limited to knocks and bangs, it is just as possible that in the charade, they indicated applause and approval for King George.

The case is one of the best-documented of its kind. The evidence is contained in letters from both parents and two sisters to the eldest son; and the personal accounts of Samuel Wesley and the Rev. Mr Hoole. The accuracy of these was later verified by their manservant and John Wesley himself. Mr Hoole's witness is somewhat limited because, although called on by the Rector for help and support, he fled after staying just one night. Some may regard his departure as a testimony as eloquent as his writing.

The disturbances could not only be seen and heard, but also touched. Dennis Bardens in *Ghosts and Hauntings* writes:

> Sometimes the door latch would lift itself, and when Emily, one of Wesley's daughters, tried to hold it down, it would be beyond her strength. The latch would go up and the door burst open, sending the girl flying.

The Rector wrote in his journal that when he knocked back with his stick that it was once answered by other knockings corresponding in number and volume to his own. This would not have been possible if there was some natural or geological cause, and it is generally true that poltergeist phenomena cannot be explained by mere 'forces' such as gravity or electricity.†

---

† The movements of objects in such cases are often contrary to rules governing such forces: objects *slowly* falling; trajectories of objects thrown *around* corners; the tying of a handkerchief in a knot, etc.

The disturbances ended abruptly after about a month, a time which, as Emily wrote, '. . . was sufficient to convince anybody of the reality of the thing and to try all ways of discovering any trick, had it been possible for any such to have been used'.

The Wesley family used to refer to it as 'Old Jeffrey', a name given it by Emily after someone who had died in the house, but the house was then new and had no ghostly associations whatever. I regard the nickname as something of a red herring, and am inclined to the opinion expressed by Eric Maple in *The Realm of Ghosts* when he says that the Rectory had

> . . . been haunted . . . by Old Jeffrey who was regarded by the family as one of themselves. Old Jeffrey was a very human ghost and by no means a poltergeist and it was possibly unkind of the family to hold him responsible for certain poltergeist disturbances which began to take place in the house.

Notwithstanding Mr Maple's criticism of the family's interpretation, it seems to have been John Wesley who had the clearest understanding of the possible cause. After the death of his parents, he disclosed that his father had once actually left his wife because she had *refused to pray for the King*. In revealing this, Wesley obviously felt that the underlying resentment and tensions may have been a contributory factor. That the nineteen-year-old Hetty seems to have been the 'centre' of the activities merely explains the source of energy, and does not make her a fraud or a trickster as some have maintained—not least because she was frequently asleep during these times.

The *Epworth Poltergeist* seems accurately named. An 'imprint' or 'place-memory' has no energy to move things or to cause noises; a true ghost's actions would be communicative and purposeful.

Contemporary theories of poltergeist activity as an externalised 'working off' of emotional tension could certainly fit the situation in a household so divided in its political loyalties, while at the same time—particularly over the Christmas season —under such pressures to appear united.

It is difficult to say if there was anything demonic in the affair. Everyone, except the dog, seems to have become accustomed to the situation, which suggests that the early fear of the children was largely the fear of the unknown rather than the fear of evil. But it must be remembered that the Curé D'Ars was haunted by what A. R. G. Owen calls, 'a strong resemblance to poltergeist activity'. These incidents are usually taken to have a predominantly spiritual significance because of the Curé's stature as a man of God and as an evangelist. When similar happenings occur in the home of John and Charles Wesley it may not be without spiritual significance either. Even if no demon were involved, the Enemy would have been pleased if the intervention of the unknown had opened the door to fear which might distort and undermine the spiritual lives of the young boys; the greatest danger—then as now.

It is quite possible to dismiss the case altogether, as did Coleridge, as the result of 'contagious epidemic hallucination of witnesses', but to dismiss *all* such cases in this way would be a formidable task, as well as undermining almost completely the validity of any personal testimony about anything.

A close parallel to the Epworth Poltergeist may be read in the *Proceedings of the Society for Psychical Research*, Vol. XXV, 1911, in what is known as the 'Derrygonnelly Case'. This was investigated by Sir William Barrett himself, Professor of Physics at Dublin University and a prominent member of the Society.

A farmer with his wife and family of one son and four daughters lived in a small cottage in which, so the report reads 'objects began to move about without any visible cause, stones to fall, candles and boots repeatedly thrown about the house'. Like the Wesley family they at first thought the cause was rats, but with the increase in the noise and nature of the disturbances, the 'rat theory was abandoned and general terror took possession of the family'.

The report continues:

Several neighbours urged them to send for a priest, but they were Methodists, and their class leader advised them to lay an open Bible on the bed. This they did in the name of God, putting a big stone on the top of the volume; but the stone was lifted off by an unseen hand and the Bible placed on top of it. After that 'it', as the father called the unseen cause, moved the Bible out of the room and tore seventeen pages right across.

Professor Barrett reported 'knocks were going on everywhere around; on the chairs, the bedstead, the walls, and ceiling . . . Suddenly a large pebble fell in my presence on the bed; no one had moved to dislodge it even if it had been placed for the purpose . . . the knocks became still louder, like those made by a heavy carpenter's hammer driving nails into flooring.'

The conclusion of the incident is interesting, and is another reminder against making classifications which are too 'water-tight'.

The farmer, not surprisingly, begged his investigators not to finish the case without ridding his family of the trouble. The Rev. Maxwell Chase, one of the investigators, conducted a short service. Sir William described it thus:

> The noises were at first so great we could hardly hear what was read, then as the solemn words of prayer were uttered they subsided, and when the Lord's Prayer was joined in by us all, a profound stillness fell on the whole cottage. The farmer rose to his knees with tears streaming from his eyes, gratefully clasped our hands, and we left . . . I am afraid this does not sound a very scientific account, but it is a veracious one.

The report concluded that there were no further disturbances from that night. In forming even a tentative theory about the cause it must be remembered that the Lord's Prayer is not only a plea for deliverance from evil, but in its supplications a prayer for the coming of God's Kingdom; for the doing of his will; for our needs to be met; for our sins to be forgiven; and for us not to be put to the test. An answer to any single *one* of these petitions would undoubtedly make a substantial difference to the disturbance, whatever its causes.

## SPIRITISTIC CAUSES

Without doubt, the most common causes of disturbances in places are practices in them, or near them, which either deliberately or unintentionally open the door to psychic tension and spirit interference. The following has been transcribed from the Rev. Arthur Dean's account of a case, available on tape from Summer Crusades, York. The account will be neither startling nor unfamiliar to those who work among young people, and it provides a clear example of the interreaction of people and places.

> . . . the 'phone rang. It was the university chaplain explaining that there were two students who had called on him who had been dabbling around with a ouija board, and desperately

needed help. The chaplain admitted himself that he had not had much experience in these things, and he didn't really think he could help them—at least he was honest and open . . .

An hour later these two students arrived and told us that a few months before they . . . had begun to play around with a ouija board, thinking that it was just a joke.

. . . At first they thought that it was one of the others in the group pushing the glass . . .

One day as a test to the 'spirit' they asked it to break the glass. The glass shattered like a car windscreen into little crystals, and instead of deterring them, they asked for further proof. In the room was a two-bar electric fire, and they asked whatever power it might be to put one of the bars out.

. . . not just one bar went out, but both bars went in and out almost like a Belisha beacon, until eventually the fire exploded. Later that evening I [Mr Dean] saw the 'remains' of that fire, for that is the best way to describe it.

When the students later asked for proof *outside* the house, the spirits informed them of Satanic rituals in the nearby grave-yard—the animal remains of which they found on their first visit there.

Soon after, the spirits began to use one of them as a medium; she 'had become really possessed, and at times she became quite violent, and the three boys in the house had to hold her down on a number of occasions'. She attacked one of the boys twice and tried to kill him.

One day when they were sitting in the living room, they saw horseshoes flying around the ceiling, and at another time, a green 'X' appeared on it. But one day:

a yellowy-grey cloud formed in the room from ceiling to floor. It was like a pillar. When they got up to waft it away, it just kept coming back together again. That night . . . [the girl] who was also an unmarried mother, went to bed, but in the middle of the night she woke up. This yellowy-grey cloud was enveloping the cot in which her little baby son was lying. Natur-ally she jumped out of bed and began to waft the cloud away, but as she did the cot fell to bits—I don't just mean it was British made! In an uncanny way each of the different struts around the side came out. I saw . . what remained of the cot, and naturally it couldn't fall to bits as it did. If it had broken and smashed I could understand this, but *each* hinge and *each* part fell apart.

It is not the place in this chapter to recount the exorcism of the students, except to say that during the exorcism of the girl there was a crash behind the Methodist ministers. 'Afterwards, when he had finished the service, we picked up from the floor a little wooden gonk . . . When we found it it was about a yard and a half away from the mantelpiece. My minister friend when he had heard the crash had looked up and he said he saw it *fly* off the mantelpiece, it didn't just drop . . . and it landed with the head broken off. It was a type of fetish in which evil was personified, so we burnt it after the service.'

I have related this story at some length because had it been approached purely in terms of a disturbed *place*, the cause of the trouble would have been missed. Had the house *alone* been exorcised on account of the yellowish cloud and other phenomena, the life-style of the students was such that the last state would have been worse than the first (Matthew 12:45).

While it is a convenient distinction to divide the Church's Ministry into 'People' and 'Places', in practice they are complementary aspects of *one* ministry to the situation. In recent years there has been a drawing together of ministers who in the past had a particular ministry either to people *or* to places, and it has been found in learning from each other that it is a *both . . . and* ministry.

I remember visiting one home where the child was in need of exorcism. The minister with me sensed also an evil presence in the home, which he subsequently exorcised, after his exorcism of the child. In this instance, since the boy's condition had been the same in the previous house, it was likely that his demonic state was influencing the home. In this, as in so many cases, the case-history of the family concerned shed light on the trouble, for they had gone to a healer who enlisted the aid of spirits. Those who enlist the aid of spirits frequently get what they ask for, and that is why the disturbances of so many places originate from spiritistic séances held in them or nearby. In blocks of flats, in particular, the cries for help come frequently from those who live adjoining or above practising mediums, however much the mediums themselves may be claiming to make contact only with 'good' spirits.[1] Unfortunately the intentions and integrity of the people involved seems to be little check on the nuisance value of their practices, while amateur dabbling, as in the case above of the students, invites psychic and spiritual disturbance for its own sake.

## HUMAN SIN

A house or site used for sexual misbehaviour (in the countryside often the ancient fertility-cult site), but equally the office of an organisation devoted to greed or domination, can often incur trouble or act as a dispersal centre. Human sin also opens the door for other forces to enter in.

Thus the *Exorcism* Report indicates a basic cause for disturbances in places, and incidentally in people also, for all too frequently unconfessed sin lies behind the psychic disturbances of which a person appears to be the victim, but is in fact the cause. A minister friend of mine related to me how a couple who were living together came to him for advice on how to be rid of the various psychic pains from which they frequently suffered. They were living together, although not married, and he pointed out to them that wholeness cannot be built on a distortion, it can only replace it. They agreed to live apart, but unknown to the minister at the time soon cohabited again. Their troubles never really ceased until they married, when their distorted life-style ended. There will be differing views about whether their extra-marital relationship should be called 'sin', but it was clearly their distorted way of living which contributed to psychic disturbance.

Similarly it is a distortion to attribute to powers which God has created, the worship and honour which is rightly due only to the Creator. This is the distortion in so many occult practices, coupled, alas, with the 'domination' and 'greed' of which the Report speaks. This is why Magicians are listed by the Report as one of six possible causes of disturbed places. I do not think they deserve a separate heading, not because I doubt their power, but they are simply one group among a very wide range who set out to manipulate powers and people, and it

---

[1] See *I Talked with Spirits* by Victor Ernest (Coverdale).

would be all too easy to underrate the 'sin' of more socially respectable groups, simply because they do not resort to secret rituals. Doctor Theodor Bovet in *That They May Have Life* has some wise words in this connection:

> It is especially important to take a firm stand in cases where the occult has become a substitute for religion, or indeed a full-blown religion in its own right, as happens with many Europeans, such as Theosophists and Anthroposophists . . . The pastor can only do this, however, if he is to some extent acquainted with occult phenomena, and knows that like everything else they are placed under the sovereignty of God. At the same time he will be cautious, and test all other possibilities before ascribing any particular disturbance to magic. A purely exorcistic pastoral treatment may be nothing more than a device of the devil to make us more easily overlook the real sin.

The late Fr Gilbert Shaw in his important essay 'Angels and Demons in Human Life'[1] says that the infestation of places may be 'either through some human wickedness done there whereby the demon has entered, or through an idolatrous worship, particularly connected with lust or violence; or again the demon may have been planted by the deliberate purpose of man'. The latter is obviously a reference to the activity of magicians. In considering 'Satanism and Black Magic' (in Chapter Four) I quoted the comment in *Black Magic Today* that in extreme cases where a magical group cannot rid itself of a curse from another group, a clergyman is called in to exorcise the 'poltergeist'. The magician Aleister Crowley records that he had to use electric light even on the brightest days because of the darkness that surrounded him as he prepared for his Abramelin Magic. C. R. Cammell writing of this period in Crowley's life states that the 'phenomena which occurred were certainly enough to test a man's nerves . . . The sinister influence was not confined to the house. Crowley's lodge-keeper, "a total abstainer for twenty years" became "raving drunk for three days" and "tried to kill his wife and children".'

---

[1] In *The Angels of Light and the Powers of Darkness*, E. L. Mascall (ed.) (Faith Press).

## Pagan Sites

The activities of occultists and magicians often centre on Celtic
sites, such as tumuli, circles and snake-paths, and such places,
which with or without the encouragement of ritual, may suffer
from a psychic 'hangover' from previous usage. This is particularly true of sites that have been desecrated. One theory is
that stone circles, for instance, were constructed to attract
energy, whether this is so remains a matter of opinion, but it
does seem that such centres act as distribution points for occult
forces, however created or whatever their nature, forces which
appear to run on power-lines or 'leys' between each centre. The
assessment by young people of a place by its good or bad
'vibes' (vibrations) and their willingness to spend hours at such
ancient sites as Glastonbury Tor, stems probably from an
instinctive awareness of such things.

Whatever the truth of the matter, we are no more to live by
the dictates of our history than we are to live by the dictates
of contemporary magicians, and the reality of either must never
detract from the responsibility of the individual so to order his
life in relation both to God and others, that he can say with
St Paul, 'I am certain of this . . . nothing that exists, nothing
still to come, nor any power . . . nor any created thing, can
ever come between us and the love of God made visible in
Christ Jesus our Lord' (Romans 8:38–9).

The proximity of ancient pagan sites may, however, be the
only explanation of places of disturbance which are not
centred on a home. Readers of Donald Omand's *Experiences of a
Present Day Exorcist* will be familiar with the possible influence on
motorists of psychic or demonic forces. Following the publication of his book, Mr Omand was asked to exorcise a notorious
'accident black spot' selected by the police of the county concerned; an exorcism which was televised. Mr Omand kindly
invited me to assist him, and contrary to some claims in the
Church press that such things are ridiculed by what we rather
arrogantly call 'outsiders', both the camera crew and the
famous producer were more willing than many Christians I
have met, to consider the reality of what was done. Indeed the
presence of a herd of pigs close by caused merry speculation
about whether they would rush down the hill as a result of our
actions!

## THE CHURCH'S MINISTRY

It must be stressed that not only is there an interaction between people and places, but that the possible causes of disturbance and strain frequently occur together. It is usually not possible to diagnose a single cause to the exclusion of all others. Fortunately the scope of the Gospel is wide enough to be relevant to all situations whatever their components, whether centred on people or places.

There would seem to be three different types of force which may be operating in any given place: (i) The *impersonal*—'place memories', and perhaps also in some cases the 'poltergeist phenomena'; (ii) the *demonic*—invited either deliberately or accidentally by spirit-inviting, or spiritistic actions, including magic ritual; (iii) *human* influence—in some cases the 'poltergeist'; forces instigated by magicians; and the whole spectrum of sin and greed and domination to which humans are so prone.

In *all* cases I would put the 'prayer and pastoral care of the persons involved' (to use the *Exorcism* Report phrase) *first*—even in those which are clearly demonic. It will be realised that *exorcism*, the binding and expelling of evil powers by the triumph of Christ, is the ministry only to states which are demonic. Only Satan binds *people*, neither God nor his Church will do so, however great a temporary nuisance people exercising their free will may create. In the long term, as the biography of Aleister Crowley and others makes abundantly clear, such people invariably become bound by the very powers with which they had hoped to manipulate others. There is no need for such people to be bound even if it were allowable for they afford no menace or danger to those who are 'in Christ' while their activities which start as a threat to others frequently open these same people to a new awareness of the Gospel's relevance.

It seems that an exorcism in the place can be undertaken without any problem 'to remove at least one possible factor from the situation'. 'Exorcism' here is used as a shorthand word for the whole ministry of exorcism-and-blessing, the latter of which must always follow the former whatever the situation.

The Church's Ministry is not a counter-magic, nor must it be thought that the use of Christian symbols, as for instance the alleged issue of crucifixes to police when searching for maniacs known to be involved with magic, is sufficient in itself to warrant the adjective 'Christian'. Such externals may be expressions of a living faith, but are no substitute for it.

The use of holy water in the blessing of places is similarly magical unless it is in fact, and understood to be, an outward expression of the prayers of the Church. Some Christians find the use of such externals dangerous precisely for this reason. But it is interesting that a number of Pentecostalists and others on the basis of Acts 19:12 will bless 'handkerchiefs' and take them to the sick as expressions of the Church's prayer for them. Their term *prayer cloths* neatly expresses the theology of such actions— perhaps if holy water were called *prayer water*, as well it might be, its use would be more widely accepted.

But it is not simply the prayers of the Church, but the whole saving Gospel of Christ which needs to be expressed in such cases. '. . . Every time you eat this bread and drink this cup you are proclaiming his [the Lord's] death . . .' (1 Corinthians 11:26). It is not surprising, therefore, that a celebration of the Holy Eucharist is so frequently the most appropriate action, not least because it re-establishes the Lordship of Christ in a situation where fear has ruled.

In places where it seems that the trouble may be caused by an earth-bound spirit, prayers for the departed linked with the place are appropriate, not prayers or commands of expulsion, but confession on their behalf, and a compassionate commending of them to find their peace in God. Those in Catholic traditions will find this no new aspect of ministry, and it is to be hoped that others will appreciate it as, in the most literal sense of the word, truly 'evangelistic'.

Those who wish to undertake an exorcism, or to consider the possibility of it, are referred to the *Exorcism* Report (SPCK) for guidance of the exorcism of both places and people.

By way of a supplement to that essential document, the following is a summary of part of Dom Robert Petitpierre's privately printed notes on the subject, and is headed 'A general pattern for the cleaning up of places, especially where the trouble is ill-defined.'

(i) General Exorcism, beginning with the main part of the building and then proceeding through it to all rooms and cupboards, using holy water.

(ii) A celebration of the Eucharist with special prayers for the departed.

(iii) Blessing of the building and each room.

(iv) Later, another celebration of the Eucharist in honour of the Patron, or of St Michael and All Angels, concluding with the praise of the Te Deum or Gloria.

The exact form of ministry undertaken will be influenced not simply by the pastor's own spiritual tradition and resources, but by the spiritual maturity and preparation of the people concerned. It is as bad to combat magic with magic as it is to be *thought* to do so, and nothing should be done until the persons in the situation are clear about what is being done and what is *not* being done. While there may legitimately be some ignorance about the exact nature both of the disturbance and its cure, there is never any doubt, in Christian ministry, of the Power at work. As Dom Robert concluded in *The Times*, April 26th, 1972:

People should not panic when they encounter this kind of thing. It is all quite simple really, you say your prayers and the Lord deals with it.

# A POSTSCRIPT

I HAVE DELIBERATELY avoided the heading 'Conclusion' for this section, because the range of topics and their implications in this study has been so wide that to offer conclusions would be rather presumptuous. There are, however, some implications and pointers that can and ought to be shown.

The newspapers on the day I write this are full of a brutal three-child killing in which one had a broken skull by being dashed against a wall, another was strangled with curtain wire, and the third had his throat cut; what was left of them after being bludgeoned with a pick axe and mutilated with a razor blade was impaled on spiked iron railings. The defence stated that they had studied the reports of three psychiatrists 'and there cannot be any evidence to support legal insanity'. The doctors said that there was a risk of the crimes being repeated. The father of the murderer said 'We cannot begin to account for . . . his behaviour. He was always so fond of children'. The person concerned received a minimum twenty-year sentence. He had pleaded *guilty*, saying, 'Everything caved in . . . I don't know what possessed me.' I do not take the view of some that psychological studies are so narrow, or psychiatrists so insular and inhumane that in such a case, for instance, they would presume to account for all causes, or not be grateful for any further insights from whatever quarter. The contemporary Church is immeasurably the better because of the exposure by medicine and psychiatry of the false demons within her and her history; I am certain that the time will come when these disciplines will begin to be thankful to the Church if she has a return of nerve and ventures to offer *some* explanation of events beyond the scope of their dedicated study.

Not only are there implications for studies of mental health and behaviour, but also for theology, and the status of the *New Testament records*. I have not bothered to mention the possibility of possession of animals as it is of no pastoral significance. Donald Omand's book *Experiences of a Present Day Exorcist* has an account of lions becoming possessed immediately following the sudden falling unconscious of a man, resulting in the two animals attacking and killing their trainer. Mr Omand later exorcised the animals by going into the cage himself. Other less dramatic cases of animal possession occur in books on this subject. I mention it here simply to enable me to state that there are a number of contemporary incidents parallel to *everything* in the story of the Gerasene demoniac, including the implied 'possession' of the swine (Mark 5:11-13). Commentators may employ various methods of criticism and deduce that the story has been changed in various ways. It is not necessary, however, to feel obliged to change it—and *then* find means for doing so—on the ground either that such things did not or that such things do not happen.

The Rev. John Nevius in his classic work on demonic possession wrote:

The testimony of the Scriptures on this subject, and that which we derive from sources outside the Scriptures, are mutually confirmatory. To one in whose mind doubts have risen as to the possibility of occurrences which are declared in the Scriptures to have taken place, the appearance in the present age, and in ordinary life, of facts similar to or identical with those to which the Bible bears witness tends to solve his doubts. The very statements which were the means of shaking his faith in the Bible become to him convincing evidence of its truth.[1]

Oesterreich, as we noted in Chapter Seven, concluded that the New Testament records 'even should they be recognised as of little or no historical value, bear in themselves the stamp of truth. They are pictures of typical states exactly reproduced.' To my knowledge Nevius' and Oesterreich's works are the fullest studies of the subject † and ought to be regarded as authoritative on it until another scholar presents either the same or opposite conclusions based on a similarly thorough treatment. The energy in linguistic and mental gymnastics which commentators have sometimes displayed in 'accounting for' these stories might have been better used in finding and critically evaluating alleged contemporary phenomena which appear to be so similar. I for one would not be in the least worried if they came to opposite conclusions to the ones I hold,

[1] *Demon Possession* (Kregel).
† Available in English.

providing they were *genuine conclusions* and not presuppositions, supported by an arbitrary selection of facts.

The following story carries its own lesson when the implications of *clergy training* are considered. (I have omitted the source, so as not further to publicise what is something of a confession, although it does appear in print, and the source is mentioned in my bibliography.)

> I know of a teenage lad in our own experience who apparently was trying to fight this spirit of hate. He came into our Church one night and ran out from the congregation with a knife in his hand pointing at the preacher. As he came forward the power of the Holy Spirit struck him down to the ground, where he lay until the end of the service almost like a dead man. One of the deacons had already taken the knife away from him.
>
> At the close of the service I took hold of the young man and tried to understand him as I told of Jesus Christ's power to save and redeem. He told me of his past life, and at the end of the conversation, said 'I must murder somebody'. But alas, the story is almost too sorrowful to record, for he went out into the park in our own locality and murdered a young boy. The reason for this was that this spirit of murder, whether you believe it or not, had overcome him and taken advantage . . .

A less grim story might do less to waken people to the reality of these things, for humanly speaking, this tragedy came about because while the minister concerned 'told him of Jesus Christ's power to save and redeem'—he did not act on Jesus' authority to deliver us from evil.

There is certainly some interest among clergy and ordinands about exorcism, but, it seems, not in its context. I have always refused to speak on the subject unless it was within a course on the healing ministry of the Church. Of the two theological colleges which (when I was free to do so) asked me to speak, the condition I imposed meant that in one I had to introduce the healing ministry myself, and that the other was unable to invite me.

The reluctance to give the deliverance ministry its due attention has many causes: a misunderstanding of what comes within (or outside) psychology; a healthy fear of returning to the atrocities of the Middle Ages; an uncritical acceptance of interpretation of New Testament healings as unhistorical or of dramatic or mythical language, etc. An important factor is the *theological climate* (as distinct from the 'religious climate') of today. In 1934 William Temple, as we noted in Chapter Five, wrote of his belief in evil caused by evil spirits. The following year in an article 'The Reality of the Demonic Powers Further Considered',[1] E. Langton made this plea: 'the time has come when the Church's attitude to the belief in the reality of the demonic powers should be fearlessly re-examined in the light of all the evidence available to the modern student . . . Having recently had occasion to review the evidence for the belief in demons, historically and critically from the Middle Ages to the present time, we have been forced to the conclusion that there is far more evidence for the belief in the reality of evil spiritual powers than has been recognised in recent years by Christian theologians.' If this study provokes theologians to take up this challenge after so long a delay and 'fearlessly re-examine' the matter 'in the light of all the evidence' I would be honoured that my short introduction had accomplished what Langton's immense scholarship has failed to do.

I have distinguished between the 'theological climate' and the contemporary *religious climate*. While theological trends enthusiastically deny the spiritual, social trends enthusiastically affirm it:

> The progression of topics ran from Asian philosophy to meditation, yoga, Zen, then to *I Ching* (a book presenting an ancient Chinese divination device . . .), to yang-yin, macrobiotic diet, Meher Baba, astrology, astral bodies, auras, U.F.O.s, tarot cards, parapsychology, witchcraft and magic. He [the Professor who related this of his group] added that the students were not dallying with these subjects, but involved in them . . .

Which group was this? A seminar of students having two or three years of saturation in science at the Massachusetts Institute of Technology, and described by their professor as 'intellectual . . . aristocrats, with the highest average maths scores in the land.'[2]

In Britain, the Professor of Anthropology at the London School of Economics says that upsurge of occult interest is a symptom of living in an age of 'marginal mystical recrudescence, a world where humanists seem positively archaic', and in

---

[1] *Hibbert Journal*, July 1935.
[2] H. Lindsey, *Satan is alive and well on planet earth.*

which the shamans (possessed priests) of primitive areas would find a ready welcome. (*Ecstatic Religion—An Anthropological Study of Spirit Possession and Shamanism*, Penguin.)

I hold a very dim view of being 'with-it' purely for the sake of it, yet some move in this direction by the theologians would decrease the gulf between their contemporary thinking and life around them. For reasons which others will be able to deduce better than I, their 'movement' has been towards the 'secular' society which is fast becoming a thing of the past, and not towards the 'religious' society of the last decade. Theology is, as the Editor of *Theology* kindly reminded us,[1] 'the specific pastoral tool of the Church'. If it is permissible to divide the role of pastor and theologian, it would seem that provided the pastor is truly of the Church, and not some heretical crank, he is not answerable to the theologians for aspects of genuine Christian experience, but rather the theologians must evaluate and interpret such experiences. For this reason I have not attempted to give a theological critique of demons or deliverance, I have instead drawn together a good deal of contemporary Christian experience of men and women of all denominations, and have not provided a theology, but the raw stuff about which theology must be hammered out. That is the theologians' job, not mine. I have presented nothing that is not to be found in life, and it is with life that the theologian has to deal, not selections from it.

A theological readjustment to accommodate the facts presented here would encourage the Church, and be an advance for it, not a setback. For four major aspects of the deliverance ministry are (i) its *pastoral relevance*—it meets people's needs; (ii) it is, in Prebendary Cooper's phrase,[2] 'a kind of John the Baptist to Jesus'—it is *evangelistic* in that it prepares the way and points to Christ, and in practice is often followed by commitment to him; (iii) it knows *no denominational barriers*—as the sources I have quoted so clearly show, and (iv) it *breaks down linguistic barriers*—by uniting together those of different traditions and terminologies (either inherited or invented) where the realities behind the clichés are very clear.

The deliverance ministry, as well as contributing to the unity, effectiveness, and relevance of the Church must, above all, drive the Church anew to The Exorciser—the Holy Spirit

[1] Vol. LXXVI, No. 633, March 1973.
[2] 'Bible and Exorcism', *Chrism*, Vol. XVII, No. 2, May, 1973.

—and to be no less spiritual than society is religious. The charismatic movement seems to be that part of the Church which is moving parallel to society rather than away from it. Whether it was intentional or not, James Dunn's conclusion to his article 'Rediscovering the Spirit' (*Expository Times*, Vol. LXXXIV, No. 2, November 1972) was completely in harmony with the 'religious' society.

> What Christians today must rediscover is God the Holy *Spirit* —not just the God in whom we believe, not just the God who was one of us, but the God whom we *experience*.

The growth—the phenomenal growth—of 'Pentecostal' Churches is well known. John Taylor in *The Go Between God* writes:

> I want to state categorically that I believe the time has arrived when we must take into account all that is positive in the witness of the pentecostal movement if we hope to press further forward along any of the various roads of liturgical renewal, inter-faith dialogue, the indigenization of Christianity . . . the ministry of healing, especially towards psychotics and addicts . . .

The reason, he states, that so many young graduates in Latin American universities are drawn to the Pentecostal healing sects is that they seem to be more relevant to human needs and conditions than the Protestant or Catholic congregations. 'After all, these students argue, for every person who feels an immediate concern for politics or social change, there are ten who feel the need for help in some sickness of body or mind . . .' And yet, the consideration of the Church's ministry of healing in theological colleges seems at best to be an 'optional extra'— as if relevance could ever be optional.

For the *individual* there are many implications, but they do not include reintroducing the Devil in his music-hall guise or in viewing his life as the helpless target for the Devil's fiery dart-throwing practice. Alec Vidler in a sermon entitled 'The Devil' concluded:

> You have not really to bother whether the devil is best described as a person, or as a power, or as a supernatural agency—so long as you take him seriously. What you have to do, is not to define him but to renounce him. And if you imagine that he is leaving you alone at present, and that what I have been saying

does not somehow apply to you, remember that will be the greatest feather in his cap. The devil is your opponent, not only your neighbour's.[1]

Brother Max Thurian of Taizé in *Modern Man and the Spiritual Life* (a title which may partly account for the modern significance of Taizé) says:

The conflict, then, which is the concern of Christian self-discipline, must not be understood in terms of an inner battle between the spirit and the body. The conflict is against the powers of evil, not against flesh and blood. This is to be taken quite objectively. The whole universe is the scene of this conflict. When it is understood in this way, the Christian is free from anxious pre-occupation with himself; instead he is summoned by his Lord, he is enlisted by the Church, to serve in a battle which is raging in the world, the aim of which is to make effective in the world that victory which God has already won.

[1] *Windsor Sermons.*

# APPENDIX

# EXORCISM OF THE POSSESSED

A PRIEST—ONE who is expressly and in special wise author-ized by the Ordinary—when he intends to perform an exorcism over persons tormented by the devil, must be properly distinguished for his piety, prudence, and integrity of life. He should fulfil this devout undertaking in all constancy and humility, being utterly immune to any striving for human aggrandizement, and relying not on his own, but on the divine power. Moreover, he ought to be of mature years, and revered not alone for his office but for his moral qualities.

2. In order to exercise his ministry rightly, he should resort to a great deal more study of the matter (which has to be passed over here for the sake of brevity) by examining approved authors and cases from experience; on the other hand, let him carefully observe the few more important points enumerated here.

3. Especially, he should not believe too readily that a person is possessed by an evil spirit; but he ought to ascertain the signs by which a person possessed can be distinguished from one who is suffering from melancholy or some other illness. Signs of pos-session are the following: ability to speak with some facility in a strange tongue or to understand it when spoken by another; the faculty of divulging future and hidden events; display of powers which are beyond the subject's age and natural condition; and various other indications which, when taken together as a whole, pile up the evidence.

4. In order to understand these matters better, let him inquire of the person possessed, following upon one or the other act of exorcism, what the latter experienced in his body or soul while

the exorcism was being performed, and to learn also what particular words in the form had a more intimidating effect upon the devil, so that hereafter these words may be employed with greater stress and frequency.

5. He will be on his guard against the arts and subterfuges which the evil spirits are wont to use in deceiving the exorcist. For often-times they give deceptive answers and make it difficult to understand them, so that the exorcist might tire and give up, or so it might appear that the afflicted one is in no wise possessed by the devil.

6. Once in a while, after they are already recognized, they conceal themselves and leave the body practically free from every molestation, so that the victim believes himself completely delivered. Yet the exorcist may not desist until he sees the signs of deliverance.

7. At times, moreover, the evil spirits place whatever obstacles they can in the way, so that the patient may not submit to exorcism, or they try to convince him that his affliction is a natural one. Meanwhile, during the exorcism they cause him to fall asleep, and dangle some illusion before him, while they seclude themselves, so that the afflicted one appears to be freed.

8. Some reveal a crime which has been committed and the perpetrators thereof, as well as the means of putting an end to it. Yet the afflicted person must beware of having recourse on this account to sorcerers or necromancers or to any parties except the ministers of the Church, or of making use of any superstition, nay any sort of forbidden practice.

9. Sometimes the devil will leave the possessed person in peace and even allow him to receive the Holy Eucharist, to make it appear that he has departed. In fact, the arts and frauds of the evil one for deceiving a man are innumerable. For this reason the exorcist must be on his guard, lest he fall into this trap.

10. Wherefore, he will be mindful of the words of our Lord (Matt. 17:20), to the effect that there is a certain type of evil spirit who cannot be driven out except by prayer and fasting. Therefore, let him avail himself of these two means above all for imploring the divine assistance in expelling demons, after the example of the holy fathers; and not only himself, but let him induce others, so far as possible, to do the same.

11. If it can be done conveniently, the possessed person

should be led to church or to some other sacred and worthy place where the exorcism will be held, away from the crowd. But if the person is ill, or for any valid reason, the exorcism may take place in a private home.

12. The subject, if in good mental and physical health, should be exhorted to implore God's help, to fast, and to fortify himself by frequent reception of penance and Holy Communion, at the discretion of the priest. And in the course of the exorcism he should be fully recollected, with his intention fixed on God, Whom he should entreat with firm faith and in all humility. And if he is all the more grievously tormented, he ought to bear this patiently, never doubting the divine assistance.

13. He ought to have a crucifix at hand or somewhere in sight. If relics of the saints are available, they are to be applied in a reverent way to the breast or the head of the person possessed (the relics must be properly and securely encased and covered). One will see to it that these sacred objects are not treated improperly or that no injury is done them by the evil spirit. However, one should not hold the Holy Eucharist over the head of the person nor in any way apply It to his body, owing to the danger of desecration.

14. The exorcist must not digress into senseless prattle nor ask superfluous questions or such as are prompted by curiosity, particularly if they pertain to future and hidden matters, all of which have nothing to do with his office. Instead, he will bid the unclean spirit keep silence and answer only when asked. Neither ought he to give any credence to the devil if the latter maintains that he is the spirit of some saint or of a deceased party, or even claims to be a good angel.

15. But necessary questions are, for example: about the number and name of the spirits inhabiting the patient, about the time when they entered into him, the cause thereof, and such like. As for all jesting, laughing, and nonsense on the part of the evil spirit—the exorcist should prevent it or contemn it, and he will exhort the bystanders (whose number must be very limited) to pay no attention to such goings on; neither are they to put any question to the subject. Rather they should intercede for him to God in all humility and urgency.

16. Let the priest pronounce the exorcisms in a commanding and authoritative voice, and at the same time with great confidence, humility, and fervor; and when he sees that the spirit is

sorely vexed, then he oppresses and threatens all the more. If he notices that the person afflicted is experiencing a disturbance in some part of his body or an acute pain or a swelling appears in some part, he traces the sign of the Cross over that place and sprinkles it with holy water, which he must have at hand for this purpose.

17. He will pay attention as to what words in particular cause the evil spirits to tremble, repeating them the more frequently. And when he comes to a threatening expression, he recurs to it again and again, always increasing the punishment. If he perceives that he is making progress, let him persist for two, three, four hours, and longer if he can, until victory is attained.

18. The exorcist should guard against giving or recommending any medicine to the patient, but should leave this care to physicians.

19. While performing the exorcism over a woman, he ought always to have assisting him several women of good repute, who will hold on to the person when she is harassed by the evil spirit. These assistants ought if possible to be close relatives of the subject, and for the sake of decency the exorcist will avoid saying or doing anything which might prove an occasion of evil thoughts to himself or to the others.

20. During the exorcism he shall preferably employ words from Holy Writ, rather than forms of his own or of someone else. He shall, moreover, command the devil to tell whether he is detained in that body by necromancy, by evil signs or amulets; and if the one possessed has taken the latter by mouth, he should be made to vomit them; if he has them concealed on his person, he should expose them; and when discovered they must be burned. Moreover, the person should be exhorted to reveal all his temptations to the exorcist.

21. Finally, after the possessed one has been freed, let him be admonished to guard himself carefully against falling into sin, so as to afford no opportunity to the evil spirit of returning, lest the last state of that man become worse than the former.

# BIBLIOGRAPHY

ONLY A HANDFUL of people—Dr W. M. Alexander, Dr Kurt Koch, Rev. J. L. Nevius, Professor T. K. Oesterreich —have written whole books (available in English) which are devoted to possession, deliverance or exorcism. Most writers' healthy approach to these subjects is reflected in their treatment of them, where they are dealt with briefly but not lightly. Thus the majority of books listed do not dwell on the subject, but such treatment is usually more useful than the few standard works—Kurt Koch excepted. Familiar examples will be the mere twelve pages devoted to the Problem of Demon Possession in Leslie Weatherhead's *Psychology, Religion and Healing*, and George Bennett's chapter 'Casting out Devils' in his more recent *The Heart of Healing*.

Another major source of material is the booklets and leaflets which ministers have published, and which are the main means of drawing on the experience and teaching of such authorities as Daphne Buckley, Rev. Leslie Giddens, W. V. Grant, Derek Prince, Peter Scothern and H. A. Maxwell Whyte—although an increasing number of such ministers are making available tape-recordings of their talks, some of which I have listed. In most fields of study leaflets supplement books; in this study, the reverse is nearer the truth, because those most qualified to write about Deliverance are those actively engaged in such ministry with little or no time to put pen to paper. Derek Prince's *Expelling Demons* is not alone in having an importance quite disproportionate to its size of eight pages. For this reason I have not distinguished between leaflets and books because of the position of importance which the former hold in this instance.

I have omitted almost entirely standard works of reference, whether theological or not, biblical commentaries and standard theological works. Thus Oesterley's entry under 'Demon, Demoniacs' in *Hasting's Dictionary of Christ and the Gospels* is so obvious a source of reference to the Biblical student that I have not listed it, although I have for convenience listed some of the more important articles, like Langton's 'The Reality of

Demonic Powers Further Considered', which appear from time to time in theological and other journals, but are less well known. If a book is mentioned contrary to these general principles it is to draw particular attention to it, e.g. Loos' *The Miracles of Jesus*, which is indispensable in a way that many more familiar books on the same subject are not.

I have only listed a few books on the occult as my purpose in writing about it was not to encourage further study, but rather to provide the background to make such study unnecessary for the busy minister and general reader.

Further bibliographies, that I have taken no steps to duplicate, will be found in Kurt Koch's, *Christian Counselling and Occultism*, and Merrill Unger's *Biblical Demonology*. I. M. Lewis' *Ecstatic Religion* draws together some useful material, particularly from anthropological studies, while a review of psychiatric literature can be found in *The Journal of Mental Science*, Vol. 106, No. 442, following Dr Yap's article 'The Possession Syndrome'.

*Administration of Holy Unction and the Laying on of Hands.* SPCK.

AHMED, Rollo, *The Black Art*. Hutchinson, 1936.

ALEXANDER, Dr W. M., *Demonic Possession in the New Testament: its relations Historical, Medical and Theological*. T. & T. Clarke, Edinburgh, 1902.

ALLEN, A. A., *Demon Possession Today*. Allen, Dallas.

BACON, B. W., 'The Markan Theory of Demonic Recognition', *Zeitschrift für die Neutestamentliche Wissenschaft, etc.*, No. 6, 1905.

BAELTZ, Prof. Peter, 'Old Wine in New Bottles', *Theology*, LXXVI, No. 633, March 1973.

BARDENS, Dennis, *Ghosts and Hauntings*. Zeus Press, 1965.

BARKER, Dr J. C., *Scared to Death*. Muller, 1968.

BASHAM, Don W., *Can a Christian Have a Demon?* Whitaker Books, Pennsylvania, 1971.

BAUER, Paul, *Christianity and Superstition*. Marshall, Morgan & Scott, 1966.

BENNETT, Dennis and Rita, *The Holy Spirit and You*. Logos, New Jersey, 1971.

BENNETT, Rev. George, *About Exorcism*. Divine Healing Mission, Crowhurst.

BENNETT, Rev. George, *The Heart of Healing*. A. James, Evesham, 1971.

BENNETT, Rev. George, *Miracle at Crowhurst*. A. James, Evesham, 1970.
BENNETT, Rev. George, *Spiritual, Psychic and Radiesthetic Healing*. Divine Healing Mission, Crowhurst.
BENSON, Carmen, *Supernatural Dreams and Visions*. Logos, New Jersey, 1970.
BOLT, Pastor Richard, *Casting Out Devils* (tape). Richard Bolt Tapes, London.
BONNER, Gerald, *The Warfare of Christ*. Faith Press, 1962.
BOOM, Corrie ten, *Defeated Enemies*. Christian Literature Crusade.
BOVET, Theodor, *That They May Have Life*, trans. J. A. Baker. Darton, Longman & Todd, 1964.
BRACE, Reginald and WINTER, Geoffrey, 'The Men Who Fight The Devil', 'How To Treat A Ghostly Lodger' etc., *Yorkshire Post*, November 16th, 17th, 18th, 20th, 21st, 1970.
BRO, Dr Harmon Hartzell, 'Dangers of Psychic Development', *Fate*, Feb. and March, 1972.
BRUNO DE JESUS-MARIE, OCD (ed.), *Satan*, Sheed & Ward, 1951.
BUCKLEY, Daphne G., *Exposure of Seducing Spirits*. Full Gospel Deliverance Crusade, 1966.
BUCKLEY, Daphne G., *The Ministry of Exorcism*. Full Gospel Deliverance Crusade, 1971.
BUTT, A. *et al.*, *Trances*. Allen & Unwin, 1967.

CARRIGAN, Robert L., 'The Revival of Astrology—its implications for pastoral care', *Pastoral Psychology*, Vol. 21, No. 209, December, 1970.
CARRINGTON, Hereward and FODOR Nandor, *The Story of the Poltergeist Down the Centuries*. Rider, 1953.
CARRINGTON, Dr W. L., *A Medical View of Spiritual Healing*. T. & T. Clarke, Edinburgh (Reprint from *Expository Times*, Vol. LXXXI, No. 3, December 1969).
CATHERINET, Mgr F. M., 'Demoniacs in the Gospel', *Satan*. Sheed & Ward, 1951.
CHADWICK, G. A., 'Some Cases of Possession', *Expositor*, 4th Series, No. 6, 1892.
CHAFER, Prof. L. S., *Satan—His Motives and Methods*. Zondervan, Michigan, 1964.
*Christianity and Mental Health*. Christian Personal Workers' Assoc., 1971.
*Church's Ministry of Healing, The.* (Report) Church Information Office, 1958.
CLARK, Walter Houston (ed.), *Pastoral Psychology—Religion and Parapsychology*, Vol. 21, No. 206, September 1970.

CLAXTON, Dr E. and McKAY, Dr H. A. C. (eds), *Medicine, Morals and Man*. Blandford, 1969.

CONYBEARE, F. C., 'The Demonology of the New Testament' and 'Christian Demonology', *Jewish Quarterly Review*, VIII, 1896, and IX, 1897.

CONYBEARE, F. C., *Myth, Magic and Morals*, Watts, 1925.

COOPER, Preb. Henry, 'The Biblical Justification for Exorcism', *Chrism*, Vol. XVII, No. 2, May 1973.

COOPER, Preb. Henry, *Deliverance and Healing—The Place of Exorcism in the Healing Ministry*. Guild of Health & Guild of St Raphael, 1972.

COOPER, Preb. Henry, *Holy Unction—A Practical Guide to its Administration*, Guild of St Raphael, 1966.

'CORTE, Nicolas', *Who is the Devil?* Burns & Oates, 1958.

CREHAN, Fr J. sj, 'Exorcism', *Man, Myth, and Magic*. Purnell, 1971.

CREHAN, Fr J. sj, *Spiritualism*. Catholic Truth Society, 1967.

CRISTIANI, Mgr L., *Satan in the Modern World*, trans. C. Rowland. Barrie & Rockcliff, 1959.

CROW, W. B., *A History of Magic, Witchcraft and Occultism*. Aquarian Press, 1968.

CROWLESMITH, J. (ed.), *Religion and Medicine*. Epworth, 1962.

CULLMANN, O., *Christ and Time*. SCM, 1951.

DAILY, Starr, *Recovery*. A. James, Evesham, 1948.

DARNALL, Jean, *Divine Deliverance—The Devil's Devices* (Tape). London Healing Mission.

DEHAAN, Richard W., *Satan, Satanism and Witchcraft*. Zondervan, Michigan, 1972.

*Demon Experience in Many Lands* (A Compilation). Moody Press, Chicago, 1960.

DOLPHIN, Lambert T. Jnr, *Astrology, Occultism and the Drug Culture*. Good News Publishers, Illinois, 1970.

DOWDY, Homer E., *Christ's Witchdoctor*. Hodder & Stoughton, 1964.

DUNCAN, Rev. A. D., *The Christ, Psychotherapy and Magic*. Allen & Unwin, 1969.

EDMUNDS, Dr Vincent and SCORER, Dr C. Gordon, *Faith Healing*. Christian Medical Fellowship, Tyndale, 1956.

ELLIOT, G. Maurice., *The Psychic Life of Jesus*. Spiritualist Press, 1938.

EPP, Theodore H., *How to Resist Satan*. Lincoln, USA, 1958.

ERNEST, Victor H., *I Talked With Spirits*. Coverdale House, Illinois, 1970.

*Exorcism—a simple way of dealing with alleged infestation by evil.* Guild of St Raphael.

FISHER, The Most Rev. G. *et al.*, *Is There Life After Death?* A. James, 1960.
FITZHERBERT, Dr Joan, *Introductory Notes on Psychiatry for Christian Workers*. Mackay Graphics, Chatham, 1969.
FOX, Rev. A. H. Purcell, *The Church's Ministry of Healing*. Longmans, 1959.
FREEDLAND, Nat, *The Occult Explosion*. Michael Joseph, 1972.
FREEMAN, Hobart E., *Angels of Light?* Logos, USA 1969.
FRIDRICHSEN, Prof. A., 'The Conflict of Jesus with Unclean Spirits', *Theology*, Vol. XXII, No. 129, March 1931.
FROST, Evelyn, *Christian Healing*. Mowbray, 1940.

GAGE, Rev. George, 'The Laying on of Hands', *Way of Life*, May/June 1971.
GASSON, Raphael, *The Challenging Counterfeit*. Logos, New Jersey, 1966.
GEE, Donald, *Concerning Spiritual Gifts*. Gospel Publishing House, Missouri, 1947.
GIDDENS, Rev. Leslie, *Christ's Healing Ministry* (film-strip). Giddens, Hayes.
GIDDENS, Rev. Leslie, *The Ministry of Deliverance* (Exorcism). Giddens, Hayes.
GIDDENS, Rev. Leslie, *What is Exorcism?* Giddens, Hayes.
GOULDTHORPE, Martin J., 'Deliver us from Gullibility', *Renewal* A6, Aug-Sep, 1073.
GRACE, Dr Roy E., 'Parapsychology and Biblical Religion', *Pastoral Psychology*, Vol. 21, No. 206, September 1970.
GRAD, Dr Bernard, 'Healing by the Laying on of Hands—Review of Experiments and Implications', *Pastoral Psychology*, Vol. 21, No. 206, September 1970.
GRAHAM, Billy, *The Jesus Generation*. Hodder & Stoughton, 1971.
GRANT, W. V., *Demon Suppression and Possession*. Grant, Texas.
GRAYMONT, Dr B., 'Counseling and Epilepsy', *Pastoral Psychology*, Vol. 22, No. 217, October 1971.
*Great Things*. St Jude's Church, Herne Hill.
GUINNESS, Oswald, *Dust of Death* IVP, 1973.

HADFIELD, Dr J. A., *Psychology and Mental Health*. Allen & Unwin, 1950.
HADFIELD, Dr J. A., *Psychology and Morals*. Methuen, 1923.

HARDING, Rev. G. C., 'Exorcism or Psychotherapy?', *Concible*, Sep-Oct, 1973.

HARPER, Rev. Michael, *None Can Guess*. Hodder & Stoughton, 1971.

HARPER, Rev. Michael, *Spiritual Warfare*. Hodder & Stoughton, 1970.

HARRIES, John, *The Ghost Hunter's Road Book*. Muller, 1968.

HARRIS, Charles, 'Visitation of the Sick—Unction, Imposition of Hands, and Exorcism', *Liturgy and Worship* (ed. Lowther Clarke). SPCK, 1932.

HARRIS, Pastor Leo, *Victory over Satan*. Crusader Publications, Australia.

HAYS, Peter, *New Horizons in Psychiatry*. Penguin, 1964.

HEILPERN, John, 'The Church and the Jesus Trip', *Nova*, November 1972.

HEUVEL, Albert van den, *These Rebellious Powers*. SCM, 1966.

HEYWOOD, Rosalind, *The Sixth Sense*. Chatto & Windus, 1966.

HILL, Douglas, *Return From The Dead*. Macdonald Unit 75, 1970.

HILTNER, Prof. Seward, 'Christian Understanding of Sin in the Light of Medicine and Psychiatry', *Pastoral Psychology*, Vol. 19, No. 187, October 1968.

HOARE, Dorothy E., *More Than Conquerors*. Hoare.

HOCH, Dorothee, *Healing and Salvation*. SCM, 1958.

HOLE, Christina, *Haunted England*. Batsford, 1940.

HUEGEL, F. J., *That Old Serpent—The Devil*. Zondervan, Michigan, 1954.

HUXLEY, Aldous, *The Devils of Loudon*. Chatto & Windus, 1970.

HYATT, Jean, *The Concept of Demonic Possession in Mental Illness* (unpublished dissertation). Birmingham University.


IRVINE, Doreen, *From Witchcraft to Christ*. Concordia, 1973.


JAHODA, Gustav, *The Psychology of Superstition*. Lane/Penguin, 1969.

JAMES, Prof. William, 'Report on Mrs. Piper's Hodgson-Control', *Proceedings of the American Society for Psychical Research*, Vol. III, 1909.

JAMES, Prof. William, *The Varieties of Religious Experience*. Longmans Green, 1911.

JEEVARATNAM, Lam, *Concerning Demons*. F. J. Lamb, 1949.

JEREMIAH, Rev. F. Roy, *Venture Into Healing*. Lakeland, 1972.

JOHN OF THE CROSS, St, *Ascent of Mount Carmel*. T. Baker, 1906.

JOHNS, June, *Black Magic Today*. New England Library, 1971.

JONES, Dr D. Martin Lloyd, *The Supernatural in Medicine*. Christian Medical Fellowship Publications, 1971.


KELLY, Henry A., *Towards the Death of Satan*. Chapman, 1968.

KERR, John Stevens, *The Mystery and Magic of the Occult*. SCM, 1971.

KIMBER, W. J. T., *The Healing Church*, SPCK, 1962.

KELSEY, Morton T., *Healing and Christianity*. SCM, 1973.

KNAPP, Martin Wells, *Impressions from God or . . . ?* Voice Christian Publications Inc., California, 1963.

KNIGHT, Walker I., *The Weird World of the Occult*. Tyndale House, Illinois, 1972.

KOCH, Dr Kurt E., *Between Christ and Satan*. Evangelization Publishers, W. Germany.

KOCH, Dr Kurt E., *Christian Counselling and Occultism*. Evangelization Publishers, W. Germany, 1972, and Kregel, Michigan, 1965.

KOCH, Dr Kurt E., *The Devil's Alphabet*. Evangelization Publishers, W. Germany.

KOCH, Dr Kurt E., *Occult Bondage and Deliverance*. Evangelization Publishers, W. Germany.


LAING, Dr R. D., *The Divided Self*. Pelican, 1960.

LAING, Dr R. D. and ESTERSON, Dr A., *Sanity, Madness and the Family*. Penguin, 1964.

LAMBOURNE, Dr R. A., *Community, Church and Healing*. Darton, Longman & Todd, 1963.

LANDAU, Rom, *We Have Seen Evil*. Faber & Faber, 1941.

LANG, Andrew, *The Making of Religion*. Longmans Green, 1900.

LANGTON, Edward, *Essentials of Demonology*. Epworth, 1949.

LANGTON, Edward, *Good and Evil Spirits*. SPCK, 1942.

LANGTON, Edward, 'The Reality of Demonic Powers Further Considered', *Hibbert Journal*, July 1935.

LANGTON, Edward, *Satan—A Portrait*. Skeffington, 1945.

LANGTON, Edward, *Supernatural: The Doctrine of Spirits, Angels, and Demons from the Middle Ages to the Present Time*. Ryder, 1934.

LAW, Dr Robert, 'Mental Illness and Demon Possession', *Man, God and Magic (Viewpoint* 16), D. Wood (ed.). Inter School Christian Fellowship, 1970.

LECHLER, Dr Alfred, 'Disease and the Demonic', *Occult Bondage and Deliverance*. Evangelization Publishers, W. Germany.

LEECH, Rev. Kenneth, 'Drugs, Youth and Spirituality', *New Fire*, Vol. 11, No. 1.

LEECH, Rev. Kenneth, *Keep the Faith, Baby*. SPCK, 1973.

LEECH, Rev. Kenneth, *A Practical Guide to the Drug Scene*. SPCK, 1973 (published also as *Pastoral Care and the Drug Scene*: SPCK, 1970).

LEECH, Rev. Kenneth, *Youthquake*. Sheldon, 1973.

LESLIE, Anne, 'Turn on to Jesus, Baby', *Nova*, February, 1971.

LEWIS, Prof. I. M., *Ecstatic Religion—An Anthropological Study of Spirit Possession and Shamanism*. Pelican, 1971.

LHERMITTE, Dr Jean, *Diabolical Possession—True and False*. Burns & Oates, 1963.

LHERMITTE, Dr Jean, 'Les possédés sont-ils des fous?', *Ecclesia*, No. 67.

LHERMITTE, Dr Jean, 'Pseudo-possession', *Satan*. Sheed & Ward, 1951.

LINDSAY, Gordon, *Satan*, Vols. I–III. Christ for the Nations, Texas, 1967, 1972.

LINDSAY, Gordon, *Sorcery in America*, Vols. I–III. Christ for the Nations, Texas.

LING, Trevor, 'Christ's conquest of Satan, and its Relation to the Individual', *Theology*, Vol. LVI, No. 399, September 1953.

LING, Trevor, 'The Enemy of Holiness', *Theology*, Vol. LXVII, No. 525, March 1964.

LING, Trevor, *The Significance of Satan*. SPCK, 1961.

LLOYD, G. A. Lewis, 'The After Life', *Chrism*, Vol. XV, No. 1, February 1971.

LOOS, H. van der, *The Miracles of Jesus*. Brill, Leyden, 1965.

LYONS, Arthur, *Satan Wants You*. Mayflower, 1972.


MACLACHLAN, Lewis, *Miracles of Healing*. A. James, Evesham, 1968.

MACMILLAN, J. A., *Modern Demon Possession*. Christian Publications Inc., P.A.

*Man, Myth and Magic*, special articles in *Frontiers of Belief*: 'A Company of Devils', 'The Flesh and the Devil', 'Grave Robbing in Suburbia', 'London's Graveyard Ghouls', 'Occultism—The Future', 'The Rise of Modern Witchcraft', etc., Purnell, 1971.

MANUEL, Frances D., *Though an host should encamp*. Christian Literature Crusade, Fort Washington, Pennsylvania, 1971.

MAPLE, Eric, *The Dark World of Witches*. Hale, 1962.

MAPLE, Eric, *The Domain of Devils*. Pan, 1966.

MAPLE, Eric, *Magic, Medicine and Quackery*, Hale, 1968.

MAPLE, Eric, *The Realm of Ghosts*. Pan, 1964.

MAPLE, Eric, *Superstition and the Superstitious*. Allen, 1971.

MAQUART, F. X., 'Exorcism and Diabolical Manifestation', *Satan*. Sheed & Ward, 1951.

MARTIN, Bernard, *Healing for You*. Lutterworth, 1965.

MARTIN, Bernard, *The Healing Ministry of the Church*. Lutterworth, 1960.

MARTIN, Walter R., *The Kingdom of the Cults*. Marshall, Morgan & Scott, 1965.

MASCALL, Prof. E. L. (ed.), *The Angels of Light and the Powers of Darkness*. Faith Press, 1954.

MASCALL, Prof. E. L., *The Christian Universe*. Darton, Longman & Todd, 1965.

MAULEVERER, Rev. W., *The Prayer of Affirmation (A New Way to Pray)*. A. James, Evesham, 1952.

MAY, Dr Rollo, *Love and Will*. Souvenir Press, 1969.

McALL, Dr Kenneth, 'Demonosis or the Possession Syndrome', *International Journal of Social Psychiatry*, Vol. XVII, No. 2, 1971.

McCASLAND, S. V., *By the Finger of God—Demon possession and exorcism in the light of modern views of mental illness*. Macmillan, NY, 1951.

McDOUGALL, William, *An Outline of Abnormal Psychology*. Methuen, 1926.

METCALFE, J. C., *The Great Enemy*. Overcomer Literature Trust, Parkstone.

METCALFE, J. C., *Satan*. The Overcomer Book Room, Parkstone.

MICKLEM, E. R., *Miracles and the New Psychology*, Oxford University Press, 1922.

MILLER, Russell, 'The Ghost Hunters', *Mirror Magazine*, January 31st, 1970.

MORRISON, Clinton D., *The Powers That Be*. SCM, 1960.

MULLINS, Rev. A. G. OP, 'The Sinister Cult of Witchcraft'. *HM Prisons Chaplains' Newsletter*, November 1972.

MURPHY, Prof. Gardner, 'Phantasms of the Living and the Dead', *Pastoral Psychology*, Vol. 21, No. 206, September 1970.

MYERS, F. W. H., *Human Personality and the Survival of Bodily Death* (abridged). Longmans Green, 1907.

NEE, Watchman, *The Spiritual Man*. Christian Fellowship Publications Inc., New York, 1968.

NEEDHAM, G. C., *Angels and Demons*. Moody Press, Chicago.

NELSON, Dr M. H., *Why Christians Crack Up*. Moody Press, Chicago, 1960.

NEVIUS, Rev. John, *Demon Possession*. Kregel Publications, Michigan, 1968. (Previously published as *Demon Possession and Allied Themes*. Redway, 1897.)

*Non-Medical Use of Drugs* (Interim Report). Canadian Government Commission of Enquiry, Penguin, 1971.

NYGREN, Bishop Anders, 'Christ and the Forces of Destruction, and a word concerning the De-mythologising of Christianity', *Scottish Journal of Theology*, No. 4, 1951.

OBEYESEKERE, Prof. G., 'The Idiom of Demon Possession', *Social Science and Medicine*, Vol. 4, No. 1, July 1970.

OESTERREICH, Prof. T. K., *Possession, Demoniacal and Other*. Paul, Trench & Trauber, 1930.

OMAND, Rev. Donald, *Experiences of a Present Day Exorcist*. Kimber, 1970.

ORR, William W., *Are Demons For Real?* Scripture Press Publications, Illinois, 1970.

ORR, William W., *The Mystery of Satan*. Scripture Press Publications, Illinois, 1966.

OSBORN, T. L., *Healing The Sick*. T. L. Osborn Evangelistic Assoc., Okla/Birmingham/Toronto, 1959.

PALMS, Roger C., *The Jesus Kids*. SCM, 1972.

PALMS, Roger C., *The Occult: A Christian View*. Oliphants, 1973.

PATERNOSTER, Rev. Michael, 'The Theology of Death', *Chrism*, Vol. XV, No. 1, February 1971.

PEARCE-HIGGINS, Rev. Canon John, *A Letter to a Schoolboy about Ouija Boards, Glass and Alphabet and Psychic Experiments*. Churches' Fellowship for Psychical and Spiritual Studies.

PEARCE-HIGGINS, Rev. Canon John, *Review article of 'Thirty Years Among the Dead', by K. Wickland* (CFPSS).

PEARCE-HIGGINS, Rev. Canon John, 'The Unseen World' (series), *Home Words*, January, etc., 1971.

PENN-LEWIS, Jessie, *The Spiritual Warfare*. Overcomer Literature Trust, Poole/Christian Literature Crusade, Pennsylvania.

PENN-LEWIS, Jessie, *War on the Saints*. Overcomer Literature Trust, Poole/Christian Literature Crusade, Pennsylvania.

PENTECOST, J. Dwight, *Your Adversary The Devil*. Zondervan, Michigan, 1969.

PERRYMAN, F. J., *He Must Reign till——*. Perryman, Bournemouth, 1966.

PERRYMAN, F. J., *Whom Resist*. Perryman, Bournemouth, 1970.

PETERSON, Robert, *Roaring Lion*. Overseas Missionary Fellowship, 1968.

PETITPIERRE, Dom Robert OSB, (ed.), *Exorcism—The Findings of a Commission Convened by the Bishop of Exeter*. SPCK, 1972.

PETITPIERRE, Dom Robert OSB, (ed.), *Notes on Christian Exorcism*. Petitpierre, Nashdom.

PETITPIERRE, Dom Robert. OSB, 'Spirits in Prison' (unpublished ms.).

PHILLIPS, J. B., *Ring of Truth*. Hodder & Stoughton, 1967.

PIKE, Bishop James and KENNEDY, Diane, *The Other Side*. Allen, 1969.

*Prayer and the Department* (Report). SPCK, 1971.

'A Prevalence of Witches', *Life Magazine*, Vol. 36, No. 9, May 18th, 1964.

PRINCE, Derek, *Expelling Demons*. Prince, Florida.

PRINCE, Derek, *Exorcism and Deliverance* (tape). Prince, Florida.

PRINCE, Dr Morton, *The Dissociation of Personality*. Longmans, 1906.

PRINCE, R. (ed.), *Trance and Possession States*. Montreal, 1967.


RAMSEY, I. T., *Our Understanding of Prayer*. SPCK, 1971.

RÉGINALD-OMEZ, Fr OP, *Psychical Phenomena*. Burns & Oates, 1959.

RICHARDS, Rev. John, *The Demonic Dimension in Pastoral Care—a paper*. Richards, Cambridge.

RICHARDS, Rev. John, 'The Minister and the Demonic', *Regina*. Birmingham, 1971.

RICHARDS, Rev. John, *Synopsis of 1972 Exorcism Conference*. Richards, Cambridge.

RICHARDS, Rev. John, 'The Victory Given', *Renewal*, No. 40, August/September 1972.

*Roman Ritual, The*, Vol. 11. Bruce, Milwaukee, 1950.

ROBBINS, Rossell Hope, *The Encyclopaedia of Witchcraft and Demonology*. Crown, New York, 1959.

ROBERTS, Estelle, *Fifty Years a Medium*. Corgi, 1959.

ROGERS, Prof. Clement F., *Astrology and Prediction*. SCM, 1948.

*The Role of Religion in Mental Health*. National Assoc. for Mental Health, 1967.

ROSS, Fr Kenneth N., *Spiritualism*. SPCK, 1965.

RUSSELL, Eric, *Ghosts*. Batsford, 1970.

RUSSELL, Ray, *The Case Against Satan*. Souvenir, 1963.


SANDERS, J. Oswald, *Heresies and Cults*. Oliphants, 1962.

SANDERS, J. Oswald and WRIGHT, J. Stafford, *Some Modern Religions*. Inter Varsity Press, 1956.

SANFORD, Agnes, *Healing Gifts of the Spirit*. A. James, Evesham, 1966.

SARGANT, Dr William, *Battle for the Mind*. Heinemann, 1957.

SARGANT, Dr William, 'Possession', *Man, Myth and Magic*. Purnell, 1971.

SARGANT, Dr William, 'Possession and Trance', *Man, Myth and Magic*. Purnell, 1971.

SAVA, George, *Strange Cases*. Faber & Faber, 1950.

SCHLIER, Prof. Heinrich, *Principalities and Powers in the New Testament*. Burns & Oates, 1961.

SCOTHERN, Peter, *Casting Out Demons Today*. Voice of Deliverance, Nottingham.

SCOTHERN, Peter, *Prayer and Fasting*. Voice of Deliverance, Nottingham.

SHAW, Fr Gilbert, 'Angels and Demons in Human Life', *The Angels of Light and the Powers of Darkness*. Faith Press, 1954.

SHAW, Fr Gilbert, 'Exorcism and the Ministry of Healing', *The St Raphael Quarterly*, Vol. 4, No. 6, May 1961.

SHAW, Fr Gilbert, 'Exorcism: Its Application', *The St Raphael Quarterly*, Vol. 4, No. 7, August 1961.

SHAW, Fr Gilbert, 'Exorcism: Its Occasions', *The St Raphael Quarterly*, Vol. 5, No. 1, February 1962.

SHAW, Fr Gilbert, A letter, *St Raphael Quarterly*, Vol. 4, No. 5, February, 1961.

SHEED, F. J. (ed.), *Soundings in Satanism*, Morbrays, 1972.

SIGERIST, Henry E., *Primitive and Archaic Medicine* (A history of Medicine Vol. 1). Oxford University Press, New York, 1967.

SMITH, David R., 'Divine Healing in Relation to the Devil', *Be Thou Made Whole* (ed.) D. R. Smith. Rushworth Literature Enterprises, 1961.

SMITH, David R., *Some Light on Deliverance*. Rushworth Literature Enterprises.

SMITH, Maurice, *Five, Five, Fifty-Five*. Christian Literature Crusade, 1969.

SMITH, Maynard, *Frank, Bishop of Zanzibar*. SPCK, 1926.

SMYTH, Frank, *Modern Witchcraft*. Macdonald Unit 75, 1970.

SMYTHIES, J. R. (ed.), *Science and ESP*. Routledge & Kegan Paul, 1967.

SPENSER, F. A. M., 'Demonic Powers: the Case for their Reality', *Hibbert Journal*, Vol. XXXIII, No. 3, April 1935.

STETTNER, Prof. John W., 'Pastoral Counseling in the Age of Aquarius', *Pastoral Psychology*, Vol. 21, No. 207, October 1970.

STEWART, Prof. James, 'On a Neglected Emphasis in New Testament Theology', *Scottish Journal of Theology*, Vol. 4, September, 1951.

STRACHAN, Françoise, *Casting out the Devils*. Aquarian, 1972.

STREETER, B. H. *et al.*, *Immortality*. Macmillan, 1925.

SUMMERS, Montague, *The History of Witchcraft and Demonology*. Routledge & Kegan Paul, 1926.

TAYLOR, Mrs H., *Pastor Hsi*. Overseas Missionary Fellowship, 1949.

TAYLOR, John V., *The Go Between God*. SCM, 1972.

THIELICKE, Helmut, *Between God and Satan*. Oliver & Boyd, 1958.

THIELICKE, Helmut, *Man in God's World*. James Clarke, 1967.

THURSTON, Fr Herbert sj, *Ghosts and Poltergeists*. Burns & Oates, 1953.

THURSTON, Fr Herbert sj, *The Physical Phenomena of Mysticism*. Burns & Oates.

THURSTON, Fr Herbert sj, *Surprising Mystics*. Burns & Oates, 1955.

TOMLINSON, Mgr G. A. *et al.*, *Christianity and Addictions*. The Church's Ministry of Healing, Personal Workers Assoc., 1970.

TOURNIER, Dr Paul, *A Doctor's Case-Book in the Light of the Bible*. SCM, 1954.

TOYNBEE, Prof. Arnold, PRICE, H. H., HAYWOOD, R. *et al.*, *Man's Concern with Death*. Hodder, 1968.

TROWELL, Rev. Dr H., 'Co-operation Between Doctors and Clergy', *Theology*, Vol. LXVII, No. 523, January 1964.

TROWELL, Rev. Dr H., *Diseases of Strain and Stress—a Review of Psychosomatic Disorders*. Institute of Religion and Medicine, 1970.

TROWELL, Rev. Dr H., *Faith Healing*. Institute of Religion and Medicine, 1969.

UNGER, Merrill F., *Biblical Demonology*. Scripture Press, Illinois, 1952.

UNGER, Merrill F., *Demons in the World Today*. Tyndale House, Illinois, 1971.

UNGER, Merrill F., *The Haunting of Bishop Pike*. Tyndale House, Illinois, 1968.

USHER, Charles H., *Satan—a Defeated Foe*. Christian Literature Crusade, Pennsylvania.

Various—'Growth of the Occult' (correspondence). *Church Times*, January–February, 1971.

VEITH, Dr Ilza, *Hysteria—The History of a Disease*. Univ. of Chicago, 1965.

VOGL, Rev. Carl, *Begone Satan!* (trans. C. Kapsner, osb). Collegeville, Minnesota, 1935.

WALKER, J. B., *Christianity an End to Magic*. Darton, Longman & Todd, 1972.

WALL, J. Charles, *Devils*. Methuen, 1904.

WALLIS, Arthur, *God's Chosen Fast*. Victory Press, 1968.

WALLIS, Arthur, 'The Real and the Counterfeit' (*Renewal* reprint). Fountain Trust.

WARDEN, Dr J. William (Gen. ed.), 'The Theology and Psychology of Death', *Pastoral Psychology*, Vol. 23, No. 225, June 1972.

WATSON, Rev. David, *Spiritual Warfare* (tape). Gateway Fellowship.

WEATHERHEAD, Leslie D., *Life Begins at Death*. Denholm House Press, Redhill, 1969.

WEATHERHEAD, Leslie D., *Psychology, Religion and Healing*. Hodder & Stoughton, 1951.

WEATHERHEAD, Leslie D., *Wounded Spirits*. Hodder, 1962.

WEBSTER, Douglas, *The Healing Christ*. Highway Press, 1963.

WELBOURN, Rev. F. B., 'Exorcism', *Theology*, LXXV, No. 629, November, 1972.

WHEATLEY, Dennis, *The Devil and All His Works*. Hutchinson, 1971.

WHITE, Anne S., *Healing Adventure*. A. James, Evesham, 1969.

WHITE, Fr Victor OP, *God and the Unconscious*. Harvill, 1952.

WHYTE, H. A. Maxwell, *Dominion Over Demons*. Whyte, Toronto, 1969.

WHYTE, H. A. Maxwell, *Hidden Spirits*. Whyte, Toronto, 1970.

WICKLAND, Dr Karl, *Thirty Years Among the Dead*. Spiritualist Press, 1924.

WIESINGER, Alois, *Occult Phenomena in the Light of Theology*. Burns & Oates, 1957.

WILKINSON, Dr J., 'The Case of the Epileptic Boy', *Expository Times*, Vol. LXXIX, No. 2, November 1967.

WILLIAMS, Arthur, *Demonology—A Bible Truth*. Barrett & Williams.

WILSON, Jim, *Go Preach the Kingdom—Heal the Sick*. James Clarke, 1962.

WILSON, Jim, *Healing through the Power of Christ*. James Clarke, 1946.

WILSON, Dr Michael, *The Church is Healing*. SCM, 1966.

WILSON, Peter J., 'Status Ambiguity and Spirit Possession', *Man*, Vol. 11, No. 3, September, 1967.

WINSLOW, Jack C., *The Gate of Life*. Hodder, 1970.

WINSLOW, Jack C., *Modern Miracles*. Hodder, 1968.

WOOD, Derek and Maureen (eds), *Man, God and Magic*, Viewpoint 16. Inter School Christian Fellowship, 1970.

WOODARD, Dr Christopher, *A Doctor's Faith Holds Fast*. Parrish, 1955.

WOOLLEY, Canon R. M., *Exorcism and Healing of the Sick*, SPCK.

WORCESTER, Dr Elmwood and McCOMB, S., *Body, Mind and Spirit*. Hodder & Stoughton, 1931.

*The Work of the Holy Spirit* (Report to 182nd General Assembly United Pres. Church, USA). Philadelphia, 1970.

WRIGHT, J. Stafford, *Christianity and the Occult*. Scripture Union, 1971.

WRIGHT, J. Stafford, 'Encounter with the Cults' (four articles), *Outreach*. Scripture Union, April, July, October, 1970 and January 1971.

WRIGHT, J. Stafford, *Mind, Man and the Spirits* (formerly published as *What is Man?*). Paternoster Press, Exeter, 1968.

WRIGHT, J. Stafford, *Spiritualism*. Church Book Room Press, 1959.

WYATT, Thomas, *The Work of Demons*. Wings of Healing, California, 1948.

YAP, Dr P. M., 'The Possession Syndrome', *The Journal of Mental Science*, Vol. 106, No. 442, January 1960.

# INDEX

After-Care, 190–1
Anointing with Oil, 16–17
Astrology, 47–54

Binding, 169–70
Black Magic, see Satanism and Black Magic

Case-History, see Diagnosis
Confession, 10–11
Curses, see Ill-wishing

Deliverance, 119–54
distinguished from exorcism, 119
'programmes' of, 174–6
Demonic, The, 132–3
and demons distinguished, 134
Demons, 134–5
manifestations, see 'Possession'
reaction to Christ, 144–6
demonic attack, summary of symptoms, 156
Demythologising, 31–2
Diagnosis, 124 ff.
Case-History, 121–4
of the spiritual, 127 ff.
Dualism, 148

Epilepsy, 98–105
Exorcism, 155–91
see also Pseudo-exorcism context of, 120–1
Christian exorcism, 160–77
at a distance, 164
distinguished from deliverance, 119
failures, 164–77
distinguished from healing, 163
'major' and 'minor', 164
more than once?, 174
words of, 164–7
Exorcism, Non-Christian, 159–60
Exorcism (Report), 117, 183
Exorcist, The (Christian), 176–90
authority of, 184 ff.
dangers facing, 181–2

Fasting, 186–8
Fortune-telling, 55–7

Ghosts, 197–200; see also Place-memories

Healers, Eight types of, 7–9
Holy Communion, 12–13
Hysteria, 112–14

Ill-wishing, 85–6
Implications (of this study) for Biblical interpretation, 215–17
for the Church, 219–20
for clergy-training, 217
for the individual, 220–21
for mental health, 215
for theology, 215–19

Jesus Christ
Ministry of, 163
Victory of, 188–90

Laying-on of hands, 13–15
in exorcism, 170–1

Occult Explosion, The, 19–37
Causes:
Churches' spiritual bankruptcy, 30–2
historical, 27
psychical research, 28
death of rationalism, 28
science, changing view of, 28
spiritual need, 30–1
writers' influence, 28–9
Ouija, 59–66

Pike, Bishop James, 74–6; see also Spiritualism
Place-memories, 195–7
Places, Disturbed/Infested, 192–214
Church's Ministry to, 212–14
and human sin, 209–10
and pagan sites, 211
and spiritist activities, 206–9
Planchette, see Ouija
Poltergeist Activity, 200–6
'Possession', 91 ff.; see also Epilepsy, Hysteria, Pseudo-possession, Schizophrenia, etc.

'Possession' – *Contd.*
of animals, 215–16
cases of, 136–50
and the Christian, 129, 171–3
demonic manifestations
physical, 136–43
'mental', 143–50
by departed spirits, 152–3
by invitation/mediums, 129–31
by the living, 153–4
and mental illness, 158–9
multiple, 151
following occult involvement, 132
summary of true/false, 157–8
terminology, 129
theiromania, 148–9
uninvited, 131–2
voluntary and involuntary, 129–30
Possession and
abnormal psychology, 95
anthropology, 93–4
history, 92–3
the law, 96–7
medicine, 97–105
mental illness, 105–14

psychic research, 95
Spiritualism, 94–5
theology, 114–18
Prayer, 9–10
of affirmation, 189–90
for the departed, 199–200
Prediction, 51–4
Pseudo-exorcism, 114
Pseudo-possession, 107–8
Psychic Development, 39–45

Roman Ritual, Rubrics on Exorcism, 222–5

Satanism and Black Magic, 80–90
Schizophrenia, 110–12
'Spirit of the Glass', *see* Ouija
Spiritism, 66–77
Spiritualism, *see* Spiritism
Superstition, 45–7

Unction, *see* Anointing with Oil

Witchcraft, 77–80

# INDEX OF BIBLICAL REFERENCES

| Genesis | page | Mark | page |
|---|---|---|---|
| 3:1 ff. | 82 | 6:5 | 13 n. |
| 3:5 | 23 | 6:7 | 163, 183 n. |
| Deuteronomy | | 7:25–30 | 163 |
| 18:9–14 | 22 | 7:32–7 | 103 |
| 18:10 | 140 n. | 8:22–5 | 103 |
| 1 Samuel | | 8:33 | 134 |
| 28. | 23 | 9. | 15 |
| Isaiah | | 9:2–8 | 23 |
| 61:1 | 2 | 9:14–27 | 100 |
| Matthew | | 9:17–18 | 100 |
| 6:31–4 | 24 | 9:18 | 101 |
| 8:16 | 163 | 9:20 | 101 |
| 11:5 | 2 | 9:21–2 | 102 |
| 12:19–21 | 198 | 9:21–7 | 102 n. |
| 12:22 ff. | 103 | 9:22 | 121 |
| 12:24 | 182 | 9:25 | 101, 166 |
| 12:28 | 166 | 9:26 | 101, 139 |
| 12:29 | 169 | 9:26–7 | 103 |
| 12:45 | 208 | 9:27 | 101 |
| 15:21–8 | 163 | 9:28 | 186 |
| 16:18 | 173, 185 | 9:29 | 104 |
| 16:19 | 169 | 9:38 | 165 |
| 17:12 | 187 | Luke | |
| 17:15 | 100 | 4:39 | 163 |
| 19:13–15 | 15 | 6:17 | 163 |
| 26:63 | 160 | 7:22 | 2 |
| 28:18 | 185 | 8:2 | 151, 160 n. |
| Mark | | 8:36 | 3 n. |
| 1:23–4 | 139 | 9:1–2 | 150, 184 |
| 1:23 ff. | 172 | 9:39 | 100, 101 |
| 1:27 | 162 | 9:42 | 101, 103, 163 |
| 1:32 | 163 | 10:17 | 181 |
| 1:34 | 168 | 11:15 | 182 |
| 1:41 | 13, 13 n. | 11:22–3 | 169 |
| 2:1–12 | 11 | 11:24–6 | 119, 120 |
| 3:11 | 160 n. | 13:10–13 | 170 n. |
| 3:11–12 | 139 | 13:16 | 169 |
| 3:22 | 182 | 19:9 | 3 n. |
| 3:27 | 169 | 22:3 | 162 n., 184 |
| 3:29–30 | 182 | John | |
| 5. | 94 | 3:8 | 179 |
| 5:8 | 163 | 5:6 | 190 |
| 5:9 | 94 n. | 5:14 | 190 |
| 5:11–13 | 216 | 8:36 | 37 |
| 5:12 | 94 n. | 12:31 | 162 |
| 5:23 | 13 n. | 13:2 | 162 n. |

| *Acts* | *page* | *Ephesians* | *page* |
|---|---|---|---|
| 3. | 165 | 6:10–20 | 90 |
| 3:5 | 2 | 6:11 | 173 |
| 3:12 | 9 | 6:12 | 132 |
| 10:30 | 186 | 6:14–17 | 134 |
| 16. | 150 | 6:16 ff. | 188 |
| 16:16–18 | 23 | *Philippians* | |
| 16:17–18 | 163 | 2:6 (NEB) | 191 |
| 19:12 | 163 n., 213 | 2:9–11 | 189–90 |
| 19:13 | 161 | 4:4–9 | 87 |
| 19:13–20 | 142 | 4:7 | 87 |
| 19:18–20 | 22 | *Colossians* | |
| *Romans* | | 1:16–17 | 162 |
| 8. | 134 | 2. | 54 |
| 8:38–39 | 211 | 2:15 | 90, 162, 188 |
| 12:2 | 185 | 3:1–3 | 188 |
| 12:11–14 | 133–4 | *1 Timothy* | |
| 13:12 | 173 | 4:1 | 72 |
| *1 Corinthians* | | *2 Timothy* | |
| 7:5 | 186 | 2:3 | 189 |
| 9:26b | 173 | *Hebrews* | |
| 11:26 | 213 | 4:15 | 43–4 |
| 11:27 | 199 | *James* | |
| 12:4 ff. | 44 | 2:19 | 162 |
| 12:9 | 8 | 5:14–16 | 16, 121 |
| 12:10 (Moffat) | 8 | *1 Peter* | |
| 12:10 | 124 | 3. | 200 |
| 12:26 | 126 | 5:8 | 82 |
| 15:29 | 200 | *1 John* | |
| *2 Corinthians* | | 4:1 ff. | 72 |
| 5:17 ff. | 54 | 4:1–3 | 63 |
| 5:18–19 | 4 | *Revelation* | |
| 11:13 ff. | 72 | 3:20 | 82 |
| *Galatians* | | 13:11 | 188 |
| 2:19 | 153 | 20:1–3 | 167 |
| | | 22:2 | 3 |